"This book offers a very fascinating collection of chapters that represent Nordic research in the Institutional Ethnography (IE) tradition. It provides a very impressive view of the network c ̇ ̇ ̇ involved in such research, and also of the range and quality of th ̇ ̇ ̇ ̇ship
—*Marjorie DeVa*
and P

CW01096286

Institutional Ethnography in the Nordic Region

Developed in response to the theoretically driven mainstream sociology, institutional ethnography starts from people's everyday experiences, and works from there to discover how the social is organized. Starting from experience is a central step in challenging taken-for-granted assumptions and relations of power, whilst responding critically to the neoliberal cost-benefit ideology that has come to permeate welfare institutions and the research sector. This book explicates the Nordic response to institutional ethnography, showing how it has been adapted and interpreted within the theoretical and methodological landscape of social scientific research in the region, as well as the institutional particularities of the Nordic welfare state. Addressing the main topics of concern in the Nordic context, together with the way in which research is undertaken, the authors show how institutional ethnography is combined with different theories and methodologies in order to address particular problematics, as well as examining its standing in relation to contemporary research policy and university reforms. With both theoretical and empirical chapters, this book will appeal to scholars and students of sociology, professional studies and anthropology with interests in research methods and the Nordic region.

Rebecca W. B. Lund is an Academy of Finland postdoctoral researcher in Gender Studies at the University of Tampere, Finland.

Ann Christin E. Nilsen is an Associate Professor of Sociology at the Department of Sociology and Social Work, University of Agder, Norway.

Routledge Advances in Research Methods

For more information about this series, please visit: www.routledge.com/
Routledge-Advances-in-Research-Methods/book-series/RARM

Institutional Ethnography in the Nordic Region

Edited by Rebecca W. B. Lund
and Ann Christin E. Nilsen

Routledge
Taylor & Francis Group

LONDON AND NEW YORK

First published 2020
by Routledge
2 Park Square, Milton Park, Abingdon, Oxon OX14 4RN

and by Routledge
52 Vanderbilt Avenue, New York, NY 10017

Routledge is an imprint of the Taylor & Francis Group, an informa business

First issued in paperback 2021

British Library Cataloguing-in-Publication Data
A catalogue record for this book is available from the British Library

Library of Congress Cataloging-in-Publication Data
Names: Lund, Rebecca W. B., editor.
Title: Institutional ethnography in the Nordic region / edited by Rebecca
W. B. Lund and Ann Christin E. Nilsen.
Description: Abingdon, Oxon; New York, NY: Routledge, 2020. |
Series: Routledge advances in research methods | Includes
bibliographical references and index.
Identifiers: LCCN 2019039161 (print) | LCCN 2019039162 (ebook) |
ISBN 9780367030353 (hbk) | ISBN 9780429019999 (ebk)
Subjects: LCSH: Ethnology—Scandinavia. | Sociology—Scandinavia. |
Welfare state—Scandinavia.
Classification: LCC GN308.3.S34 I57 2020 (print) |
LCC GN308.3.S34 (ebook) | DDC 305.800948--dc23
LC record available at https://lccn.loc.gov/2019039161
LC ebook record available at https://lccn.loc.gov/2019039162

ISBN: 978-0-367-03035-3 (hbk)
ISBN: 978-1-03-208644-6 (pbk)
ISBN: 978-0-429-01999-9 (ebk)

Typeset in Times New Roman
by codeMantra

MIX
Paper from
responsible sources
FSC
www.fsc.org FSC™ C013985

Printed in the United Kingdom
by Henry Ling Limited

Contents

Figures

Table

Contributors

Siri Yde Aksnes is a social anthropologist and holds a PhD in social policy. She works as a researcher at the Work Research Institute, Oslo Metropolitan University. Her research interest includes IE and work and welfare studies.

Janne Paulsen Breimo is a Professor of social work at Nord University, Norway. She holds a master's in political science and a PhD in sociology. She has published on several issues of social policy, including collaboration and the organization of services related to rehabilitation and child protection services. She was the coordinator for the Nordic network of IE from 2015 to 2017. She is currently chair of the European Sociological Association's (ESA) Research Network 26 (Sociology of Social Policy and Social Welfare) and the coordinator for the Center for Welfare Innovation at Nord University.

Naomi Curwen completed her master's in development management at University of Agder, Department of Global Development and Planning, in 2016. She wrote her thesis on child marriage in Nepal, a study inspired by IE. Her research interests include social injustice, gender and development and research methods in sociology.

Hanne Haaland is an Associated Professor at the Department of Global Development and Planning, University of Agder, Norway. She holds a PhD in development studies. Her research interests include local responses to development projects and intervention, resistance, mobilization as well as discussions of knowledge in a development context. She also does research on citizen initiatives within aid and relief work and lately she has engaged in integration research. Her research is published in international journals such as *Third World Quarterly*, *Forum for Development Studies*, *Journal of Sustainable Tourism*, *Women, Gender and Research* as well as in books and journals in Norwegian and Spanish.

Helle Cathrine Hansen is an Associate Professor at VID Specialized University in Oslo. She currently holds a postdoc position at NOVA, Oslo Metropolitan University. Her research interests are within social work, social policy and the welfare state. Her works include research on activation policy and practice, coordination of services to vulnerable children and adolescents, and integrated and person-oriented services to elderly. She has published articles in several social work and social policy journals, e.g. *British Journal of Social Work*, *International Journal of Social Welfare*, *Social Policy & Society* and *Nordic Social Work Research*.

Riikka Homanen is an Academy Research Fellow in Gender Studies at the Tampere University, Finland. She is also the Principal Investigator for the Kone Foundation-funded project "Technology, Ethics and Reproduction: Controversy in the Era of Normalisation". Her research explores social relations and valuation in (assisted) reproduction. More recently, she has inquired into the marketization of reproduction and reproductive healthcare. Her work is ethnographic and firmly grounded in gender studies, sociology and feminist STS. She is also currently the editor-in-chief for the Finnish peer-reviewed journal on sociology, *Sosiologia*, and co-founder and co-leader of the Finnish Reproductive Studies Network (FiResNet).

Kjeld Høgsbro has since 2008 been Professor of social work, Department of Sociology and Social Work at Aalborg University in Denmark. He got a PhD in 1991 with a dissertation on social problems and self-help organizations in Denmark. He has published books on disabilities, mental illness, social work and community development in Denmark between 1991 and 2015. As Senior Research Fellow at The Danish Institute of Governmental Research (2000–2008) he conducted evaluations of programmes for people with mental illness, substance abuse, homelessness, brain injury and pervasive developmental disorders. He is a board member of two ISA research groups on sociology of mental health and IE.

Marjo Kuronen is Professor of social work at the University of Jyväskylä, Finland, and currently PI of the research project *"Transforming welfare service system from the standpoint of women in vulnerable life situations"* (Academy of Finland 2016–2020, project no. 294407). Her research interests include the relationships between women, family and the welfare state, feminist social work, local welfare policies and IE. She has been the editor of three books including *Local Welfare Policy Making in European Cities*. Social Indicators Research Series 59. Springer 2015, together with Dagmar Kutsar.

Rebecca W. B. Lund works as a postdoc and researcher at the Centre for Gender Research at the University of Oslo, Norway. She is moreover joint editor-in-chief for *NORA: The Nordic Journal for Gender and Feminist Research* and acts as coordinator for the International Sociological Association (ISA) Thematic Group of IE. Her research interests are academic work, activism, knowledge production, feminist theory and epistemology. She has published in journals such as *Organization: The Critical Journal of Organization, Theory and Society*, and *Gender & Education.*

Kjetil G. Lundberg is as an Associate Professor at the Department of Welfare and Participation, Western Norwegian University of Applied Sciences. Previously he worked as a senior researcher at the Rokkan Centre, Bergen, and as a visiting scholar at King's College, London. He holds a PhD and a master's in sociology. His research interests include welfare encounters, activation, social care, social policy, social work professions and sociological perspectives on power and social interaction. His research is published in journals such as *Social Policy & Administration, Journal of Sociology & Social Welfare, Comparative Journal of Social Work* and *Ethics & Social Welfare.*

May-Linda Magnussen holds a PhD in sociology from the University of Oslo and works as an Associate Professor at the Department of Sociology and Social Work, University of Agder, Norway. Her research interests are gender in family- and work-life, migration, everyday life and welfare state and gender in the academia. Methodology is a key issue in her writing. She is currently one of the coordinators of the Nordic network of IE.

Ann Christin E. Nilsen is an Associate Professor of sociology at the Department of Sociology and Social Work, University of Agder, Norway. She is currently one of the coordinators of the Nordic network of IE. Her research interests include childhood and families, gender, early intervention, early childhood services and interdisciplinary collaboration. Her research is published in international journals such as *Childhood, Gender Issues, Nordic Social Work Research, Comparative Social Work, Contemporary Issues in Early Childhood, European Early Childhood Education Research Journal* and *Journal of Research in Childhood Education*, as well as in diverse journals and books in Norwegian.

Nina Olsvold is a registered nurse, sociologist and holds a PhD in sociology from the University of Oslo. She works as an Associate Professor at VID Specialized University where she teaches research methods and theory of science for master students. Her work includes research on topics related to care, responsibility and the organization of professional work.

Hogne Lerøy Sataøen is Docent at the School of Humanities, Education and Social Sciences, Örebro University. His research interests include communication practices, professionalization and public sector organizations. His research is rooted in the interpretive and sociological tradition, and in particular he has been interested in (neo)-institutional theories. His research is published in international journals such as *Corporate*

Communication, International Journal of Strategic Communication, British Journal of Management, Public Management Review, Scandinavian Journal of Management and *Scandinavian Journal of Educational Research.*

Majken Jul Sørensen is an Associate Professor of sociology at Karlstad University, Sweden. Her research interests include everyday and constructive resistance, nonviolent social movements, conflict transformation as well as humour and political activism. In this intersection between sociology and peace and conflict studies, she focusses on participants' experiences and people's agency and ability to create change from below. She has published books and articles on these topics in a wide range of academic journals, such as *Journal of Resistance Studies, Humor: International Journal of Humor Research*, and *Peace and Change.*

Cathrine Talleraas is a senior researcher at the Peace Research Institute Oslo (PRIO). Her research focusses on the governance of migration and transnationalism, welfare policy and institutional analysis. She holds a PhD and an MA in human geography from the University of Oslo, and an MSc in migration studies from the University of Oxford. Her research is published in international journals such as *Ethnic and Racial Studies* and *Journal of Ethnic and Migration Studies.*

Ann-Torill Tørrisplass is a PhD candidate with particular interests in gender, migration, youth and welfare research. She holds a master's in sociology from Nord University, Norway. She is currently writing a dissertation on unaccompanied refugee minor girls and their transition to adulthood, using IE as methodology. She is currently chair of the local sociology association (Nordland sosiologforening) and member of the board in the National Research School for Gender Research.

Hege Wallevik is an Associated Professor at the Department of Global Development and Planning, University of Agder, Norway. She has a PhD in development studies. Her research interests include gender and development with a focus on everyday life practices. She has also done research on integration issues in a Norwegian context and lately she has been concerned with civil society and citizen initiatives within aid and relief work. Her research is published in international journals such as *Third World Quarterly, Forum for Development Studies, Environment and Urbanization, Women, Gender and Research* as well as in international and Norwegian books and Norwegian journals.

Karin Widerberg is Professor of Sociology at the Department of Sociology and Human Geography, University of Oslo, Norway. Her main research fields are theory of science and methodology, understandings of gender and the role of the welfare state. Time, work and work-life, the body, family life and sexual violence have been empirically investigated. Among her books *In the Heart of the Welfare State. An Invitation to Institutional Ethnography* (2015) (in Norwegian) should be mentioned here. Methodology is a key issue in all her writings and exploring qualitative approaches, such as IE and Memory Work, is a main concern and activity.

Guro Wisth Øydgard is an Associate Professor of social work at Nord University, Norway. She holds a master's in rehabilitation and a PhD in sociology. Her research interests are rehabilitation, welfare and collaboration systems – especially the interconnection between the individual and the welfare state, and between different levels and areas of welfare services.

Part 1

Contextualizing IE in the Nordics

1   Introduction

Conditions for doing institutional ethnography in the Nordics

Rebecca W. B. Lund and Ann Christin E. Nilsen

What is institutional ethnography?

Institutional Ethnography (IE) is a methodology-of-inquiry associated with the Canadian sociologist Dorothy E. Smith (e.g. Smith (ed.) 2006). IE is designed to discover, unpack and challenge the social organization of everyday life and involves commitment to doing research *with* and *for* people, rather than *about* them (Smith 1987, 2005). Ontologically, people are understood as essentially social beings and the social, in turn, is understood as people coordinating activities. Speaking of the social as "coordination", rather than "structure", "rules" or "system", implies people's *actual activities*. This ontology is central to understanding the development of IE as a sociological method-of-inquiry which does not end with individual experience, but never loses sight of it either. In this way, IE challenges structure-agency, macro-micro and individual-society distinctions and dualisms.

The theoretical, methodological and onto-epistemological underpinnings of IE have grown in and responded to debates in sociology and feminist studies, particularly the methodological discussions related to the linguistic turn, the critique-of-representation and processes of objectification in mainstream sociology. Smith developed a thorough critique of theory-driven research as well as positivist ideals and principles in knowledge production (Smith 2005). In her book *The Conceptual Practices of Power: A Feminist Sociology of Knowledge* (1990a), Smith noted how theory-driven knowledge production involves the reproduction of institutional orders, of ideology, and ultimately societal orders and inequity in terms of whose experiences and interests gain representation:

> The categories structuring data collection are already organized by predetermined schema; the data produced becomes the reality intended by the schema; the schema interprets the data [...] though it is perfectly possible to prove or disprove statements, issues of objectivity must be framed within established structure. Issues, questions, and experience that do not fit the framework and the interrelated relations of categories and schemata do not get entry to the process, do not become part of the textual realities ...
> (Smith 1990a, 93–94)

In her critique of objectifying processes, she notes how it happens in at least four ways. (1) The *subject disappears* and is replaced by social facts or social phenomena, e.g. through the nominalization of verbs. (2) *Agency is transferred* from the subject to the social phenomenon. Hence the social phenomenon, rather than people and their actual relations, becomes the object of study. (3) People's actual sayings and doings are translated into an expression of discourse or category, and the researcher's theoretical narrative. People are *held accountable to discourse and categories*, but discourse or categories are not held accountable to people. (4) The subject is *reconstructed as a category* identified through looking for discursive attributes (e.g. gender, class and ethnicity) (Smith 1999).

Smith developed IE in order to understand processes of objectification in research and other institutions, and to challenge such processes, *not* to overthrow them. Indeed, no form of research can overthrow processes of objectification "that would be a contradiction". Rather, by acknowledging that all knowledge claims are embedded in values and are essentially contested, Smith suggests that we can challenge dominant knowledge claims by starting inquiry from the *standpoint* of people whose "knowing" and "interests" have hitherto been downplayed in institutional representations. The epistemic privilege ascribed to a particular experience and standpoint is not automatic but empirically and contextually justified (e.g. Lund 2015). Through people's everyday embodied experience and *work-knowledge*, understood generously as *"everything people do, from they get up till they go to bed, that takes time, effort and emotion, as they participate in or resist institutional orders"* (see Smith 2005), we may learn how institutions are made to work and shape people's lives in ways that are not necessarily in their own best interests. In learning from what people know, the institutional ethnographer should avoid *institutional capture*, that is, avoid treating concepts and discourses *as if* they are *descriptive* of experience rather than *organizers* of experience.

As with all Smith's concepts, *institutions* or the *institutional* are understood in a manner that privileges inquiry above theory. There is

> ... a complex of relations forming part of the ruling apparatus, organized around a distinctive function – education, health care, law and the like. In contrast to such concepts as bureaucracy, "institution" does not identify a determinate form of social organization, but rather the intersection and coordination of more than one relational mode of the ruling apparatus.
>
> (Smith 1987, 160)

The relational modes occur on at least two levels: the local and the translocal. While the *local* is the immediate site of our embodied practice (e.g. the act of writing, teaching, sitting in a meeting, engaging with a client), *some* of the *translocal* social relations that organize and regulate our lives in contemporary society operate in objectified forms (e.g. the discourses, concepts, rules and regulations that shape the local activity and coordinates across space and time). The objectified relational mode is captured in Smith's concept of *ruling relations* (see 1999, 73), developed through a reinterpretation of Marx (2004, 1999, 1990a). Ruling relations are:

> ... text-mediated and text-based systems of 'communication', 'knowledge', 'information', 'regulation', 'control' and the like. The functions of 'knowledge, judgment, and will' that Marx saw as wrested from the original 'producer' and transferred to capital become built into a specialized complex of *objectified* forms of organization and relationship [...] Knowledge, judgment, and will are less and less properties of the individual subject and more and more of objectified organization. They are constituted as actual forms of concerting and concerted activities and *can be investigated as such.* 'Objectivity', the focus of postmodern critique, is only one form of objectification, though objectified organization relies extensively on text-mediated virtual realities [...] Social consciousness exists now as a complex of externalized or objectified social relations through which people's everyday/everynight activities organize and coordinate contemporary society [...] The concept of the ruling relations identifies a historical development of forms of social consciousness that can no longer be adequately conceived as arising in the life conditions of actual individuals.
>
> (Smith 1999, 77–78)

The fact that local and translocal modes are *relational* highlights how individuals and agency never disappear. People coordinate their activities, produce and change institutional relations. Institutional relations, in turn, involve the coordination of activities. Discovering the ruling relations should hence return us to the standpoint – the experience – from which we started.

Why a book about IE in the Nordic countries?

IE, as a school of thought, emerged in North America and has primarily been shaped in scholarly debates in Canada and USA. Gradually it has spread across the world, becoming recognized as an important contribution to the social sciences in, for example, Australia, Argentina, Taiwan, Japan, UK and the Nordic countries. When IE is taken up and activated in other contexts, it necessarily responds to the legacies and characteristics of social inquiry wherever that might be. Distinct characteristics define the institutions explored, new methodological issues arise, indeed the context of debate and justification differs. Our motivation for writing this book has emerged out of a recognition that the debates and usage of IE take a particular form in particular contexts.

With the books *The Everyday World as Problematic. A Feminist Sociology* (1987), *Texts, Facts and Femininities: Exploring Relations of Ruling.* (1990a), *The Conceptual Practices of Power: A Feminist Sociology of Knowledge* (1990b) and *Writing the Social. Critique, Theory and Investigations* (1999), Smith set the stage for IE, providing theoretical reflections on the production of knowledge and the conceptual apparatus fundamental to the approach. A more thorough methodology was outlined and developed in her books *Institutional Ethnography. A Sociology for People* (2005) and *Institutional Ethnography as Practice* (2006). The most recent books, *Incorporating Texts into Institutional Ethnographies* (Smith and Turner 2014) and *Under New Public management. Institutional Ethnographies of Changing Front-line Work* (Griffith and Smith 2014), both co-edited by Smith, include several empirical chapters from scholars using IE in their research. Foundational to IE as a school of thought, these books – predominantly authored by North American and Canadian scholars and anchored in North American and Canadian scholarly debates and specific social problematics – have acquired an instructive position as to how people understand, evaluate and use IE across the world. This is despite of the fact that Smith emphasizes that "there is no one way of conducting institutional ethnography" (2006) and that concepts within IE have been developed to privilege inquiry above theory. Hence, the above-mentioned books have contributed, unintentionally, to a certain IE jargon and meticulousness that appears to be institutionally capturing, leaving little room for contextual and linguistic variation. Given the ontological grounding of IE and the intention of questioning objectification in knowledge production, IE scholars in other contexts should take part in the wider discussion of how IE could be developed and used in diverging ways, drawing attention to legacies, controversies, and characteristics of its use in other contexts.

In the Nordic countries, and particularly Norway, IE has increasingly gained recognition over the past decade. The first well-known article about IE in Norwegian was written by Karin Widerberg, Professor of Sociology at the University of Oslo, in 2007. Published in one of the leading sociological journals in Norway, the article title proposes that IE offers a new possibility for qualitative research, and since then Widerberg has been an important proponent of IE in the Nordic countries. In 2011 she established the Nordic network for institutional ethnographers, which has been growing ever since. The responsibility for coordinating the network has travelled between Norwegian universities, engaging scholars in different disciplines and departments. The network has initiated and facilitated PhD courses, book-projects, seminars and conference streams, and meets twice annually to discuss the latest research. This book is a product of the joint effort of scholars who are part of the network. The predominantly Norwegian presence in the network is reflected among the authors of this book, whereof 15 are affiliated to Norwegian universities, 3 to Finnish universities (Homanen, Kuronen and Lund), 2 to Swedish universities (Sataøen and Sørensen) and 1 to a Danish university (Høgsbro).

The first collection on IE in and about the Nordic region was also a product of the network. Edited by Karin Widerberg, *I hjertet av velferdsstaten. En invitasjon til institusjonell etnografi* [At the Heart of the Welfare State. An Invitation to Institutional Ethnography] (2015) consists of chapters authored by Norwegian, Swedish, Danish and Finnish early career academics, engaged in exploring the changing nature of Nordic welfare state policies and institutions. The book covers a wide range of empirical explorations into the ruling relations of and dilemmas existing within childcare, family support, rehabilitation, working life and disability, care for the elderly, refugee policy, isolation in jails and academia. Although it is a significant contribution to knowledge about the changing welfare state and provides insight into how IE is interpreted in different ways by different scholars, the book does not engage in an explicit positioning of Nordic IE as a contribution to the broader debates on the conceptual, theoretical and methodological interpretation and development of IE. Moreover, the book is written in Norwegian, rendering it inaccessible to an international audience.

The aim of this book is to depict Nordic use of, and responses to, IE. What characterizes IE in the Nordic context? How is it justified? Which topics do institutional ethnographers address in the Nordics, and how do they go about doing their research? How do they combine IE with different theories and other methodologies in order to address particular problematics? And finally, and most importantly, what insights can the Nordic IE studies contribute to the development of the approach as such?

The Nordics – some characteristics

The Nordics refers to a region in Northern Europe, known as "Norden", which literally translates to *the North*. The region consists of five countries: Denmark (including Greenland and the Faroe Islands), Finland (including the Åland Islands archipelago), Iceland, Norway (including the Svalbard archipelago) and Sweden. In sum, it encompasses almost 27 million people, spread across 3.5 million square kilometres. Sweden is the most populous country, with almost 10 million citizens, followed by Denmark, Finland and Norway, all comprising of 5–6 million people. Iceland is the smallest of the five countries, with a population of less than 500,000. Whilst Denmark, Finland and Sweden have joined the European Union (EU), Norway and Iceland have opted to stay out.

The majority of the people in the Nordics are Scandinavian, i.e. Danish, Norwegian or Swedish. Indeed, Scandinavia/Scandinavian are terms that are often used interchangeably with the Nordics/Nordic, despite the fact that Scandinavia only refers to the three monarchies of Denmark, Norway and Sweden. The Scandinavian languages are mutually understandable both orally and in writing, and have their roots in the old Norse language, as is also the case with Icelandic. The Nordic region, however, also comprises of Finns, who form the majority of Finland, and the indigenous Sami people and Greenlandic Inuits. Like the Sami languages and Greenlandic, Finnish is a non-Germanic language bearing no similarities to the Scandinavian languages. However, Swedish is, alongside Finnish, recognized as an official language in Finland, and it is compulsory to learn Swedish at school.

"Nordic" is usually used as an identity marker that complements, rather than stands in opposition to, national identity markers, such as Swedish, Finnish, Norwegian, Icelandic, Danish etc. Indeed, Nordic assumes some taken-for-granted similarities between the Nordic countries, which, of course, often involve the downplaying of contestations, contradictions and changes over time and place (e.g. Dahl et al. 2016). Nordic and Nordicness often refers to common political and cultural projects (e.g. Pan-Scandinavianism), institutions (e.g. the Nordic Council), a particular family and gender system (dual earner/dual carer family), the social-democratic welfare, work and employment models and state religion (the national Protestant church). These institutions have resulted in a region that, at least according to metrics, can be perceived as prosperous and successful. Indeed, the Nordic countries cluster near the top in several rankings of national performance, such as education, economic competitiveness, civil liberties, gender equalities, happiness, quality of life and human development, just to mention some. Praised by politicians, social scientists and economists across the world, the Nordic welfare model is acknowledged as highly successful.

Seen from the outside, the Nordic region may also appear rather homogeneous. However, the Nordic countries all have their distinct characteristics, policies and challenges. For instance, the increasing migration to Europe has led to different policies in the Nordic countries; Sweden favouring liberal immigration policies while Denmark has adopted one of the strictest immigration policies in Europe. Indeed, the Nordic region has a heterogeneous population; indigenous peoples (Sami and Inuit), considerable Romani populations as well as second and third-generation immigrant groups, all holding distinct cultural traditions. Sweden has the highest ratio of foreign-born citizens, whereas Finland and Iceland have the lowest. Nevertheless, Nordic countries continue to conceive of themselves as culturally homogeneous, with a relatively high degree of gender equality, income redistribution (although this can be challenged) and little social unrest. The relative success of the Nordic countries has been referred to in titles such as *The Scandinavian Utopia* (Booth 2014) and *The Next Supermodel* (*The Economist*, February 2, 2013), not least fuelled by the emergence of the new *Scandi Noir* in popular culture, which has drawn the attention of Western media. Although academics and journalists have made efforts to question the utopian myth of the Nordics, e.g. by pointing at the high consumption rate of anti-depressants, the high taxes, the insurmountable bureaucracy, the continuous horizontal and vertical gender segregation of the job market, and the seemingly modest, unwelcoming and reserved character of the Nordic people, there is little doubt that the Nordic countries enjoy great social stability, democratic freedom and thriving economies.

However, Nordic/Nordicness is also, as this book is an example of, a category of academic analysis. Nordic scholars question the taken-for-granted goodness of the Nordic model; explore the construction of the Nordic; and are concerned with how societal changes impact our values and ways of life, such as increasing globalization and migration, increasing social inequalities, the evolving distrust in democratic institutions, the influx of new organizational logics and so on. In particular, Nordic social scientists are questioning the neoliberal cost-benefit ideology that increasingly permeates both our welfare institutions and higher education and research, raising concerns about the future of the welfare state.

The emancipatory or transformational allegiances that are inherent in IE provide an opportunity to respond to these challenges. The legacy and current developments of the Nordic welfare states, university reform and contemporary tensions within the research sector call for studies that can strengthen our understanding of the characteristics and consequences of these developments in the Nordics. Within this context, IE has become a favoured approach for several Nordic scholars. Yet the questions the scholars raise and the ways they go about their studies have to be seen in light of current controversies that preoccupy social scientists in the Nordics. Two topics are particularly worthwhile addressing: the development and future of the Nordic welfare model and the legacy of the social sciences in the Nordics.

The Nordic model

In his seminal work, *Three Worlds of Welfare Capitalism* (1990), Danish sociologist Gøsta Esping-Andersen outlines a typology of welfare capitalism, defining three types of welfare regimes. The UK, the USA and Australia are examples of what he calls liberal regimes, giving allegiance to a market economy. These regimes are characterized by a high degree of privatization and modest state intervention, primarily targeted at people in low-income or disadvantaged groups. Conservative regimes, on the other hand, such as Italy and Spain, are characterized by a strong appreciation of family values, encouraging family-based solutions to social problems, with limited state intervention. The Nordic countries are examples of what Esping-Andersen called social-democratic regimes. Characterized by universalistic systems aimed at promoting equality of high standards, the level of state intervention is high compared to the other regimes, implying comprehensive, de-commodified public welfare services.

Esping-Andersen's typology can serve as a starting point in depicting the so-called *Nordic model*. This term is used with reference to the commonalities in political, economic and social structure between the Nordic countries. Politically, the Nordic, social-democratic model is facilitated by what may arguably be referred to as *consensual democracy* (Arter 2006), characterized by a political system that enjoys a high degree of legitimacy, relatively small social divisions, and where political deliberation is compromising and neutralizing. Economically, the model can be understood as a kind of fusion of capitalism (free market, globalization, outsourcing) and socialism (high tax rates, universalistic welfare arrangements, strong trust in labour unions), yet with unique features. Important in this respect, is the tripartite arrangement between market economy, strong labour unions and a comprehensive and universalistic welfare sector, financed by heavy taxes. Together, these features have resulted in some of the world's most stable societies, distinguished by a characteristic *stateness*. Indeed, in the Nordic countries *the state* is a word with positive connotations; i.e. the trust and legitimacy of the state is high. According to the Norwegian social anthropologist Halvard Vike (2018), people in the Nordics tend to perceive the state as an essential part of everyone's environment and not as something people need to avoid or seek protection from. The idea that the state can solve major collective problems, and that its bureaucracy generates freedom rather than deprives people of it, is still quite robust in the Nordic countries, despite international trends towards increasing distrust in the state. Hence, and in contradiction to liberal democracies, there is no need for an extensive civil society to oppose state power and grant individual freedom. Quite the contrary, voluntary activity is an integral part of the state. Socially, then, the Nordic welfare states are both individualizing and collectivist.

Although the establishment of modern welfare institutions in the Nordics is normally dated to the post-war period, the emergence of a Nordic welfare model can be traced all the way back to the pre-industrial area. In contrast to many other European countries at the time, the social transformations of the Nordic countries were not impaired by major class divisions, but by a peaceful transformation in which the peasantry had a strong position. The peripheral position of the Nordics made it difficult to sustain an urban, noble elite, dependent on international trade. Instead, peasants organized themselves in social movements, gradually seizing power within political institutions. These grassroots movements were fundamental to the state formation of the Nordic countries and led to a compromise between social classes (Esping-Andersen 1990). This was particularly the case in Norway which, until 1905, was under Danish and subsequently Swedish rule and consequently did not have a bourgeois elite of its own. The situation was different in Denmark and Sweden, where up until recently class divisions have been more manifest. Nevertheless, parliamentarism emerged in all of the Nordic countries as a result of compromises where the peasantry, then the working classes and finally women and poor people legitimately seized the power to vote and be elected alongside landowners and nobility. With the transition from an agricultural subsistence economy to industrialization, the seeds of the contemporary welfare model were sown. The 1930s were particularly important in this respect, as financial hardship led to compromises between industrial and agricultural sector interests, and between labour and capital. It was during this decade that labour unions gained increased political influence. The importance of work, mediated by the role of peasants and workers, has been foundational for contemporary Nordic welfare and employment policies that focus on enabling people to participate in the workforce.

This work-line policy emerging in the 1930s has also been foundational for the high rate of female work participation in the Nordics. In response to the low fertility rates of the 1930s, the Swedish couple Alva and Gunnar Myrdal launched the book *Kris i befolkningsfrågan* [Population Crisis] in 1934, where they outlined a set of policy reforms aimed at facilitating female participation in the workforce. The purpose was to create better financial conditions for families in order to enhance fertility rates. The reforms included both different forms of cash benefits for families and welfare services, such as organized day care, which eventually became common in all the Nordic states. The Nordic *care regime* is thus characterized by generous public care services targeting children, families and the elderly, and the high work participation of women (Leira 2012). Referred to as "a woman-friendly welfare state", a term coined by the Norwegian sociologist Helga Hernes in 1987, it depicts a welfare model characterized by extensive family policies and a normative dual earner/dual carer model. The high tolerance for female work participation in the Nordic countries has been an important condition – and engine – both for comprehensive gender equality and for the state economy. Indeed, on the occasion of the International Women's Day in 2012, the then Norwegian prime minister, Jens Stoltenberg, asserted that the high participation of women in the workforce has been a more important prerequisite for the financial success of the Norwegian state than the discovery of the North Sea oil.

The state formation and emergence of the Nordic model was rendered possible by two principles that are still firmly embedded in the Nordic welfare mentality: *universalism* and *equality*. In the Nordic countries, the principle of universal social rights comprises the whole population and is not only targeted at the poor or marginalized. The idea is that in order to maintain the legitimacy of the welfare state, everyone should benefit and everyone should feel responsible. In Esping-Andersen's words: "All benefit: all are dependent; and all will presumably feel obliged to pay" (1990, 27–28). Therefore, state income (through taxes) is redistributed in order to promote social equality. Historically, the differences in income, class and gender have, in relative terms, been rather small in the Nordic countries. This is largely due to the historically strong position of the peasants and workers – in terms of both policy and economy – giving rise to an intolerance of social inequality and poverty. This is also reflected in the family and gender policy, as mentioned above. The Nordic countries are accordingly rated among the highest in the world when it comes to gender equality. Nevertheless, gender inequalities are still present, both in work life, in the family, academia, media and politics, and this is a matter of concern for social scientists.

The priority of universalism and equality has also been a leading principle in the international relations of the Nordics, extending the arm of the

Nordic welfare model beyond its borders. With their weak colonial ties, the self-image of the Nordic countries is one of "good agents", specifically pronounced in the development aid and peace building policies of Norway and Sweden (Keskinen et al. 2016). Indeed, this self-image is fuelled by the fact that the Nordic countries have been world leading in terms of state expenditure on international development, also involving an export of ideas and notions of "good". For instance, the enchanting notion of "folkhemmet" (people's home) and the "harmonic imperative" turned Sweden into an epitome of benign and socially sensitive modernity in the 1990s. The term "regime of goodness", coined by Norwegian foreign policy expert Terje Tvedt captures (mockingly) the Norwegian self-image of an aspiring moral superpower on the stage of development aid (Witoszek 2011).

The universalism and comprehensiveness of Nordic welfare states requires a large public sector. Indeed, in the Scandinavian countries almost 30% of the workforce is employed in general government (OECD 2017). As the extended arm of the state, the street-level bureaucrats (Lipsky 1980) working within the different welfare services (schools, hospitals, kindergartens, social services etc.) possess great power. They are responsible for putting policy into practice, thus enforcing the democratic power of the state. Indeed, the Norwegian political scientist Erik O. Eriksen has referred to the power of the professionals employed within the bureaucratic institutions of the state as the "dark hole of democracy", implying that their extensive power is not sufficiently democratically grounded (Eriksen 2001). The alliance between the state and the professions has traditionally been strong in the Nordic countries, much owing to the role of the trade unions. However, the neoliberal turn and the introduction of new public management principles, accompanied by novel requirements pertaining to evidence and accountability, has given rise to an increasing mistrust towards professionals. As tools of the welfare state, professionals often find themselves squeezed between bureaucratic rules and regulations at the top and a moral obligation to care for the most vulnerable citizens at the bottom of society. Professionals play a crucial role in the creation and reproduction of specific categories of people, identifying and distinguishing between needs that are constitutive for the different welfare institutions. As this collection bears witness, the role of professionals in the welfare state and their interaction with citizens with different needs is a matter of concern for many institutional ethnographers. The import of new ideas and ways of thinking which has accompanied the neoliberal turn, increasing globalization and migration, and the high expenditures of the welfare state, reinforced by an ageing population, have caused both scholars and politicians to question the future of the welfare state. Is the Nordic welfare model in crisis? Some critics claim that the high taxes and the comprehensive public sector are prohibitive for innovation and economic growth. Nevertheless, the Nordic countries are thriving economically. Building on the case of the economic cutbacks in Sweden in the early 1990s, Lindbom (2001) points out two contradictory hypotheses regarding the future of the welfare state. One hypothesis predicts that the irresistible force of globalization will ultimately lead to a dismantlement of national autonomy and welfare arrangements. The other hypothesis points at the resilience of the welfare state to cutbacks. Lindbom's analysis gives prominence to the second hypothesis, indicating that, despite the cutbacks, the major attributes of the, in this case, Swedish welfare state, e.g. its generosity, universality and developed welfare services, remains intact. The handling of the financial crisis in 2007 indicates the same. In other words, the ideology of the welfare model seems to enjoy substantial support. To repeat, if one can speak of a particular kind of welfare mentality in the Nordics, it is one that values both individual autonomy and collectivism.

The conditions for doing sociology are shaped in a wide range of social and ruling relations, historical and material processes. Some translocal processes can be characterized as "international", while others may be perceived as connected more to societal and political particularities, such as the Nordic welfare state. The position of IE, as well as the debates around and use of IE which the present anthology covers, should be seen in this light.

Placing institutional ethnography in context

While sociological thinking and research has a long history in the Nordics, as elsewhere, it was historically often fragmented and tied to a few isolated individuals.[1] The discipline was first properly institutionalized and established in the Nordic universities post-World War II (WWII), when sociological research became a source of data and ideas for rebuilding, rethinking and planning a modern society and welfare state. The discipline of sociology developed rapidly in Denmark, Sweden, Norway and Finland,[2] combining traditions from American sociology with those of national intellectual traditions, resulting in distinct features (Allardt 1989; Lindbekk and Sohlberg 2000; see also Andersson and Dabrowski 1996; Hansson and Aagaard Nielsen 1996; Hansen 1997; Gundelach 2000; Tepora and Roselius 2014; Larsson and Magdalenić 2015). Proponents of both a quantitative positivist sociology and qualitative cultural sociology could be found in the Nordics throughout the 1950s. The latter traditions, however, established a stronger foothold from the 1960s and onwards. These forms of sociology were often grounded in the study of everyday life, social problems and inequality, and had a massive impact on the development of disciplines such as social work, organization studies, media and communication studies, gender studies and human rights research (Ahrne et al. 2010), all of which can be seen represented in this book.

The anti-positivist, qualitative and cultural sociology traditions in the shape of what has been named "problem-oriented empiricism" (Aubert 1969; Mjøset 1991) had a particularly strong standing in Norway from early post-WWII. We argue that this, combined with the strong institution building work of Karin Widerberg, at least in part explains why IE has been so widely embraced in Norway, both in sociology and other disciplines as this book, with contributions from 15 Norwegian scholars, is a testimony to. We also think that the particular history of Norwegian sociology has meant that IE does not necessarily stand out as an alternative sociology in Norway, but rather builds upon and contributes to existing debates and research practices. In contrast, IE has not been embraced widely by sociologists and social science in Finland but is still perceived as an explicitly feminist method of inquiry, considered an alternative to mainstream social science and usually used by gender scholars (cf. Chapter 9).

In Norway the first Department of Sociology was founded at the Faculty of Humanities at the University of Oslo in the 1950s and, simultaneously, the Institute for Social Research (ISF) was founded in Oslo as an independent research institute made possible by a private donation. Sociology, from the very beginning, had status as a critical discipline in Norway, engaging with the consequences of social change and voicing the needs of less privileged members of society.[3] The term "problem-oriented empiricism" (Aubert 1969) was coined to describe the legacy of Norwegian sociology: as one that gives allegiance to everyday experience, makes use of qualitative as well as quantitative methods (but with a preference for qualitative methods) and is explicitly committed to solving social problems (Kalleberg 2000; Næss and Pedersen 2012). The legacy of "problem-oriented empiricism" has also shaped contemporary Norwegian sociology. From the earliest days of its institutionalization, Norwegian sociology held a clear identity, with a strong professional profile and legitimacy, also in comparison to other Nordic countries (Allardt 1973, 1989; Mjøset 1991). Today, this is reflected by the prevalence of applied research and the presence of many independent sociological research institutes, as well as the fact that many sociologists work interdisciplinary. Similar forms of sociology, with a focus on experience, everyday life and social transformation, can of course be found in Denmark (e.g. Charlotte Bloch, Birthe Bech-Jørgensen), Finland (e.g. Liisa Rantalaiho) and Sweden (e.g. Ahrne 2007) but cannot be characterized as a *defining feature* of Finnish, Swedish or Danish sociology, where there is much less of a common disciplinary identity.

In the latest national evaluation of Norwegian sociology (Norwegian Research Council 2018), conducted by an international evaluation committee, the interdisciplinary feature of sociology and the relatively high prevalence of commissioned work in the sector, as well as the "lack of theorizing" and "advancement of theory" is problematized. The critiques should be seen in light of the overall neoliberalization of academia, where interdisciplinary and applied research is increasingly being put under pressure and devalued.

Despite these critiques, "problem-oriented empiricism" continues to serve as a shared heritage. Moreover, the position of sociology as a discipline remains strong in Norway, compared to other Nordic countries. This argument is often expressed in terms of numbers when it is claimed that there are more sociologists in Norway than in any other Nordic country

(Kalleberg 2000, 400). Others see this strength in paradigmatic terms: sociology as a discipline has an established legitimacy and there is widespread consensus around its core object of study and usefulness (Engelstad 2000; Ahrne et al. 2010, 20).

The age of "excellence", internationalization, quantification and big data

IE connects with and develops the strong legacy of qualitative research in the Nordic region, particularly in Norway. The hegemonic position of positivism has been challenged successfully over several decades in the Nordic countries, and Nordic sociology has largely distanced itself from American positivist traditions, functionalism and a priority given to quantitative methods. Empirically driven critical, cultural and feminist sociology as well as qualitative and action-oriented methods have held a relatively strong position in the Nordic countries. Due to this, IE has not thus far been perceived as a radically different or less legitimate methodology, particularly not in Norway. In fact, we are often asked to explain how IE differs from other frequently used methods-of-inquiry. Therefore, in the Nordic context, the position, use of and debates related to IE appear to be quite different from the situation in North America.

There are, however, certain contemporary tendencies worth turning a critical and cautious eye towards. The widespread neoliberalization of higher education and the implementation of standardized quality indicators that emphasize international publications in top-journals have also made their way into the academia of the Nordic countries (Lund 2012, 2015). These tendencies are often associated with the American and positivist or pragmatist orientation, as opposed to the tradition within central Nordic journals. Sociologists and peers in other disciplines face the pressure that they have to produce article manuscripts quickly and in English, which is not conducive to experience-based research or to conveying cultural particularities and nuances (see e.g. Widerberg 1998). Furthermore, they often have to justify the quality of their research in accordance to positivist notions of "validity", "generalizability" as well as convincing reviewers as to why they should be interested in data from the Nordic countries (Lund and Tienari 2019).

Furthermore, the reforms of higher education and the usage of international and external evaluation committees force departments to be increasingly narrow in their definition of their discipline and to formulate strategic focus areas, which, in turn, shape who is considered eligible for a faculty position. The evaluation of Norwegian sociology[4] referred to above and which was carried out by internationally renowned Nordic sociologists concluded that while "problem-oriented empiricism is a strength", Norwegian sociology does not sufficiently touch upon "core issues of sociology", and these are not sufficiently theorized. Moreover, the evaluators argue that sociology in Norway is not sufficiently "strong and coherent"; it is, in other words, too interdisciplinary. This conclusion has been critiqued for promoting "orthodoxy" and "positivist" sociology and for challenging the multiplicity of Norwegian sociology and its ability to respond to current societal and environmental challenges.[5]

In the context of Denmark, we also note that when positions open in Sociology, which remains a small discipline in Denmark, it is explicitly requested that the applicant should be strong in terms of quantitative methods and big data. This does, in a way, make sense given that "data has become a currency of power" (D'Ignazio 2017) and understanding these methods is a prerequisite for understanding and scrutinizing the use and power of data in contemporary society. However, Inge Henningsen et al. (2017) remind us, *"The emerging interest in quantitative methodologies and big data, reflects the growing hegemony of evidence-based views in neoliberal policy-making, which has turned statistics and quantitative methodologies into key data with wide-ranging effects at both the individual and institutional level"* (2017, 3–4). The problem with this, Catherine D'Ignazio argues, is that these forms of data are more often used to discriminate against and surveil people, than they are used for the benefits of civil society and democratization (D'Ignazio 2017). In light of these points, we would argue that big data and quantitative methods are not necessarily in opposition to IE, but neither are they easily compatible with IE's emphasis on experience, doing and maintaining that sociology should be *for* rather than *about* people.

In this book we will focus attention on the ways in which IE is and can be relevant for exploring contemporary societal issues in the Nordic countries, and how IE engages in debates with different methods and theories.

About this book

IE's critique of objectification in mainstream sociology has often been misunderstood as taking a dislike to theory in general, and as if it makes claims to having overcome objectification. This ultimately leads to treating IE's concepts as if they are descriptive, rather than organizers of knowledge. Smith herself recognizes that it would be a contradiction to treat IE as if it could overcome objectification due to the fact that it is itself a theorized practice. Overcoming objectification is not the goal; the goal is to *challenge* objectification (Smith 2005). Of course, the theories we should engage with as institutional ethnographers have to be aligned with the ontological ambition of IE, which is to unpack social relations rather than prematurely categorize and define them. Against this backdrop, we find it crucial to show how IE fruitfully can be combined with other theories. As noted above, there is a strong legacy of qualitative and participatory perspectives in social research in the Nordic countries, which have contributed substantially to the development of theory and scientific discourse. The Nordic response to IE has accordingly been to engage in discussing how and to what extent IE can engage with these perspectives and contribute to the development and improvement of social research. As such, this book serves two purposes: It displays how IE is *used* in the Nordic context, and it contributes to *a development* of IE by explicitly bringing into view and discussing how it can be combined with other approaches and theories.

This book is divided into four sections. In the first section, which this chapter is a part of, the aim is to contextualize IE in the Nordics, specifically focussing on how IE fits into the legacy of social sciences in this region and how *Nordic Public Welfare Objectification* (see Chapter 2 by Widerberg) represents a backdrop against which social sciences in the Nordics, including IE, evolve. The chapters in the subsequent section share a commitment to engaging in dialogues between IE and other theories. With their individual take, all the chapters address how IE and other theories and methodologies may mutually inform and converse with each other, highlighting the relevance of such an enterprise within the Nordic case. This includes conversations between Scandinavian Neo-Institutional Theory and IE (Chapter 3 by Lundberg and Sataøen), Organization Theory and IE (Chapter 4 by Talleraas); Actor Network Theory and IE (Chapter 5 by Tørrisplass and Breimo); Feminist Studies of Technoscience and IE (Chapter 6 by Homanen); IE, discourse and interactionist approaches (Chapter 7 by Nilsen); and finally IE, Nordic Postcolonial and Critical Race Studies (Chapter 8 by Lund). The third section consists of chapters presenting empirical cases and applications of IE in the Nordic countries, focussing on social work research (Chapter 9 by Kuronen), gender and family policy (Chapter 10 by Magnussen), work inclusion (respectively, Chapter 11 by Aksnes and Olsvold, Chapter 12 by Hansen and Chapter 13 by Øydgard) and development aid (Chapter 14 by Curwen, Wallevik and Haaland). Finally, in the last section, we address the transformative potential of IE in the Nordics, addressing pedagogical approaches in care facilities (Chapter 15 by Høgsbro) and everyday resistance (Chapter 16 by Sørensen, Nilsen and Lund).

Notes

1 18th, 19th and early 20th centuries: Carl Linnäus and Gustaf Steffen in Sweden; Eilert Sundt in Norway; Johannes Peter Anchersen, Joseph Davidson and Theordor Geiger in Denmark; Edward Westermarck, Lilius & Gebhard in Finland.

2 In Iceland, Sociology was first established as a university discipline in 1970 (Thórlindsson 1982).

3 Despite a strong influence from American sociology, and notably Columbia University Professor Phil Lazarfield, Norwegian sociologists were from the outset engaged in both qualitative and quantitative research, but with a strong preference for the qualitative. And a particular tradition developed drawing on American and Norwegian thought and practice. The so-called "golden age of sociology" originated in a small group of eminent Norwegian sociologists, such as Vilhelm Aubert, Yngvar Løchen, Johan Galtung, Nils Christie, Sverre Lysgaard and Thomas Mathiesen. In addition, despite being educated a psychologist, Harriet Holter had an important impact on sociology as a pioneer for

methodologically innovative feminist research, which later came to flourish in Norway (Widerberg 2000; Ahrne et al. 2010, 20).
4 Ahrne, Esseveld, Gundelach, Riska & Boja. *Sociological Research in Norway: An Evaluation.* Norwegian Research Council Publications.
5 See the article "Norway: Fears for future of sociology" in *University World News* (accessed 04.01.2019) at www.universityworldnews.com/post.php?story= 20110122090031817

References

Ahrne, G. 2007. *At se samhället [To See Society]*. Stockholm: Liber.
Ahrne, G., J. Essevald, P. Gundelach, E. Riska, and T. Boje. 2010. *Sociological Research in Norway: An Evaluation.* Oslo: The Research Council of Norway.
Allardt, E. 1973. *About Dimensions of Welfare: An Exploratory Analysis of Comparative Scandinavian Survey.* University of Helsinki reports.
Allardt, E. 1989. "Recent Developments in Scandinavian Sociology." *Annual Review of Sociology* 15: 31–45. doi: /10.1146/annurev.so.15.080189.000335
Andersson, B. and A. Dabrowski. 1996. "Sociologiens akademiske, administrative og kommercielle felter 1950–1970." [The Academic, Administrative and Commercial Fields of Sociology, 1950–1970]. *Dansk Sociologis Historie [The History of Danish Sociology]*, edited by K. Aagaard and F. Hansson, 113–189. Frederiksberg: Forlaget Sociologi.
Arter, David. 2006. *Democracy in Scandinavia. Consensual, Majoritarian or Mixed?* Manchester: Manchester University Press.
Aubert, V. 1969. *Det Skjulte Samfunn [The Hidden Society]*. Oslo: Pax.
Booth, M. 2014. *The Almost Nearly Perfect People: Behind the Myth of the Scandinavian Utopia.* New York: Picador.
Dahl, U., M. Liljeström and U. Manns. 2016. *The Geo-Politics of Nordic and Russian Gender Research 1975–2005.* Södertörn: Södertörn University.
D'Ignazio, C. 2017. "Creative Data-Literacy: Bridging the Gap between the Data-Haves and Data-Have Nots." *Information Design Journal* 23(1): 6–18. doi: 10.1075/idj.23.1.03dig
Engelstad, F. 2000. "Norsk Sosiologi ved 50-årsmerket." [Norwegian Sociology on its 50 Years Anniversary] *Sosiologi i dag* 39(1): 15–24.
Eriksen, E.O. 2001. *Demokratiets sorte hull [The Dark Hole of Democracy]*. Oslo: Abstrakt forlag.
Esping-Andersen, G. 1990. *The Three Worlds of Welfare Capitalism.* Princeton: Princeton University Press.
Griffith, A. and D.E. Smith, eds. 2014. *Under New Public Management. Institutional Ethnographies of Changing Front-Line Work.* Toronto: Toronto University Press.
Gundelach, P. 2000. "Kaare Svalastoga: The Unceasing Positivist." *Acta Sociologica* 43(4): 365–373. doi: 10.1177/000169930004300409
Hansen, L. 1997. *Sociologi i Tiden: Backgrund, utveckling, framtid [Sociology in Time: Background, Development, Future]*. Göteborg: Daidalos.
Hansson, F. and Aagaard, K. 1996. "Dansk Sociologis Historie. En historie om brud og lidt kontinuitet." [The History of Danish Sociology. A History of Disruption and Some Continuity]. In *Dansk Sociologis Historie [The History of Danish Sociology]*, edited by K. Aagaard and F. Hansson, 9–34. Frederiksberg: Forlaget Sociologi.

Henningsen, I., T. Steffensen, and H. Rømer Christensen. 2017. "Quantitative Methodologies and Big Data." *Women, Gender and Research* 26(1): 3–7. doi: 10.7146/kkf.v26i1.97083

Kalleberg, R. 2000. "The Most Important Task of Sociology is to Strengthen and Defend Rationality in Public Discourse: On the Sociology of Vilhelm Aubert." *Acta Sociologica* 43(4): 339–411. doi: 10.1177/000169930004300412

Keskinen, S., S. Tuori, S. Irni, and D. Mulinari. 2016. *Complying with Colonialism: Gender, Race and Ethnicity in the Nordic Region.* London: Routledge.

Larsson, A. and S. Magdalenić. 2015. *Sociology in Sweden.* Basingstoke: Palgrave Pivot.

Leira, A. 2012. "Omsorgens institusjoner, omsorgens kjønn." [Institutions of Care, Gender of Care]. In *Velferdsstatens familier: Nye sosiologiske perspektiver [Families of the Welfare State: New Sociological Perspectives]*, edited by A.L. Ellingsæter and K. Widerberg, 76–98. Oslo: Gyldendal Akademisk.

Lindbekk, T. and P. Sohlberg. 2000. "Introduction: The Nordic Heritage." *Acta Sociologica* 43(4): 293–298. doi: 10.1177/000169930004300401

Lindbom, A. 2001. "Dismantling the Social Democratic Welfare Model? Has the Swedish Welfare State Lost its Defining Characteristics?" *Scandinavian Political Studies* 24(3): 171–193. doi: 10.1111/1467-9477.00052

Lipsky, M. 1980. *Street-Level Bureaucracy: Dilemmas of the Individual in Public Services.* New York: Russell Sage Publications.

Lund, R. 2012. "Publishing to Become an Ideal Academic: An Institutional Ethnography and a Feminist Critique." *Scandinavian Journal of Management* 28(3), 218–228. doi: 10.1016/j.scaman.2012.05.003

Lund, R. 2015. *Doing the Ideal Academic: Gender, Excellence and Changing Academia.* Helsinki: UniPress.

Lund, R. and J. Tienari. 2019. "Passion, Care and Eros in the Gendered Neoliberal University." *Organization* 26(1): 98–121. doi: 10.1177/1350508418805283

Mjøset, L. 1991. *Kontroverser i Norsk Sosiologi [Controversies in Norwegian Sociology]*. Oslo: Universitetsforlaget.

Myrdal, A. and G. Myrdal. 1934. *Kris i befolkningsfrågan [Crisis in the Population Question]*. Stockholm: Albert Bonniers.

Næss, H.E. and W. Pedersen. 2012. *Merkesteiner i Norsk Sosiologi [Milestones in Norwegian Sociology]*. Oslo: Universitetsforlaget.

Norwegian Research Council. 2018. *Evaluation of Social Science Research in Norway: Report from the Principal Evaluation Committee.* Oslo: The Research Council of Norway.

OECD. 2017. *Government at a Glance 2017.* Paris: OECD Publishing. doi:10.1787/gov_glance-2017-en

Smith, D.E. 1987. *The Everyday World as Problematic: A Feminist Sociology.* Boston: Northeastern University Press.

Smith, D.E. 1990a. *Texts, Facts and Femininities: Exploring Relations of Ruling.* London: Routledge.

Smith, D.E. 1990b. *The Conceptual Practices of Power: A Feminist Sociology of Knowledge.* Boston: Northeastern University Press.

Smith, D.E. 1999. *Writing the Social: Critique, Theory and Investigations.* Toronto: University of Toronto Press.

Smith, D.E. 2004. "Ideology, Science and Social Relations: A Reinterpretation of Marx's Epistemology." *European Journal of Social Theory* 7(4): 445–462.

Smith, D.E. 2005. *Institutional Ethnography: A Sociology for People.* Lanham: AltaMira.

Smith, D.E. ed. 2006. *Institutional Ethnography as Practice.* Lanham: Rowman and Littlefield.

Smith, D.E. and S. Turner, eds. 2014. *Incorporating Texts into Institutional Ethnographies.* Toronto: Toronto University Press.

Tepora, T. and A. Roselius. 2014. *The Finnish Civil War 1918: History, Memory, Legacy.* Boston: Brill.

Thórlindsson, T. 1982. "Icelandic Sociology: National Conditions and the Emergence of a New Discipline." *Acta Sociologica* 25(1): 79–89.

Vike, H. 2018. *Politics and Bureaucracy in the Norwegian Welfare State: An Anthropological Approach.* Basingstoke: Palgrave Macmillan.

Widerberg, K. 1998. "Translating Gender." *NORA: Nordic Journal of Feminist and Gender Research* 6(2): 133–138. doi: 10.1080/08038749850167833

Widerberg, K. 2000. "Harriet Holter: A Pioneer in Gender Studies and Sociology." *Acta Sociologica* 43(4): 413–420.

Widerberg, K. 2007. "Institusjonell etnografi: en ny mulighet for kvalitativ forskning?" [Institutional Ethnography: A New Possibility for Qualitative Research?]. *Sosiologi i dag [Sociology Today]* 37(2): 7–28.

Widerberg, K. 2015. *I hjertet av velferdsstaten. En invitasjon til institusjonell etnografi* [At the heart of the welfare state. An invitation to institutional ethnography]. Oslo: Cappelen Damm akademisk.

Witoszek, N. 2011. *The Origins of the "Regime of Goodness": Remapping the Cultural History of Norway.* Oslo: Universitetsforlaget.

2 In the name of the welfare state

Investigating ruling relations in a Nordic context

Karin Widerberg

Introduction

How are we to understand the doings in and of local relations and the way these relations are hooked up to trans-local relations, if we do not have an overall, historical and theoretical understanding of the society in question? And does not the lack of such a background result in making the empirical studies from different societies quite alike, as variations on a theme, when in fact the very theme might be questioned? How can theory inform, and yet be challenged by, empirical institutional ethnographic studies?

In this chapter it is argued that an understanding of the welfare state challenges our understandings of ruling relations. Objectification in the name of welfare, aiming at equality (class, gender and ethnicity) – *Public Welfare Objectification* – results in specific experiences and reactions (characterized by ambivalence and insecurity). In the Nordic context of today such ruling permeates all aspects of everyday life to an extent that is unheard of in democracies elsewhere. As such *Nordic Public Welfare Objectification* presents a case where the more general patterns and implications of ruling can be highlighted and discussed. Within these frames a "traditional" empirical Institutional Ethnographic approach can give a content to local and trans-local relations under study that might challenge the theoretical concepts and understandings we started out with, for example of the ruling relations of the welfare state. The very aim of Institutional Ethnography (IE) is here not only to highlight "blind-spots" of welfare ruling but to investigate the taken for granted in the organization of everyday life so as to make alternative paths visible. I will start with an empirical study of academic work at a Norwegian university to illustrate and illuminate the points taken. My main argument is that we need to hook up our final empirical results to theoretical debates, so as "to make a difference" in the ongoing theoretical and political discussions. The aim of this chapter is accordingly to explore theorizing and contextualizing IE so as to improve its quality and relevance to social science research.

"That would never work with us!"

My English colleague looks at me with surprise and interest. I have just told her about "the accounting of hours" that we as scientific staff at the University of Oslo have to fill out at the end of each term, so as to document how we have fulfilled our teaching and supervision duties surmounting to 46% (880 hours/year) of our total working hours. At my faculty, the Social Science Faculty, the form has been in use since the early 1990s. Each year it is expanded and made more sophisticated, presently listing a variety of different kinds of teaching, supervision and examination, and how they are credited in terms of hours. It is this list of several pages, intending to cover it all, that intrigues my colleague. "Do all of you really fill this out?" "How do you remember all that you have done during a semester, or do you cheat?" And I start to explain why and how it is done by us teachers and how it's followed up, controlled and used in management on the levels in the university structure; the department, the faculty and the university. I tell the story of my IE study of the accounting of hours.[1] But her reactions, coming from someone who has experienced a profound change of Academia in terms of ruling in the name of marketization, takes me by surprise. Is it possible that the global mainstreaming of academia takes quite different forms in different countries? Are we, Scandinavians, in the name of welfare, maybe more easily ruled and fooled? An understanding of national responses to New Public Management (NPM) seems urgent if we are to understand what is happening locally but also globally. The fact that NPM is nationally adapted and translated, allowing for variations, can in fact be one of the reasons for its global success.

Why it works for the Norwegians – a historical explanation

Norway is a young nation. It was not until 1905 that it was proclaimed an independent kingdom. Before that, Norway was governed by Sweden and Denmark. Lacking nobility and feudal hierarchies and structures, its small population – consisting of farmers, fishermen and merchants – was less differentiated than was the case in most countries in Europe at the beginning of the previous century. The population is still small, only 5.3 million, and spread along a long coastline, where the main means of subsistence still are shipping and fishing and now also oil. Industry came late and is – with the exception of the oil industry – dominated by small- and medium-sized companies, differing in that regard from Sweden. For topographic reasons (mountains and fjords), agriculture is also small-scale compared to its other neighbour, Denmark.

This "backward" situation at the beginning of the 20th century shaped education. Higher education often meant going to Copenhagen, Denmark, and schooling was on the whole scarce and required travelling. When building a new and modern nation state, in the beginning of the 20th century, education was a key issue. The close connections between science and politics – often manifested in the very same persons – stressing education both for the burghers and for the people (that is education reforms from above was combined with education reforms from below), are cornerstones in the Norwegian house of knowledge. This combination became characteristic for the development of the Norwegian nation state. It has indeed been stated that if one were to identify *one* word to capture more recent Norwegian history for the last two centuries, it would be "educational revolution" (Slagstad 2000, 434).

This was part of the historical background from which social sciences entered the scene in the 1950s. The Norwegian sociologist Rune Slagstad (2000) claims that the social sciences were split into two: a science of ruling (economics and pedagogy) and a science of opposition. Sociology and philosophy, belonging to the latter category, got their institutional centre at the Institute for Social Research (ISF), established in 1950, where science from below, from the perspective of the ruled, was developed and used in empirical research.

The Norwegian welfare state was shaped in part through the mobilization of the social sciences. The so-called Labor Party State after 1945 was, it is claimed, "a political regime dressed in social science" (Slagstad 2000, 434). This knowledge regime was maintained even after the Labor Party lost its power, in 1965. However, in the late 1980s a new knowledge regime emerged, through comprehensive reforms in the education sector, initiated by the Minister of Education, Research and Church Affairs, Gudmund Hernes (a sociologist). The university was now to be less "populist" and more professional, with a division of labour between the university colleges, in charge of the education of the professions, and the Universities.

The Norwegian educational revolution was shaped by the combination of two traditions, the Anglo-American and the German-Continental, the first committed to respond to societal needs, while the other was committed to promoting social intellectualism or *bildung*. After World War II, the Anglo-American tradition gained the upper hand, manifesting itself through, among other things, the establishment of a variety of institutes for applied research. A division of labour regarding research was thereby established.

Summing up, the state of affairs before the more recent educational reforms. One could argue that the ideology (welfare, equality and social democracy) and scarce resources was the background for the equality-oriented organization of teaching and research at the universities. The universities, regulated by the ministry, were to be equal, non-elite- universities, i.e. public, free of charge and open to all. The teachers – professors and associate professors – should have similar and equal work tasks, responsibilities and salaries. The ideal and aim was to have teachers qualified in research (i.e. with a doctorate/PhD) and not just lecturers. Although the division of labour between research and teaching and between associate professor and professor, in practice might be less equal than intended, it is still quite a different picture in Norway compared to, for example, Sweden during the same period. In Sweden there was, and still is, a sharp division of labour between research and teaching manifested in the positions of Professor, Docent and Lecturer. Since these two countries in many ways share the same kind of ideology, the explanation for this particular difference can be sought in the longer and more feudal tradition of the Swedish University and probably also the fact of scale and resources – Sweden having twice the population, more research funding agencies and so forth. The vast majority of Norwegian professors of today were all educated in this "university of equality".

New Public Management enters the scene

The ideology of NPM, with its focus on three M's – Market, Management and Measurement – has increasingly been implemented in the public sectors of the Nordic welfare states over the past two decades. In Norway, the "modernization" began in 1990 when "management by objectives" was introduced into local public services (Forseth 1989; Rasmussen 2000, 2004; Vabø 2007), culminating in the "agencyfication" of state bureaucracy and the introduction of detailed performance measures in hospitals, the police forces, welfare bureaucracy, etc. (Christensen and Lægreid 2007).

Some areas and institutions, such as higher education and the university, are objects not only of national but also of international and more specifically European NPM policies. The desire to create a "knowledge-market" for the internal exchange of "producers and products" that can compete with the North-American "knowledge-market" is a driving force behind the Europeanization process in which NPM is a vital tool. To make a common market possible, it is considered necessary to mainstream higher education. The Bologna agreement, that is, the application of the American model consisting of 3 years (Bachelor) + 2 years (Master) + 3 years (PhD), is an example of such mainstreaming. Another example is the measurement of production systems, both in terms of education (e.g. the accounting of hours) and research (e.g. the registration of research publications (Cristin)) which represent a means of making each institution visible for competition. There is accordingly double pressure on NPM within higher education in the welfare states. One pressure comes from neo-liberalism, with arguments of a much-needed vitalizing, rationalizing and economizing of the public sector within welfare states. The other pressure comes from the Europeanization and globalization processes, in which mainstreaming and measuring ease entry into the global market. Both these pressures can be used as arguments for furthering NPM, nationally as well as internationally. The very fact that NPM is in the "good hands" of a welfare state that enjoys high public support might also contribute to its pervasiveness, speedy implementation and lack of vital opposition.[2] This is especially the case in Norway, where the close connection between academics and politicians – explicated above – is a historical and structural foundation for policymaking and policy implementation.

Previously, I used to be quite proud to be a Scandinavian academic. Educated in Sweden and working in Norway but collaborating internationally had not only made me aware of, but also appreciative of, the welfare model of Scandinavian universities. Free public education (at all levels), formal equality regarding salaries and work conditions among the academic staff and a social mission as the goal of research – could one wish for a better platform for a social scientist? When, in addition, academic knowledge is not only publicly appreciated but also made use of in policymaking for the welfare state, surely there cannot be much to complain about. Yet it is precisely this very close relationship between research and politics in Norway, where intellectuals are positioned to be politically accountable, that now seem to pose a problem. As academics we are, I would claim, more caught up in ruling relations – structurally and culturally – than intellectuals working in less egalitarian or democratic cultures. How else can one explain the rapid and profound changes within higher education and research, undertaken to mainstream and control not only the amount but also the content of both research and teaching? And just as important, how can one explain the lack of resistance and critique of this development!?

Of course, none of the reforms and changes mentioned above are unique to Norway; quite the opposite. Since the purpose is to modernize the university, novel ideas and models have been imported from other countries as well as from other branches of the state. What is striking in a Scandinavian setting, I would argue, is its very pervasiveness – its rapid, smooth and successful implementation. But let me also stress that, in themselves, none of these reforms are "bad". Quite the opposite. There are good reasons and good intentions behind every single one of them. Taken together, however, I would argue that they assume a new quality, changing both academic activities and academic culture. Registration and rating of research and teaching affect not only the tasks you do and how you do them but also your whole state of mind. You become a person who *calculates*. And if the tradition for counting and documenting is based on the individual as a unit, *individualization* will increase at the expense of a more collective working culture. When this is combined and synchronized with the policy for the mainstreaming of research in the form of strategic plans at the Research Council as well as at the university, this might prove to be the end of the university as we know it. Let me illustrate.

A case study of academic work and the role of New Public Management in Norway

A couple of years ago I decided to do an IE of the implications of NPM in academic work. Following the IE guidelines, I started out not with sociological concepts and understandings of neither NPM or academic work but with an ethnographic study of everyday academic work and the role of NPM texts herein. An example of such an NPM text is the *accounting of work hours* (in Norwegian "Timeregneskap"). At the end of each semester each scientific staff member has to document the teaching work done by filling out a form for the accounting of work hours. Since this form and the texts regulating how the counting is to be done have been much debated during the nearly two decades it has been used at my own department, the Department of Sociology and Human Geography (part of the social science faculty at the university of Oslo), I decided to make that very text central in my ethnography, in fact doing a kind of ethnography of the text.

"What do you do as a professor of sociology?"

If asked about my job by someone from outside of academia, my first answer would be that I teach and supervise, carry out research and perform administration. Most likely, I would then add that the teaching and supervision task amounts to 50%, administration 10% and research 40%. Any member of the university's academic staff could have answered almost the same, with the correct figures being 47%, 6% and 47%. This is the official picture of the duties of a professor at the University of Oslo (other Norwegian universities might have slightly different rates), manifested in general rules and regulations and translated into different departments' local texts – for example, forms to fill out for the accounting of work hours related to teaching. My first answer is simultaneously both a formal one – how it looks from the outside and from above (from a ruling perspective) – and a (partly) honest one since this time apportionment is a framework to which I am obligated and by which I am controlled. By making me *accountable* (Smith 2005, 113) to this *objectified* (Smith 2005, 27–28) job description, I reproduce the *ruling relations* (Smith 2005, 13–20) that have generated it in the first place. But of course, beneath my obedient compliance, a strategic and tactical practice might hide very different activities or prioritization of activities.

To find out about my everyday actual work, I wrote down all my work tasks – how long they took and in which relations they were involved – for a whole month. Since I found that some tasks and relations were spread out over a very long time-period, I had to use my notes and organizer for the whole year. Although I registered all daily activities, special focus was on those that were to be translated into the accounting of hours, that is, activities that counts.[3]

After registering all my daily activities during the month chosen, I used my organizer to try to get a picture of the whole semester,[4] before embarking on filling out the accounting of hours for that very semester.

Fitting it all into the text: the form for the accounting of hours

It is easy to conclude, first of all, that there are activities related to teaching and administration that are not registered as such and that are thus not recognized as work duties. Second, the hours allotted to tasks (i.e. the rating) bears little relation to the actual amount of time used on the task in question. There is no way to know if one, on the whole, uses more or less hours than one is credited for. Third, the way a task is rated affects how one reports it. When supervision of a PhD student is credited to 180 hours for the whole period of four years, that is the figure reported, not the actual and maybe lower number of hours used for supervision. Fourth, the changes in my work situation experienced over the past decade (longer semesters, more students, continuously change of courses and curricula, and more administration of it all) are not reflected in the accounting of hours. That is, the form could have been filled out in a similar way ten years ago, and *the actual increase of my workload* that has occurred in the intervening period *is not revealed.*

Finding out what tasks that are valued and how they are valued in our daily activity as professors will most surely – at least partly – affect our future behaviour. Taking on tasks and the rating of hours will become intertwined. It is not the case, I believe, that one will stop taking on intellectually demanding and time-consuming tasks but rather that one will try to combine such tasks with tasks that provide "easy hours". How this affects us will most surely also depend on the academic habitus of our generations. Future generations, raised in a culture of accounting and documentation, as both its objects and its subjects, might be less willing to do what previous generations have done for "the sake of knowledge". The accounting of hours can accordingly be expected to play an increased role both in *what* is done and in *how* it is done in future academic life. It will be an instrument used to improve the conditions of the individual employee, perhaps at the cost of benefitting the collective. As long as the ratings merit individual rather than collective activities (apart from specific duties and assignments), *the individualization of professional teaching and administration activities will be strengthened.*

Most likely this will *make us all more or less calculating and demanding* regarding teaching and administration, hereby increasing the actual activity of calculation. Personal documentation of all forms will then increase, as will the time spend on such activities. As a result, we will be more involved in the design of the accounting of hours. We will want it to be more specific or specified in other ways, *and* we will debate the ratings.

Documenting one area will most likely raise the issue of reporting in other areas. The present duty of academic staff in Norwegian higher education to annually document and report research publications (in a database called "Cristin"), which are then rated, is but a first step. The whole business of crediting the dissemination of research has been raised, but due to the variety, complexity and monstrosity of the amount of documentation involved, this task has so far been abandoned.

What I am arguing is that the accounting of hours affects not only the tasks you do and how you do them but also your whole state of mind. You become or are expected to become one who counts and reports everything.

And you start to evaluate your own work as well as the work of your colleagues in these objectified terms, that is, from the perspective of ruling relations. Even critique hereof will then tend to be formulated as well as met by adjusted but similar objectified tools and standards.

This, however, is from the perspective of the employee. The use of the accounting of hours at the level of the department, faculty and university will, of course, affect its further workings, even for its employees. Grasping this dialectic of ruling is important if we wish to fully understand the workings of NPM.

When the accounting of hours is delivered to the administration, it is checked, and the corrected data is entered into the computer system. The new version is then returned to the employee for confirmation. The head of department and the head of administration then go through all of the accounts together to gain an idea of the workload of each employee and to determine whether any action is required. Employees who have exceeded the permitted numbers of hours one is allowed to save up (equal to the teaching workload of a semester, that is 449 hours) as well as those who are in deficit will be summoned to meetings to discuss how to resolve the situation. When the faculty contacts the department to be informed of cases with heavy surplus accounts, as is routine, the department can then explain how each of these situations will be resolved. The individual account is accordingly used by those in charge at each level in the chain of command, to supervise the level below, with the ultimate aim of supervising the work situation of the employee. By this means, the work of staff members is made "proper" – in relation to rules and regulations – and mainstreamed. But this is, of course, not the only use of the accounting of hours.

At the departmental level, the accounting of hours is also used to gain an insight into the amount of time – and thus money – that is being spent on different tasks. Such insights are used in discussions of what future actions to be taken. The department's research activity – documented through the ratings of publications, research grants and so forth – is included in these discussions. At staff meetings, such facts and figures for both teaching and research are presented in such a way as to include and make the whole staff accountable in the running of the department. We are thus all invited to see the big picture and to be proud, to worry and to contribute as best as we can to the running of the department as such. And our views are heard and appreciated by the management!

The accounting of hours presents a picture of the department as the truth. Facts and figures – based on our own accounting reports – are used to draw a picture that is hard to reject. It produces a picture of how it should be, not of how it is. On paper, time and money can be saved, and the accounts can be balanced at all levels. This ideal is then made true by affecting both one's understandings and actions. We try to live up to the norms and interpret our failure or success as issues for the individual. Of course, we all know that this picture does not tell the whole truth, but we have not developed, neither individually nor collectively, alternatives that we can present. *The accounting of hours and the research registration accordingly make the employee accountable not only for her own actions but also for the actions of the collective. They are tools through which the employee – in a democratic organization such as my department – is made accountable to the management at all levels.* Opposition in the form of cheating and sabotage is accordingly done in secret, the extent of which is yet to be known.

Back to the issue of theory and history

The very starting-point in the project presented above was a text that allowed me to study objectification processes in practice. This was done thoroughly ethnographically, and here the trans-local relations of the local relation were revealed, and accordingly how objectification was done. But the whole of trans-local relations entering into the work-day of an academic, that is, of other texts regulating the work of an academic, were not made visible. This shortcoming is a result of not taking the historical background presented above as a starting ground for the design of the study. Such a historical and contextual understanding would have made the study more accurate to the actual situation of academic work of today. Academic work is much more complex, fragmented and thoroughly ruled than I have succeeded to illustrate by focussing on just one text and set of activities. And further, and just as important, an understanding of the potential specificity of public welfare state ruling relations, could and should have informed an understanding of the NPM, which in my study was instead used in an objectified way as explanation. Hereby I missed a chance not only to understand fully the ambivalence I encountered in my study but also a chance to question the general concepts and understandings of NPM as well as of the welfare state.

I would argue that the lack of negative reactions at my department, indicated in the study above, makes sense also in light of the historical and theoretical understanding of the Norwegian educational context. The small conditions and close connections between politics and politicians, and university and scientific staff have constituted a fertile ground for reforms from "above". The trust and egalitarian culture from below have, on the other hand, guaranteed a legitimate and smooth implementation. Such relations, often understood as "culture", will affect which ruling devices that can be chosen and how they can be implemented. Theoretical and general understandings of NPM accordingly need to be challenged, so as to question the very role of the general claims. This is also true for those stemming from other IE studies.

In 2014 Dorothy E. Smith, together with Alison Griffith, published a book in which several studies illuminating NPM through institutional ethnographic studies are presented. In the introductory chapter theoretical understandings – some of them documented as empirically founded – regarding the relations of the nation state are presented as a back-drop to the studies. The ones mentioned here are the globalization of the economy, the change in language, trans-national standardization of everything and NPM as something that can be taught and learned, and management as an overall governing function and authority. Characteristic NPM steps are the use of management practices in public sectors, efficiency regarding resources, from hands-off to hands-on as management and explicit and accountable standards for performance, undermining professional judgement and discretion.

The empirical studies presented in this book focus on front-line work where professional judgement and discretion previously had an important role. The aim of presenting these studies, as stated by Griffith and Smith, is to find new characteristics of NPM and to learn more of its general contours and functioning. The studies do give substance to the theoretical understandings of NPM presented in the introductory chapter of this book, but without actually challenging or specifying them. And on a more general level, these characteristics are probably true also to public welfare management. Not looking for historical and theoretical specificity of ruling relations, however, make us miss a chance to see both specific variations and specific fundamental relations informing ruling devices and their implementation. It might, for example, be argued that in public welfare management the extensive ruling from above is more dialectic, allowing for feedback from below (giving new content to categories, setting them aside, inventing new categories and so forth). Professional judgement and discretion might accordingly play a more vital and different role during public welfare management. Institutional circuits – a concept that captures how a category or concept, for example publication scores within Academia, is used as governance from global relations to local, and back again (Griffith and Smith 2014, 12–13, illustrated on page 301) – might actually be the very part of the parcel in public welfare management. But, as I have argued previously, the very fact of ruling in the name of welfare, might make opposition less likely. On the other hand, one could argue that welfare ideology might be the very foundation for such opposition. Does welfare ruling and public management imply more obedience or more resistance, or maybe both? We obviously need to know more about if and how specifying ruling relations, such as welfare state ruling, makes a difference. And that is a theoretical and historical question that needs to be raised, also within IE studies.

Summing up, one could say that the approach of IE is important so as find out how NPM is done and perceived, but a historical and theoretical linking is necessary so as to make the results of IE studies actionable, politically as well as scientifically.

Outline to a theory of ruling relations

I have argued that in order to understand the doings in and of local relations and the way these relations are hooked up to trans-local relations, we need an overall, historical and theoretical understanding of the society in question. The lack of such a background might result in making the empirical studies from different societies quite alike, as variations on a theme, when in fact the very theme might be questioned. I have tried to argue how theoretical and historical understandings can inform, and yet be challenged by, empirical institutional ethnographic studies.

Along these lines an understanding of the welfare state accordingly challenges our understandings of ruling relations. Objectification in the name of welfare, aiming at equality (class, gender and ethnicity) – *Public Welfare Objectification* – results in specific experiences and reactions (characterized by ambivalence and insecurity). In the Nordic context of today such ruling permeates all aspects of everyday life to an extent that is unheard of in democracies elsewhere. As such *Nordic Public Welfare Objectification* presents a case where the more general patterns and implications of ruling can be highlighted and discussed. This is not to underestimate the differences between the Nordic countries regarding the design of welfare ruling of different spheres, such as for example higher education. Academic work is ruled in quite different ways in Finland, Denmark and Sweden. Still, it seems as if the good intentions of welfare state ruling "make it work" smoothly in the Nordic context, where, in other countries, such ruling might be taken as the brute force of the market that silence opposition and guarantees compliance. The methodological consequences of an approach like this; as to which local and trans-local relations we start and end our studies with, will always have to be problematized and discussed. But within these frames an IE approach will give a content to local and trans-local relations under study that might challenge the theoretical concepts and understandings we started out with, for example of the ruling relations of the welfare state. The important question to answer is: does a welfare state imply specific ruling relations, as to amount of ruling/ruling ambitions, areas of ruling and forms/means/ways of ruling? And what are the implications of the different designs of the welfare state as manifested in the different Nordic countries?

So, how could we then go about when trying to outline a theory of ruling relations that could inform institutional ethnographic studies? Starting out with a definition of ruling relations as objectified forms of consciousness and organization, constituted externally to particular people and places, creating and relying on textually based realities (Smith 2005, 227), we have to proceed to specify them in relation to different means of production. Feudalism, capitalism and socialism and their different ideological paradigm, for example fundamentalism and liberalism, imply variations regarding the ruling relations. Objectification under these different headings are founded on different kinds of relations and might have different purposes and are accordingly experienced and acted upon differently. The very role of objectification within these settings will vary. Since my aim here is to argue for welfare state management as a specific ruling relation, I will just very briefly sum up the principal foundations for such a position.

In Liberalism, the individual is the unit. Historically founded on the white male as the norm, the female (due to reproduction) and the coloured individual were however made to stick out (Pateman 1988). Not considering sex, race and skin colour, so as to allow equal treatment – for the sake of freedom – has taken long to put into praxis. Relations between citizens are regulated by a private contract (marriage and labour contract, for example) and between citizen and society by a social contract. In relation to fundamentalism this is often stated as a positive characteristic of *liberalistic ruling relations*. The aim is freedom to develop and change, on all levels.

Liberalism is a foundation for Capitalism, which is its historical economic expression. *Capitalistic ruling relations* are a specification of the liberalistic ruling relations, in that the individual becomes a commodity on a market and development is understood in terms of profit. The *welfare state*, finally, represents an intervention into capitalist ruling relations, trying to recognize and act upon inequality so as to achieve equality. The equal treatment of liberalism is accordingly added by unequal treatment aiming at equality. Hereby social characteristics enter the scene (again). The areas of intervention expand with the development of the welfare state. But its political government and its changes also change the actual organization and content of the intervention. And this vary from country to country. So, although, we might find at least two characteristics of welfare ruling relations; objectification aiming at equal treatment and equality, we need to empirically state the objectification of the ruling relations of a particular country. NPM accordingly has to be approached as part of the welfare ruling relations, as *New Public Welfare Management*, due to its functioning within the welfare-context.

In the name of welfare, aiming at equality not only regarding treatment but also regarding distribution of resources (in terms of class, gender and ethnicity), can objectification be made legitimate also in the eyes of its citizens in their daily doings, at work and at home? The ambivalence and insecurity demonstrated, not only in my study presented above but also in other IE studies, such as for example in Ann Christin Nilsen's work (Nilsen 2015, 2017) on day-care personnel and how their gaze towards children at risk, is constructed. Such studies can be interpreted as illuminations of how objectification is experienced and handled in everyday work. *"Public Welfare Objectification"* then, is it to be considered a specific form of ruling relations, resulting in specific reactions (ambivalence and insecurity) or non-reactions.

Taking *Public Welfare Objectification* as a starting-point, what are then the implications for understanding NPM? Is this maybe the clue to understand why NPM works "everywhere" but for very different reasons? Compliance due to brute force or good intentions are quite different reasons calling for different political actions.

Summing up. Linking up to theory – for the sake of knowledge

Over the last couple of decades several empirical studies have been done throughout the world, illuminating the kinds of knowledge that can be gained when using IE. And it is worth noting that since concepts and theories are not given the upper hand, IE is an approach that in spite of its white-west origin still can be embraced by "the others" (Mohanty 2003). The IE studies give valuable knowledge to how for example "New Public Management", "Racism", "Socialization", "Motherhood" and so forth is actually done. As a result of thorough empirical descriptive-analytical local studies – in and of particular relations and contexts – new understandings of relations and subjects we thought we already knew all about, are made possible. Political action, especially locally, is hereby also given both direction and fuel. But what about the implications of these local studies for the understandings of trans-local relations, and for our theoretical understandings? Above, I have tried to argue, for the sake of knowledge, both why and how we can hook up to general concepts and theories and yet be true to the very idea of IE, if that is not persuasive enough maybe a blunter reason can do the trick.

The quick and blunt answer to why we should hook up to sociological concepts and theories would be; because IE studies otherwise gets boring! One after another of in-depth descriptive-analytical studies of a local or-ganization of nursing, schooling, environmental agency and so forth, un-dertaken in different countries, have been published. But in the long run, how interesting and relevant can it get when the study is kept local and this local in addition is not "your local", or when it is difficult to hook up to so-cial relations you are familiar with?! That is, the setting of the local relations studied are most often hooked up to their trans-local relations but from there to the trans-local relations of your own societal context, at the most, only implicit connections are made. Of course, one can always get input and learn from studies of local, trans-local and ruling relations, however strange the social context. That is, we can learn how to go about and what to look for when doing IE research. But after a while, you feel you have had enough of detailed descriptions and it gets boring, at least for the non-local reader.

For the local reader and researcher, it is often quite the opposite. For the local researcher it is fun to do a local in-depth empirical study – I have done them myself – and people with same or similar work knowledge as described in the study love to hear and read about it. As such, it is definitely a way to increase the interest for IE locally – among the young ones and the open-minded intellectuals. And as I have mentioned above, it is also a way to mobilize political action on the subject in question. But to academics and researchers not primarily open (-minded) to new perspectives, who rather read IE studies to see "what is in it for me", these studies might seem of limited value. The lack of connection to sociological concepts and theory makes the implicit theoretical contribution of these studies easy to neglect or oversee. The empirical IE texts do not talk to sociological theory, and therefore sociologists do not have to talk back. Hereby, both sides are left on their own, not profiting by the challenge a serious dialogue would imply.

Let me stress though that I am talking about empirical IE studies and NOT about the epistemological works by Dorothy E. Smith. Her work is founded on this very dialogue with the sociological discipline (Smith 1992,

1996, 1991, 2001, 2005, Widerberg 2004, 2008). It might be quite difficult to apprehend but is the very opposite of being boring. Her texts are ground-breaking and thought provoking to the extent that one's sociological gaze – like my own! – is forever changed (Widerberg 2015a). It is in contrast to this revolutionary epistemology and the IE method of inquiry that the empirical studies along its line come short. They might thrill locally but "out of place, out of sight" they leave few traces.

If therefore empirical IE studies are perceived as a bit boring, both among us researchers who do them and among those researchers who don't do them, something apparently needs to be done, for all of us and for the sake of knowledge. For a start, it seems as if the perceived anti-theoretical approach of IE needs to be deconstructed and an IE approach that is hooked up to sociological theory to be outlined. Here I have tried to argue for the need of a historical and contextual understanding, to inform both design and analysis of a particular IE study. And how such an understanding in its turn calls for theoretical specification, in this case of ruling relations. By choosing academic work as an illustration – a sphere considered more autonomous than other spheres in welfare state management – the issue of its ruling relations as specific, as *public welfare state management* is raised. Hopefully this effort of mine can contribute to further theoretical discussions within and between the disciplines of IE and sociology.

Notes

1 Presented in English in Widerberg (2014).
2 There are, of course, a number of critical articles and books, such as for example the book by Ahlbäck Öberg and others (2016), but these have not resulted in any articulated actions within the labour unions organizing academic staff.
3 Research activities, expressed as publications and research money, are also being registered and counted but much more roughly and the consequences (awarding of money) are more directed to the institutional than the individual level.
4 A full description of the ethnographic study can be found in two articles by Widerberg (2014, 2015b), the latter also include ethnographic studies from other positions.

References

Ahlbäck Öberg, Shirin, Li Bennich-Björkman, Jorgen Hermansson, Anna Jarstad, Christer Karlsson and Sten Widman, eds. 2016. *Det hotade universitetet* [The threatened university]. Stockholm: Dialogos förlag.
Christensen, Tom, and Per Lægreid. 2007. "Introduction – theoretical approach and research questions." In *Transcending New Public Management: The Transformation of Public Sector Reforms*, edited by T. Christensen and Lægreid, 1–16. Aldershot: Ashgate.
Forseth, Ulla. 1989. *Uten mål og mening?: Målstyring av omsorgstjenesten* [*Without Goal or Meaning?: Goal Ruling of Public Care*]. Trondheim: Norsk institutt for sykehusforskning.

Griffith, Alison, and Dorothy E. Smith, eds. 2014. *Under New Public Management: Institutional Ethnographies of Changing Front-Line Work*. Toronto: University of Toronto Press.

Mohanty, Chandra Talpade. 2003. *Feminism without Borders*. Durham: Duke University Press.

Nilsen, Ann Christin. E. 2015. "På jakt etter styringsrelasjoner ved «tidlig innsats» i barnehagen [Chasing the ruling relations of «early childhood intervention» in Norwegian kindergartens]." Chap. 2 in *I hjertet av velferdsstaten: En invitasjon til institusjonell etnografi* [*In the Heart of the Welfare-State. An Invitation to Institutional Ethnography*], edited by K. Widerberg, 32–51. Oslo: Cappelen Damm.

Nilsen, Ann Christin E. 2017. *"Bekymringsbarn blir til: En institusjonell etnografi av tidlig innsats som styringsrasjonal i barnehagen."* [*Concern Children are 'Made Up': An Institutional Ethnography of Early Childhood Intervention in Norwegian Kindergartens*]. PhD diss., University of Agder.

Pateman, Carole. 1988. *The Sexual Contract*. Stanford: Stanford University Press.

Rasmussen, Bente. 2000. "Hjemmesykepleien som grådig organisasjon" [Home-nursing as a greedy organization]. *Tidsskrift for samfunnsforskning* 41 (1): 38–58.

Rasmussen, Bente. 2004. "Between endless needs and limited resources: the gendered construction of a greedy organisation." *Gender, Work and Organization* 11 (5): 506–525. doi: 10.1111/j.1468-0432.2004.00245.x

Slagstad, Rune. 2000. *The House of Knowledge in the Norwegian System*. Appendix 1 in NOU (Norges Offentlige Utredninger) [Norwegian Public Reports] 2000: 14.

Smith, Dorothy. E. 1992. "Sociology from women's experience: a reaffirmation." *Sociological Theory* 10 (1): 88–98. doi: 10.2307/202020

Smith, Dorothy. E. 1996. "Telling the truth after postmodernism." *Symbolic Interaction* 19 (3): 171–202. doi: 10.1525/si.1996.19.3.171

Smith, Dorothy. E. 1999. *Writing the Social: Critique: Theory and Investigations*. Toronto: University of Toronto Press.

Smith, Dorothy. E. 2001. "Texts and the ontology of organizations and institutions." *Studies in Cultures, Organizations and Societies* 7 (2): 159–198. doi: 10.1080/10245280108523557

Smith, Dorothy. E. 2005. *Institutional Ethnography: A Sociology for People*. Oxford: AltaMira Press.

Vabø, Mia. 2007. "Organisering for velferd: Hjemmetjenesten i en styringsideologisk brytningstid." [*Organizing for Welfare: Home-Nursing in a Time of Changes in Ruling Ideology*]. PhD diss., Universitetet i Oslo.

Widerberg, Karin. 2004. "Institutional ethnography: towards a productive sociology. An interview with Dorothy E. Smith." *Sosiologisk tidskrift* [*Norwegian Journal of Sociology*] 12 (2): 179–184.

Widerberg, Karin. 2008. "Dorothy E. Smith". Chap. 19 in *Key Sociological Thinkers*, edited by R. Stones, 311–322. Basingstoke: Palgrave Macmillan.

Widerberg, Karin. 2014. "In the best of interests? New public management, the welfare state, and the case of academic work: an ethnographic exploration." Chap. 5 in *The Elementary Forms of Sociological Knowledge*, edited by A. Blok and P. Gundelach, 81–94. Copenhagen: Department of Sociology, University of Copenhagen.

Widerberg, Karin. 2015a. "En invitasjon til institusjonell etnografi." [An invitation to institutional ethnography]. Chap. 1 in *I hjertet av velferdsstaten: En invitasjon til institusjonell etnografi.* [*In the Heart of the Welfare-State. An Invitation to Institutional Ethnography*], edited by K. Widerberg, 13–31. Oslo: Cappelen Damm.

Widerberg, Karin. 2015b. "Akademia: Om styring i den akademiske hverdag." [Academia: on ruling in academic everyday work]. Chap. 7 in *I hjertet av velferdsstaten: En invitasjon til institusjonell etnografi.* [*In the Heart of the Welfare-State. An Invitation to Institutional Ethnography*], edited by K. Widerberg, 143–163. Oslo: Cappelen Damm.

Part 2

Conversations between IE
and other theories

3 From translation of ideas to translocal relations

Shifting heuristics from Scandinavian Neo-Institutional Theory to Institutional Ethnography

Kjetil G. Lundberg and Hogne Lerøy Sataøen

Introduction

Neo-Institutional Theory focusses on how societal ideas and concepts at the macro level shape local practice at the micro level and has become a dominant school within organisational research (Greenwood et al. 2008; Lawrence et al. 2009, 52). As a perspective for studying welfare reforms, this school has become particularly popular in the Nordic countries. A particular research tradition has also been labelled "Scandinavian institutionalism" or "Scandinavian neo-institutionalism" (SNIT) (Czarniawska and Sevón 1996). SNIT began with a few Scandinavian and American researchers who were interested in how public reforms shape organisational practices (Boxenbaum and Strandgaard Pedersen 2009, 179). At Stanford University, Scandinavian researchers initially interested in public organisations and reforms were exposed to new organisational theories, including institutional theory (180). In the Nordic countries, the relatively easy access to the public sector inspired many field studies drawing on and developing institutional theory (Czarniawska 2008, 771). Tom Christensen and Per Lægreid (2013) claim that the empirical-analytical approach to the study of organisations conducted in a Nordic context has been significant for the development of SNIT.

SNIT has dealt with theorising organisational processes, such as modifications, cultivations and translations of organisational concepts (see, e.g., Sahlin-Andersson and Engwall 2002). Despite its being an influential approach to *understanding* translation, concerns have been raised about *how* these processes (transformations, cultivations and modifications) are studied. This includes concerns about the conceptualisation of power, agency and actors (Johansson 2009; Pallas and Kvarnström 2018) as well as about *how* processes and practices are studied (e.g., Damm Scheuer 2003; Nilsen 2007). In other words, the concerns relate to epistemological and methodological aspects of grasping translation.

Institutional ethnography (IE) emphasises linking the institutional with people's everyday experience. Attention is paid to practices and experiences in people's everyday lives, and to power relations that often are embedded in textually mediated processes within them. This methodological move may contribute to SNIT's understanding of processes whereby organisational ideas and concepts are transformed, cultivated and modified into specific organisational practices. Hence, this chapter offers a critical discussion of how IE can provide fruitful avenues for SNIT. We do this by critically revisiting central components and assumptions within SNIT. Neo-liberal reforms of the public sector and social policies are reshaping Nordic welfare state organisations. This includes implementation of private-sector management tools, marketisation incentives and an emphasis on individualising responsibility. In light of such processes, we argue that SNIT must attend to the complex relations between global and local processes of transformation, as well as concepts of power. We argue that IE can provide SNIT with important tools for addressing its methodological and epistemological shortcomings. More specifically, it may provide SNIT with tools for explicating how people are actively engaged in the shaping and reshaping of institutions, and it may furthermore support the formation of "intensive, rich, process-oriented, and qualitative approaches to the study of organizational practice" (Boxenbaum and Strandgaard Pedersen 2009, 196), which was SNIT's original aim.

Theoretical background: institutional theory and the development of Scandinavian neo-institutionalism

"New institutional theory" has become an important part of organisational studies, and in the Nordic region it has been seen as *the* dominant theory (Ahrne 2009).[1] SNIT has been depicted as a promising new direction for institutional theory (Greenwood et al. 2008) and has become an established field of research (Wæraas and Nielsen 2016). A basic assumption of new institutionalism is that organisations are not only rational and goal-oriented but also influenced by normative structures and values (DiMaggio and Powell 1991). Hence, new institutional theory was developed as a critique of rational, realistic and instrumental perspectives on organisations. It is influenced by social constructivism and is sensitive to historical and sociological contexts.

SNIT sees organisational change as a process in which organisational ideas *travel*. Eva Boxenbaum and Jesper Strandgaard Pedersen (2009, 184) argue that since the mid-1990s, the Scandinavian line of research departed from standard institutional theory, as it focussed upon the "lack of a theory of action" (19). Hence, in the early 1990s, human action and agency were identified as a blind spot in institutional analysis. This was also the prelude to the development of SNIT. As we will argue, however, the question of human action and agency within organisations still needs scrutiny and theorising, especially in light of the transformations that many Nordic public-sector organisations have undergone in recent decades.

Scandinavian neo-institutionalism and the issue of explaining change

We distinguish between two different strands of SNIT: one that is oriented towards loose coupling of organisations, and another where sense-making and translations of organisational ideas are central (Boxenbaum and Strandgaard Pedersen 2009; Lægreid 2007).[2] The first strand has focussed on how different components of organisations (e.g., decisions, talk, practices and structures) are decoupled from each other. The second strand, which is the focus of this chapter, is concerned with the interpretive processes within organisations and especially with how ideas are translated in specific contexts. Translation is understood as the process by which concepts, ideas and models travel across space and time, and are adapted to local contexts and specific organisations (Czarniawska and Sevón 2003; Røvik 2016, 292; Wæraas and Nielsen 2016, 243). The translation metaphor directs attention to the process and activity by which ideas and practices pass between organisations and where "local negotiations, experiences and motivations shape and give institutions their local form" (Lövgren 2017, 56). Røvik (2016) further argues that the aspects of "translation to" and "embedding" are at the forefront of most empirical studies. Within the Scandinavian tradition, the "embedding" organisation, and hence the receiver of ideas/concepts, is understood as active and interpretive. Traditional neo-institutional analyses, on the other hand, are macro-oriented and focus more on the *mechanisms* that cause organisations to converge over time.

SNIT's view of translation relies heavily on the work of John W. Meyer (e.g., 2010) and in particular his concept of world society. In Meyer's perspective, world society refers to the presence of a set of actors (nations, organisations, individuals) which have a shared understanding. Such understandings are often expressed in widely spread and highly accepted models, scripts, ideas or theories (Pallas and Kvarnström 2018). From the perspective of world society, organisations tend to adapt to similar global structural solutions. SNIT has further developed this idea by investigating processes of decontextualisation and contextualisation of such global ideas and concepts. Translation studies have in various ways tried to describe the processes whereby (new) organisational recipes, concepts and ideas transform organisational practice, often by means of case studies and process-oriented data (Boxenbaum and Strandgaard Pedersen 2009).

However, there has been some concern that organisational studies today, including Scandinavian translation studies, do not adequately incorporate individual actors and practices (Damm Scheuer 2003; McKenley 2007; Morris and Lancaster 2006; Røvik 2007, 116). For example, Elin Anita Nielsen argues that parts of the SNIT tradition, despite having an explicit interest in the recipient side of organisations, end up analytically perceiving the organisation as a coherent unity. Hence, SNIT does not grasp processes of power and agency within organisations (2007, 41–42).

Regarding the above, concerns have been raised that SNIT neglects the *level* of actors and action in organisations: "The closer one gets to the details of practice, what people actually do, the closer to the border of institutional theory's applicability and relevance one gets" (Johansson 2009, 14, *our translation*). In a similar vein, Nilsen (2007) argues that although SNIT makes use of concepts such as translation, imitation, editing and recipes to analyse complex transformation processes and their results, detailed descriptions and analysis of *how* the translation takes place are rare (43). Nilsen goes even further when questioning whether SNIT addresses the receiving-phase of organisational ideas and concepts at all.

Within a SNIT frame of reference, ideas and concepts are not translated "as they are" in time and space. On the contrary, they are analytically dealt with as abstractions that are concretised, for example, in models, texts and visual representations (Czarniawska and Joerges 1996). When such ideas and concepts travel from one field or organisation to another, "institutional carriers" transport them. These institutional carriers can be of four types: artefacts, routines, relational systems and symbolic systems (Scott 2007). Hence, the conceptualisations of carriers of ideas are quite general, and the translation processes tend to be analysed and described without including the involvement of, or implications for, human actors.

Furthermore, the concept of world society assumes a smooth and non-conflict-ridden diffusion of ideas, norms and theories (Pallas and Kvarnström 2018). Hence, descriptions of diffusion processes often lack dimensions of power: "There could be much to gain in Scandinavian Institutionalism from an increased focus inspired by ANT on negotiations, power dynamics and micro-tactics in the translation of managerial ideas and practices" (Wæraas and Nielsen 2016, 250). While SNIT employs high levels of abstraction and a rich vocabulary when describing and analysing changing organisations, and particularly the role of (new) global concepts and ideas (e.g., reforms), relations of power often remain downplayed or uncommunicated. This results in a loss of people's experience in the theoretical scheme. The *people* described within SNIT are not assumed to be "sovereign actors with *a priori* interests that drive their behavior" (Suarez and Bromley 2016, 146). Instead, actors have been called "soft actors" (Meyer 1996), emphasising a view of actors as dependent on external sources. Although actors and actions exist in this analytical scheme, they tend to be constrained by exogenous factors: "identity and activity always involve ideas, which always have exogenous aspects, and [...] organisational behaviour involves the routine use and modification of them" (Meyer 1996, 244).

In the following sections, we argue that IE can contribute to a deeper understanding of how ideas and concepts work in and shape the local level of welfare organisations, as these ideas have concrete and practical implications for bureaucrats, professionals, front-line workers and welfare service recipients.

The introduction of institutional ethnography to Scandinavian Neo-Institutional Theory: people's standpoint, chains of actions and ruling relations

At first glance, IE may appear to be an unconventional match with institutional theory. While SNIT rests on critique of the rational and realist school of organisational studies (Pallas and Kvarnström 2018) and recognises social constructivism as a key source of inspiration. Dorothy Smith began to develop IE as response to "abstract empiricism". IE rests on a standpoint epistemology and a Marxist and feminist ontology (Hart and McKinnon 2010; Smith 2005, 2006; Tummons 2018). Smith was motivated by the idea of developing a research programme that is not only about people but also for people.

On closer examination, these differences may be harnessed to form a different viewpoint. We agree with Jonathan Tummons, who advocates for using IE together with other theoretical and methodological perspectives "through which IE can be revised or reimagined through the careful and critical use of other compatible theories of social practice or research methodologies". Tummons points to the importance of establishing the epistemological and ontological alignment between different approaches that are being used and brought together. He also draws attention to three particular affordances that IE has to offer other approaches: (1) a focus on institutions; (2) a focus on the ruling relations and the capacity to shift the researcher's gaze beyond the locally observed to the translocal; and (3) a focus on accounting for power, especially through the creation, production and distribution of texts (Tummons 2018).

To make our case for how SNIT and IE can be combined in research, we will focus on methodological issues relating to people's standpoint, and mapping chains of actions relating to translocal ruling relations.

The most fundamental idea of IE is that local and current affairs in people's lives, rather than global and abstract organisational ideas and concepts, must serve as the analytical starting point for organisational analysis. Dorothy Smith stresses that people are located knowers. Knowledge therefore needs to be grounded in what people actually do. By starting with actual work, one can explore what Smith understands as everyday problematics: "[A] problematic [...] begins in the actualities of people's lives with a focus of investigation that comes from how they participate in or are hooked up into institutional relations" (2005, 227). Empirically, the study of problematics in everyday life is a prism or "first order" analysis for understanding global ruling relations.

IE functions as an empirically oriented perspective that also encompasses a rather specific methodology. This methodology is useful for exploring how institutional conditions play out in people's experienced reality, in order to show how activities and lived life are embedded and linked to the activities of others. As in traditional ethnography, in-depth studies of social action and behaviour (as studied through analysis of interviews, observations and texts, for example) are important in IE. However, IE departs from traditional ethnography in its emphasis on understanding how actualities and problematics in people's lives are embedded in broader social relations (Smith 2006).

IE's methodology seeks to grasp the coordination of activities. Such activities are largely textually mediated, and IE often explores practices of text-mediation: how a text becomes activated – and activates – a social relation between an individual and the larger institutional apparatus. By doing this, institutional ethnographers explore how people's lives are embedded in power structures of ruling relations.

The concept of ruling relations is closely related to Smith's conceptualisation of institutions:

> I use the terms "institutional" and "institution" to identify a complex of relations forming part of the ruling apparatus, organized around a distinctive function – education, health care, law, and the like. In contrast to such concepts as bureaucracy, "institution" does not identify a determinate form of social organization, but rather the intersection and coordination of more than one relational mode of the ruling apparatus [...] We might imagine institutions as nodes or knots in the relations of the ruling apparatus to class, coordinating multiple strands of action into a functional complex.
>
> (1987, 160)

Interestingly, this understanding of institutions has a lot in common with SNIT's concept of institutions. In both IE and SNIT, institutions are understood as social constructs, in which cultural and cognitive dimensions are of importance. Institutions are viewed in both perspectives as open systems that are strongly influenced by socially constructed value systems (see Lundberg and Sataøen 2014, 39–40). As Smith (2005) stresses, the socially constructed institutions must be viewed in light of wider historical-material processes. The overlapping conceptualisations of institutions in the two perspectives create space for dialogue.

There is also a parallel between Meyer's notion of "world society" and Smith's concept of "ruling relations". Both concepts are a part of a conceptual apparatus that aims to study the linking and transfers of global – or at least, macro – processes. With its focus on transformations, cultivations and modifications of organisational concepts, SNIT has also largely concerned itself with introducing metaphors (e.g., "fashion", "virus" and "recipes"). Therefore, parts of the SNIT school can be criticised for putting analytical emphasis on concepts, ideas and recipes at the expense of the real people who activate them.

In IE, institutional and structural factors, such as organisational concepts, ideas or trends, enter into the analysis by being identified in people's everyday life experiences. Research within this tradition investigates how people's activities are connected with others and coordinated translocally through ruling relations: "The concept of ruling relations directs attention to the distinctive translocal forms of social organization and social relations mediated by texts [...] They are objectified forms of consciousness [...] constituted externally to particular people" (Smith 2005, 227). The translocal thus simultaneously structures activities at the local, observable level. The link between epistemology and methodology is the starting point and the aim of research, as well as the means of knowledge production (Widerberg 2007).

Discussion

The preceding presentation indicates both differences and similarities between IE and SNIT as research strategies. Some of these are highlighted in Table 3.1.

The integration of SNIT and IE poses several challenges. The two analytical perspectives privilege different levels of analysis and emphasise different concepts in their analytical schemes (see Table 3.1). At the same time, both require micro-level and context-sensitive analysis in order to show and discuss relations between the local and the global. We do not advocate a position where SNIT and IE are fully integrated. Instead, we argue that a modest integration of the perspectives, where concepts and methodological strategies are used eclectically, can be fruitful for empirical research. An integrative approach putting concepts, ideas and perspectives from IE to work

Table 3.1 Integrating SNIT and IE

Methodological aspects	SNIT	IE
Research focus	How ideas travel, loose couplings, translations	Translocal relations, including coordination of and implications for people
Actors and standpoint	Abstractions, "Soft actors"	People, located knowers, everyday problematics
Conceptualisations of institutions and the institutional	Socially constructed value systems	Socially constructed value systems
Mediators between different levels	Institutional carriers (artefacts, routines, relational systems, symbolic systems)	Texts and textually mediated relations
Concepts related to the macro level	World Society	Institutional ruling relations
Conceptualisation of power	Possessed by the organisation. Translation	Exercised in ruling relations. Translocal

in SNIT can be valuable for developing a more complex understanding of translational and transformational processes of management ideas. In this conclusion, we will demonstrate how concepts from IE can re-orient SNIT towards its foundation: the issue of agency in organisations.

A modest integration of IE and SNIT is especially promising in relation to questions of how ideological discourses enter the everyday life of organisations and the people acting there – where the work of translation, as well as translocal coordination, are likely to happen. Studies within IE often focus on reproduction and standardisation, whereas SNIT research tends to emphasise translation and change. As both processes are ongoing in organisational life, IE and SNIT are suitable for addressing different dimensions of social relations, the coordination of activities and what actually happens – a core ambition of IE. The two viewpoints can be combined to grasp the sometimes conflicting and ambivalent processes of change and governing in institutional complexes.

SNIT focusses on how ideas and models are adapted to local contexts, and thus how today's organisations are influenced by concepts that travel across time and space (cf. world society). In a sense, IE's area of interest also ties in with how contemporary lives are influenced by global structures and ideas, though IE uses different methodological approaches and epistemological orientations. The translations that SNIT researchers aim to study are textually mediated. IE offers a methodology that maps these transformations through the textual mediations while at the same time aiming to uncover the specific chains of actions that occur between "world society" and particular human beings. In doing so, it reveals power implications of translation work:

> For Smith, concepts and symbols do not *only* represent, rather, they are the primary means of action within text-mediated power relations [...] The coordinated effects in the real world are mediated by the hyper-real world where abstract symbols are manipulated in texts.
>
> (Hart and McKinnon 2010, 1046)

Let us illustrate this with an example. Since the turn of the millennium, individual plans, action plans and other quasi-contractual and person-centred documents have been implemented in a range of welfare organisations both in the Nordic countries and elsewhere (Breimo 2012; Lundberg 2012; Nilsen and Kildal 2009). This is part of a trend that emphasises putting the individual at the centre, tailoring services, enhancing participation and empowering service users to govern their own lives, and that involves discourses – ideas – that travel across institutions and across national borders. In Nordic unemployment programmes, individual activity plans have become central tools. In the practical use of such plans, checkboxes and categorisations of questions are used to structure administrative forms. The checkboxes and categories serve as textual instruments which the employment officers make use of in interpretation. Studies inspired by IE indicate that these figures and checkboxes become more salient than the actual problems and challenges of the clients (Åsheim 2018; Lundberg 2012). Putting the IE methodology into practice, these studies show how the plans link the activities of employees at the local level to higher levels of the work-and-welfare institutional complex.

Putting SNIT into practice, on the other hand, would involve focussing mainly on the "translation to" and "embedding" aspects of individual activity plans. Hence, particular organisations would likely be the empirical starting point, as SNIT aims to understand what is going on when global ideas and concepts "travel into" specific organisations (Røvik 2007). The strength of SNIT lies in the analysis of organising and organisations – their histories, developments and practices. With regard to activity plans, SNIT could provide an understanding of how and why different organisations translate ideas of individualisation, participation and empowerment into organisational practices, and explain potential organisational variations. For instance, studies of how the concept of LEAN has travelled into hospital organisations explain general principles for translating management concepts and provide an understanding of the logics of implementations (Andersen and Røvik 2015). IE takes this a step further, searching for the link to activities and consequences for people. Aspects of the individual plans can therefore be analysed as a particular technology of standardisation, represented through texts. These texts and the practices embedded in them subordinate the experiences and challenges of people to the institutional, as the translocal has local effects. IE's concept of translocal relations, and its methodological imperative related to following actors-as-persons, can be fruitful, as illustrated by the example of individual action plans (see also Chapter 1 in this volume). Hence, instead of SNIT's perspective on "soft actors", where individual actors "change with changing ideologies and models" (Meyer 1996, 243), knowledge must also be grounded in located knowing and work – what people actually do in everyday settings. By doing this, SNIT can become more potent in understanding "negotiations, power dynamics and micro-tactics in the translation of managerial ideas and practices", which Wæraas and Nielsen (2016) proposed as a focus for future SNIT-inspired analyses.

The example of individual activity plans also illustrates – on a macro level – how neo-liberal ideas of emphasising individualisation through "customised services" and self-government are playing out in concrete settings. It further illustrates how such global ideas are impacting on people. Within a SNIT frame of reference, neo-liberal ideas tend to be described as shifting boundaries between private and public services or in terms of the organising of decision-making processes. When ideas from IE are brought in, other effects of neo-liberalisation on welfare state organisations become visible, namely the consequences for individuals of a situation where people are valued based on their ability to adapt and adjust to rapid changes in the environment, and where people to larger extent are made responsible for the consequences of their own market-based free choices. As already discussed, IE's analytical strategies start from the standpoint of people and what they do, rather than particular pre-defined (management) concepts or ideas. By exploring such problematics, one may better understand how local practices are related to, and even embedded in, "the social", and by identifying how ideas and concepts are activated in local and observable contexts through textual mediation, IE can help us understand how institutions are shaped and reshaped by human actions. Interestingly enough, this was also a core puzzle for the first neo-institutionalists (cf. Meyer and Rowan 1977).

Notes

1 It is common to distinguish between "old" and "new" institutionalism, where the old is normatively oriented while the new is cognitively oriented (DiMaggio and Powell 1991; Scott 2003). The old institutional approach (primarily developed by Selznick 1957) emerged in response to the dominant rational and partly normative organisational theories of the 1950s and 1960s (Scott 2003).
2 See Wæraas and Nielsen (2016) for an in-depth presentation of translation theory's academic heritage in actor network theory, knowledge-based theory and Scandinavian institutionalism.

References

Ahrne, G. 2009. "Introduktion: Vad händer när nyinstitusjonell teori inte längre är ny?" *Nordiske Organisasjonsstudier* 11(3): 3–4.

Andersen, H. and Røvik, K. A. 2015. "Lost in Translation: A Case-Study of the Travel of Lean Thinking in a Hospital." *BMC Health Services Research* 15: 401.

Åsheim, H. (2018). "Aktivitetsplan som styringsverktøy." *Søkelys på arbeidslivet* 4: 242–258.

Boxenbaum, E. and Pedersen, J. S. 2009. "Scandinavian Institutionalism – A Case of Institutional Work." In *Institutional Work: Actors and Agency in Institutional Studies of Organizations*, edited by Thomas, L., Suddaby, R. and Leca, B., 178–204. Cambridge: University Press.

Breimo, J. 2012. "'Bundet av bistand' – En institusjonell etnografi om organisering av rehabiliteringsprosesser." PhD diss., Universitetet i Nordland.

Christensen, T. and Lægreid, P. 2013. "SCANCOR and Norwegian Public Administration Research Development." *Nordiske Organisasjonsstudier* 15(4): 91–110.

Czarniawska, B. 2008. "How to Misuse Institutions and Get Away with It: Some Reflections on Institutional Theory(ies)." In *The Sage Handbook of Organizational Institutionalism*, edited by Greenwood, C., Oliver, C., Sahlin, K. and Suddaby, R., 769–782. Thousand Oaks, CA: Sage Publications.

Czarniawska, B. and Joerges, B. 1996. "Travels of Ideas." In *Translating Organizational Change*, edited by Czarniawska, B. and Sevón, G., 13–47. Berlin: Walter de Gruyter.

Czarniawska, B. and Sevón, G. eds. 1996. *Translating Organizational Change.* Berlin: Walter de Gruyter

Czarniawska, B. and Sevón, G. eds. 2003. *The Northern Lights: Organization Theory in Scandinavia.* Copenhagen: Copenhagen Business Press.

Damm Scheuer, J. 2003. "Patientforløb i praksis – en analyse af en idés oversættelse i mødet med praksis." PhD diss., Copenhagen business school.

DiMaggio, P. and Powell, W. 1991. "Introduction." In *The New Institutionalism in Organizational Analysis,* edited by Powell, W. and DiMaggio, P., 1–38. Chicago, IL: The University of Chicago Press.

Greenwood, R., Oliver, C. Sahlin, K. and Suddaby, R. 2008. "Introduction." In *The Sage Handbook of Organizational Institutionalism,* edited by Greenwood, R., Oliver, C., Sahlin, K. and Suddaby, R., 1–46. Thousand Oaks, CA: Sage Publications.

Hart, R. J. and McKinnon, A. 2010. "Sociological Epistemology: Durkheim's Paradox and Dorothy E. Smith's Actuality." *Sociology* 44(6): 1038–1054.

Johansson, R. 2009. "Vid den institutionella analyses gränser: Institutionell organisationsteori i Sverige." *Nordiske organisasjonsstudier* 11(3): 5–22.

Lægreid, P. 2007. "Organization Theory – The Scandinavian Way." *Nordiske organisasjonsstudier* 9(1): 77–82.

Lawrence, T. B., Suddaby, R. and Leca, B. eds. 2009. *Institutional Work: Actors and Agency in Institutional Studies of Organization.* Cambridge: Cambridge University Press.

Lövgren, D. 2017. "Dancing Together Alone: Inconsistencies and Contradictions of Strategic Communication in Swedish Universities." PhD diss., Uppsala University.

Lundberg, K. G. 2012. "Uforutsigbare relasjoner. Brukererfaringer, Nav-reformen og levd liv." PhD diss., University of Bergen.

Lundberg, K. G. and Sataøen, H. L. 2014. "Institusjonell etnografi – Ei mogleg inspirasjonskjelde for den skandinaviske institusjonsteorien?" *Nordiske organisasjonsstudier* 16(1): 30–50.

McKenley, W. 2007. "The March of History: Juxtaposing Histories." *Organization Studies* 28(1): 31–36.

Meyer, J. 1996. "Otherhood: The Promulgation and Transmission of Ideas in the Modern Organizational Environment." In *Translating Organizational Change,* edited by Czarniawska, B. and Sevón, G., 240–252. Berlin: Walter de Gruyter.

Meyer, J. 2010. "World Society, Institutional Theories, and the Actor." *Annual Review of Sociology* 36: 1–20.

Meyer, J. and Rowan, B. 1977. "Institutionalized Organizations: Formal Structure as Myth and Ceremony," *American Journal of Sociology* 83(2): 340–363.

Morris, T. and Lancaster, Z. 2006. "Translating Management Ideas." *Organization Studies* 27(2): 207–233.

Nilsen, E. 2007. "Oversettelsens mikroprosesser. Om å forstå møtet mellom en global idé og lokal praksis som dekontekstualisering, kontekstualisering og nettverksbygging." PhD diss., University of Tromsø.

Nilsen, E. and Kildal, N. 2009. "New Contractualism in Cocial Policy and the Norwegian Fight Against Poverty and Social Exclusion." *Ethics and Social Welfare* 3: 303–321.

Pallas and Kvarnström 2018. "On Meyer: Public Relations in a Context of World Society, Soft Actors and Rationalized De-coupling." In *Public Relations and Social Theory,* edited by Ihlen, Ø., van Ruler, B. and Fredriksson, M., 1–20. London: Routledge.

Røvik, K. A. 2007. *Trender og translasjoner. Ideer som former det 21. århundrets organisasjoner.* Oslo: Universitetsforlaget.

Røvik, K. A. 2016. "Knowledge Transfer as Translation: Review and Elements of an Instrumental Theory." *International Journal of Management Reviews* 18(3): 290–310.

Sahlin-Andersson, K. and Engwall, L. 2002. *The Expansion of Management Knowledge.* Stanford, CA: Stanford Business Books.

Scott, R. 2003. *Organizations: Rational, Natural and Open Systems.* 5th edition. Englewood Cliffs, NJ: Prentice Hall.

Scott, R. 2007. *Institutions and Organizations.* Thousand Oaks, CA: Sage.

Selznick, P. 1957. *Leadership in Administration. A Sociological Interpretation.* Berkeley: University of California Press.

Smith, D. 1987. *The Everyday World as Problematic. A Feminist Sociology.* Boston, MA: Northeastern University Press.

Smith, D. 2005. *Institutional Ethnography. A Sociology for People.* Oxford: AltaMira Press, Rowman & Littlefield Publishers.

Smith, D. ed. 2006. *Institutional Ethnography as Practice.* Lanham, MD: Rowman and Littlefield.

Suarez, D. F and Bromley, P. 2016. "Institutional Theories and Levels of Analysis: History, Diffusion and Translation." In *World Culture Re-Contextualised: Meaning Constellations and Path-Dependencies in Comparative and International Education Research,* edited by Schriewer, J., 139–159. London: Routledge.

Tummons, J. 2018. "Institutional Ethnography, Theory, Methodology, and Research: Some Concerns and Some Comments." *Studies in Qualitative Methodology* 15: 147–162.

Widerberg, K. 2007. "Institusjonell etnografi – en ny mulighet for kvalitativ forskning?" *Sosiologi i dag* 37(2): 7–28.

Wæraas, A. and Nielsen, J. A. (2016). "Translation Theory 'Translated': Three Perspectives on Translation in Organizational Research." *International Journal of Management Reviews* 18: 236–270.

4 Complementing theories

Institutional ethnography and organisation theory in institutional analysis

Cathrine Talleraas

Introduction

For my PhD project I studied the Norwegian welfare state's encounter with people who lead transnational lives. I explored this through an institutional analysis where I combined concepts and tools from institutional ethnography (IE), as developed by Dorothy Smith, and organisation theory, most notably institutional theory (IT).[1] This chapter presents my journey as I discovered and applied institutional theoretical insights from both these strands of thought. The aim of this chapter is to illustrate why and how I was sensitive towards both IE and IT during the early and final stages of my research. In doing so, I seek to inspire scholars in these two fields and beyond, to explore the latent opportunities of bridging IE and IT. Through a sensitivity to both these theoretical strands, I found ways to combine and complement the two approaches. Both IE and IT thus became central to the development of my methodology and analysis and yielded insights that I might not have gained through one of the approaches alone. I term this approach "sensitive complementing".

This chapter is divided into three parts. First, I briefly describe my PhD project and explain why I decided to draw on both IE and IT within an already multidisciplinary study. Next, I explain how I integrated concepts from IE and IT in an analytical framework and briefly argue how the traditions and epistemologies of Nordic IE and Scandinavian organisational theory enable such a combination. Finally, I illustrate how sensitivity to concepts and tools from IE and IT – such as "institutional circuits", "institutional soul" and "institutionalisation" – influenced my methodology and analysis through two specific examples drawn from my PhD research.

Entering uncharted territory: using IE to study bureaucracy and transnationalism

The Norwegian welfare state and people who lead transnational lives

The overarching objective of my PhD project was to explore the encounter between the Norwegian welfare state and an increasingly mobile population.

A growing number of people lead what can be called "transnational lives". They may live in one country while they work in another, or live and work in several countries and travel between them. Some may live primarily in one country while still accessing services and collecting welfare benefits (e.g., pensions) from another. In this increasingly transnational reality, the premise for states' welfare delivery is changing. On this basis, I sought to explore how the Norwegian welfare system adjusts its services to accommodate this growing group of "transnationals". While the Norwegian social security system was created to ensure the welfare of largely sedentary citizens, the system must adapt to provide benefits and services to a mobile and diverse group of people. These transnational clients include a broad array of people, such as researchers, military personnel, students abroad, diplomats and their families, retirees living in Spain, commuters who criss-cross daily the border to Sweden, and foreign workers employed in the oil or shipping sectors – to mention just a few.

In this context, the everyday work of welfare state bureaucrats changes. These bureaucrats face a particular set of challenges in their work to assess and deliver the appropriate national social security benefits to a transnational population. In my PhD project, I analysed this situation from the bureaucrats' standpoint. I sought to explore their experiences with, and perceptions of, the relations between transnational clients and the Norwegian social security system. I did this as an IE study with the overall aim of producing knowledge not only *about* the people involved in the encounter but also *for* the people involved (Smith 2005; Widerberg 2015). I developed my inquiry from the bureaucrats' standpoint to understand the relational confines in which they operated and how the institutional and ruling relations shaped how they encountered, experienced, and accommodated transnational clients. This encounter was the problematic I wanted to explore from the standpoint of the bureaucrats – the "knowers" (Smith 2005, 38–24).

The Norwegian Labour and Welfare Administration (NAV) is the largest welfare provider in Norway, and it provides benefits to people who live within, across, and outside state borders. NAV administrates one-third of the Norwegian national budget and takes responsibility for all public social security benefits, such as pensions, child benefits, sickness benefits, unemployment benefits, work assessment allowance, and cash-for-care benefit. As many benefits are universal and not need-based, NAV's clients include all segments of the population – including those who lead transnational lives. I therefore chose to focus my research on NAV, intending to examine "the inside" through interviews, extended fieldwork, participant observations, and a collection of texts (Smith 2005, 2006). To understand NAV's encounter with transnationals, I focussed on bureaucrats working in the "international branch" of NAV – those persons who dealt with clients who had lived, were currently living, or planned to live abroad.

I selected my field sites based on my initial interest in IE and organisation theory. Drawing on the concept of translocal relations (Smith 2005), I expected that some links and power relations between units and people would be traceable only during fieldwork, through the exploration of people's work knowledge, who they contacted, and what they did. For this reason, I sought to keep my selection and number of fieldwork sites open until the end of the fieldwork. I also decided *a priori* on some sites, and some of the criteria for inclusion: being aware of the theoretical importance given to horizontal as well as vertical structures in Nordic public organisations and the importance of these concepts in both instrumental and institutional organisation theories in Scandinavia (Christensen et al. 2013), I chose fieldwork sites representing the multiple scales and localities within the institution. While awareness of structures or ruling relations is relevant in IE, I was compelled by my readings of public sector organisation theory to ensure that all hierarchical levels were included in the study from the start.

In Figure 4.1, I map out the units in which I conducted fieldwork. All of these units are part of the "international branch" of NAV, which deals with cross-border social security issues. The two large circles represent larger offices, and the medium sized circles represent the Directorate and the National Office for International Social Security. The small circles are administrative sub-units within the larger offices.

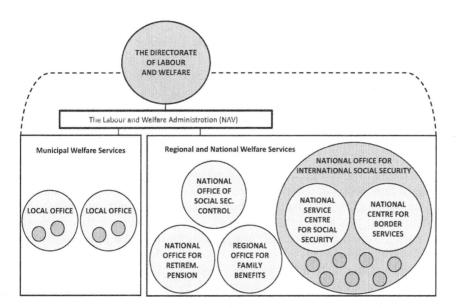

Figure 4.1 Units of the "International Branch" of NAV included in this study.

Why institutional ethnography?

As a human geographer working in the field of migration studies and welfare state research, I discovered IE by chance. During my PhD studies, I was affiliated with the Institute of Sociology and Human Geography at the University of Oslo. Due to the institutional proximity between sociologists and human geographers, I soon heard of the sociologist Karin Widerberg's work on IE. While IE has recently gained firmer footing in human geography (Billo and Mountz 2016), it was already well established among sociologists. I was introduced to IE when I stumbled across Widerberg's notes from her conversations with Dorothy Smith on the Department's website (Widerberg 2004). As an overall approach for an institutional analysis, IE appealed to me. I ordered all I could find by Smith from the university library and started exploring the vast landscape of IE.

This moment coincided with my search for an analytical framework and, until then, I had focussed my reading on organisational theory. I had become particularly inspired by the central tenet of IT: namely the idea that organisations are not necessarily rational and goal-oriented but rather develop and are influenced by norms, values and informal structures (DiMaggio and Powell 1991; Scott 1995). After examining Smith's work more closely, I found IE could add much of what I had been missing with IT: a more critical analytical approach, an orientation towards subjective standpoints, and a methodological and conceptual toolbox with which to discover the social from the standpoints of those who are ruled.

> In institutional ethnography it all seems to come together; texts and relations organising the social across time and space. Is this a sociological response to grasping globalisation?

This question, posed by Widerberg (2004, 179) in her interview with Dorothy Smith, illustrates why I pursued IE as a conceptual framework. A central aim underlying my PhD was to better understand how the social – the welfare system and its relations to transnational individuals – is organised across time and space. When I looked at how increasing transnational living patterns – a facet of globalisation – influence national structures, I also scrutinised how social and institutional relations were translocally connected to individuals "below", including both clients and bureaucrats. Moreover, I found that just as transnationals and welfare service clients experience exclusion from the relations of ruling, the work of the bureaucrats dealing with transnational cases were treated as lower ranking in the organisational hierarchy of the "nationally-oriented" NAV.

Thus, the critical feminist perspective in IE appealed to me (Smith 1987, 1) because the bureaucrats dealt with a minority group (i.e., transnationals) and because these bureaucrats were part of the "ruled" rather than the "ruling" in NAV. Indeed, during my fieldwork many of the informants underscored their subordinate position in NAV. While the focus on national casework was compared to "an 80%-capacity motorway", they said NAV's focus on international casework was deemed a mere "forest trail" in the institutional landscape.

Sensitive complementing of IT and IE

I intended to use IE as an overall analytical framework; however, as time passed, I discovered the potential to relate IE to the concepts I knew from the institutional strand of organisational theory. Taking inspiration from Pettigrew (1985), Roness (1997) has identified four modes of engaging several theories in an organisational or institutional study:

1 "prioritising" by sticking to one approach;
2 "contrasting" by comparing several;
3 "synthesising" by including theories to develop a new combination; and
4 "complementing" by combining several approaches in the same framework.

For my research, I chose the "complementing" mode, using different elements from IT and IE where I deemed them useful. I call my approach sensitive complementing as I did not rigorously apply all facets of IE and IT. In the end, my institutional analytical framework consisted of a specific and strategic selection of tools and concepts taken from IE and IT.

Nordic openness

IE and IT are complex in nature and the ways they are applied. There is not one obvious or natural way to combine these ideas in an analytical framework, and the open-endedness of both approaches enables multiple combinations. IE offers a framework of ideas, but no rules or specific guidelines that must be followed (Smith 2006). Particularly in the Nordics, researchers are encouraged to use the parts of IE that are relevant to their investigations, and there are several examples of studies where IE has been successfully combined with other methods and theories (see Widerberg 2015 for examples).

Depending on the research focus, discipline, or other factors, organisational researchers often apply different theoretical approaches. Indeed, one of the particularities of organisation theory in the Nordics – and in Scandinavian IT more specifically – is disciplinary openness. Within that approach, "dialoguing with basic disciplines has helped the organisation theory perspective to pursue a broader intellectual and societal agenda" (Thoenig 2007). The interdisciplinarity of both IE and IT in the Nordics thus allows researchers, like myself, to be sensitive to elements from both approaches as the same time.

Epistemological junctions

Epistemologically, IT and IE share some similar grounds. This similarity can be illustrated through the historical development of organisation theory, which has crossed several academic traditions and disciplines at different points in time (Christensen 2012). In general, the multiple perspectives within organisation theory can be explained as falling within one of two major approaches: a top-down (instrumental) versus a bottom-up (institutional) approach (Bogason and Sørensen 1998; Christensen et al. 2013). In pragmatic terms, these two approaches represent an historical trajectory from when organisations were studied from an economic perspective as goal-oriented entities – where "formal structure matters" (Christensen 2012) – to more recent times, when institutional values, the agency of the individuals within the organisations, and the broader organisational context have come to the fore. Instrumental organisation theory is thus informed by a functionalist kind of positivism "concerned with the generation of causal theories, as far general in scope as possible" (Donaldson 2005, 17).

Partly in parallel, and partly in response to this development, a new strand of theories emerged that enhanced the focus on the development of organisational values and informal norms. For example, critical organisation studies increased the focus on power and inequality (Burrell and Morgan 1979). In the 1950s, Selznick developed the idea of institutionalism further, combining early and new theoretical developments that fronted a view of institutions as social systems with informal norms, values, and cultures (Selznick 1949, 1957). This neo-institutional strand of institutionalism represented an anti-positivist allegiance, and the idea that there were no "social facts" found greater acceptance among scholars (Tsoukas and Knudsen 2005).

The epistemological pillars of IT resemble the feminist standpoint epistemology inherent in IE, particularly the idea that all knowledge production is value-laden and the result of historical processes (Lund 2015; Smith 2005). To understand the everyday world as it is experienced from the standpoint of the research subjects, the entry point of IE is people's everyday words and actions, and the institutional realities, including texts, that shape their experiences (Smith 2005). IE's focus on individuals within institutions, and the social relations in which they are embedded (Smith 1987, 2005), shares traits with the social-constructivist tradition in IT, with an empirical focus on the micro-level nuances, subjectivities, and "living" organisations (Christensen et al. 2013). There are, however, notable differences between the two approaches. While IT flags interpretivism, for instance, Smith argues that it is possible to minimise interpretation by allowing for "self-representation" of participants.

When looking at the specific traditions of organisational theory in the Nordics, it makes sense to argue that combining IT and IE can be particularly useful in this context. Indeed, Lundberg and Sataøen (2014) suggest that IE has a lot to offer (Scandinavian) IT and argue that IE can inspire using other types of data, which can lead to a different type of analysis, incorporate higher levels of reflection (2014), and provide fruitful avenues to address human actors and practices of power in institutional studies (see also Lundberg and Sataøen's chapter in this volume). Another argument for a local match relates to how the "Scandinavian" tradition of IT developed in relation to the nature of public organisations. In contrast to public organisations in the US, for example, Scandinavian public organisations are considered culturally and structurally homogeneous. They cater more to collective norms and values than to the rationality of the individual. Having a larger public sector than most other countries, public administration in the Nordics is characterised by strong hierarchical levels and a drive for consensus and collaborative decision making. The characteristics of Scandinavian public organisations explain why the regional research tradition has evolved to emphasise institutional facets while maintaining a focus on the structural features of public organisations (Christensen 2012; Lægreid 2007).

IE and IT: predicting or exploring?

Generally, scientific theories are concerned with exploring, explaining, and predicting phenomena. In the organisation theoretical approaches described above, however, the instrumental as well as the institutional perspectives focus more on explaining and predicting than exploring. Even though the interpretivist perspective poses a critique of the early positivist paradigm, both of these approaches can be criticised for attempting to predict outcomes. This is one of the main reasons why IE can serve as a tool to improve the theoretical foundation for inductive exploration and for explanation and prediction in organisation research.

As a method of inquiry, IE stimulates a broader, subjective, and bottom-up approach to researching social organisations, while focussing on individuals, local and translocal relations, and the interactions that comprise these relations. Through an open and ethnographic approach, the researcher can uncover the ruling relations of the institution (Smith 2005; Widerberg 2015). This perspective is not included within IT. On the other hand, perspectives from IT can be useful to contextualise the experiences of the "knowers" in public institutional complexes. For me, both instrumental and institutional theoretical elements were useful to explain and predict because they provided a systematic pathway to scrutinise the phenomena I had observed. When used in combination with IE, instrumental and institutional theoretical elements also helped to form a grounded exploration by adding a framework during the fieldwork and the analytical process.

In the next section, I describe two examples that illustrate how I complemented both theoretical approaches to produce a richer analysis than might have been yielded through one approach alone. The first example focusses on how an exploration of instrumental and cultural traits fed into my fieldwork and methodology. The second example details how the idea of "institutional circuits" and the concepts of institutionalisation, institutional soul, culture, and values to understand how bureaucrats categorised their transnational clients.

Finding "instrumental" and "cultural" traits in everyday experiences

Before entering the field, I was conscious that interview data is shaped by the informant *and* the researcher, and that objectivism is obsolete in social scientific research. Nevertheless, I sought to minimise the risk that the interviews should develop around my own pre-set expectations about bureaucrats and transnational living. I wanted to be clear-minded when I entered the everyday experiences of my informants and focus on the activities and experiences they have in their specific contexts (Smith 1987, 2006). The initial interview structure was largely inspired by my wish of staying true to IE and to my main research question: "How do bureaucrats in NAV experience and accommodate the encounter with people who lead transnational lives?" I needed to learn "how things worked" and my pilot interviews took the form of conversations loosely structured around four topics: the individual everyday work, the workplace, the transnational group of clients, and the encounter.

The first interviews moved in several different directions as the open-ended questions enabled the informants to talk about a variety of matters important to them. Following the first three conversations I had, I expanded the interview guide and brought in several topics I deemed relevant to my investigation, drawing on what had already been discussed to this point. These topics included media, regulations, client groups, work culture, practical challenges, organisational history, internal communication, differences among units, quality versus effectiveness, and immigration and the welfare state, among others. As new topics continued to arise during the ensuing interviews, I found it difficult to maintain an open and unstructured approach while also covering all the topics earlier informants had raised. So, I decided to structure the interview guide around some overarching themes, according to the underlying ideas I had from IE and my original interests and notions relevant to IT. Figure 4.2 illustrates the organisation of my final interview guide, including the eight clusters of themes to be discussed.

In clusters 1, 2, and 8, I drew on IE and focussed on the individuals, their everyday work, texts, the workplace mapped from their standpoints, and personal experiences. In clusters 3, 6, and 7, I drew on a combination of my initial interests and other topics that interviewees had raised themselves. In clusters 4 and 5, I asked about specific elements from instrumental theory and IT. Here I focussed on structure, including history, hierarchy, relationships between units, processes of reorganisation, and work culture,

Figure 4.2 My final interview guide.

including norms, values, changing perspectives, and individual experiences of such processes.

While the development of my interview guide is a methodological aspect, it very much relates to the analytical process as well. Since I drew on ideas from both IE and IT in the interviews, it became useful to build on the same theoretical concepts, and others, during the analysis. When analysing what the bureaucrats talked about in relation to cluster 4 (structure), for example, it became clear that the historical traits of the international branch of NAV influenced how the bureaucrats responded to current organisational change – much in line with the idea of "path-dependency" in organisation theory (Steinmo et al. 1992). Likewise, I found that structural changes were often driven by individual agency as well as external structures, a revelation that related closely to ideas about "institutional entrepreneurship" (Garud et al. 2007) and "myth" (Meyer and Rowan 1977). In the analysis I also built on other elements from IE and IT, which might not have been as obvious if I had not addressed them systematically in the interviews. This last idea is further illustrated by the next example, which focusses on how I analysed "institutional circuits" and found traits of the "institutional soul" within NAV.

Exploring categories through "institutional circuits" and "institutionalisation"

One of the articles from my PhD project focusses on how NAV bureaucrats categorise their transnational clients (Talleraas 2019). I was inspired by the scholarly discussion on migrant categorisation processes, in which scholars commonly blame politicians, policymakers, bureaucrats, and practitioners for using institutional categories as a top-down approach to "fix dynamic social processes into rigid structures" (Collyer and De Haas 2012). I also drew on research on institutional and bureaucratic categorisation more broadly. Here, categorisation along specific lines is seen as a useful work tool (Lipsky 2010) and as a mechanism that produces boundaries between "wanted" and "unwanted" clients. Along this line of inquiry, I explored the labels bureaucrats used to talk about their clients as a means to understand if and how transnational individuals were perceived as a specific category.

Empirically, the article on categorisation tells a story of surprise: contrary to my assumptions, it turned out that the bureaucrats shared an institution-wide approach that regarded transnationalism and cross-border mobility among clients as the "new norm". Nevertheless, although my informants aimed at avoiding generalisation and simplification, they frequently used specific labels to describe segments of their clients, ranging from formal categorisations – e.g., "EEA citizen" – to informal ones – e.g., "naïve Norwegians abroad".

Theoretically, the article is also a story of how I arrived at these findings by building on elements from IE and IT in the analysis. In short, I started to map "institutional circuits". My take on institutional circuits is inspired by Smith and Turner's (2014) understanding of the concept as sequences of text-coordinated actions that make people's actualities representable and actionable within the institutional frame. I build on this idea and view an institutional circuit as a process wherein institutional texts influence and mandate subjective action (e.g., practices of categorisation), followed by a feedback mechanism where subjective action, informed by other structural dimensions, in turn, influences institutional texts (e.g., categories in text). This work helped me discover how the modes of categorisation used in the organisation revealed what can be called an "institutional soul" – the unique culture and informal values of an institutionalised organisation (Christensen et al. 2013). I bridged these findings to other institutional traits I had found, which signalled previously undiscovered aspects institutionalised culture and shared values. I drew on these findings and traced the signs of values and culture as part of other institutional circuits within NAV.

During the interviews, I noticed that the bureaucrats used many labels when talking about transnationals in a mix-and-match approach, applying formal and informal categories, including stereotypes. Formal categories were part of the regulative framework, such as "client", "EEA citizen", and "cross-border worker". Informal categories included factual descriptions, such as "sailors" and "airline employees", and a few more unconventional ones, such as "people who live in a country with slow mail delivery". These were not recognised as legal categories, though some had an officially recognised purpose. Stereotypical presentations were oversimplified, and often negative, such as "naïve Norwegians abroad" and "single men in Thailand".

When I asked specific questions about some of the groups, the bureaucrats often referred to texts. Therefore, I investigated these texts as mediators of ruling relations and explored how they shaped the bureaucrats' use of client categories. I mapped institutional circuits and traced how and if specific categories were present in texts such as internal newsletters, unit guidelines, institutional strategy documents, and official website information. Reading through these texts, I noticed that both formal and informal categories were deployed abundantly here as well. Both formal and informal descriptions were commonly used in unofficial internal documents, but surprisingly, informal categories also occurred in the high-order texts, such as the NAV website and steering documents.

I found that all the formal categories used by bureaucrats had been derived from regulative "boss" texts, which explains why they were widespread in the institutional jargon. The text-reader conversation (Smith 2005) regarding informal categories was less clear. While some informal categories occurred in texts or speech only, others were present in both. "Fishermen", for instance, was present in texts and speech, often used to explain how specific regulations applied to transnationals. While there are no legal distinctions coupled to fishermen, there are regulative differences concerning workers on ships registered to different countries, who sail in different territories and live in different countries. "Fishermen" (and, similarly, "sailors" and "flight crew") seemed to be used as a shorthand term to encapsulate legal specificities within a group. In other words, terms like this served to simplify groups in which there were many differences between its individual members and the regulations that applied to them. I found that the use of "fishermen" in authoritative texts thus derived from spoken accounts, originating from a need to make things easier in the bureaucrats' everyday work. "Fishermen" was not a formal category in the legal sense, but it was used as if it was to point bureaucrats to a larger set of regulations and diversities that applied within a specific group of clients.

The texts and the bureaucrats' spoken accounts contrasted in that bureaucrats repeatedly said they did not want to categorise their clients unlike the texts that included formal categories. However, this did not mean there were not individual differences in opinions and perspectives among the bureaucrats. Those who worked with pensions, for instance, were likelier to use a stereotype, such as "retirees moving to sunny areas". But the bureaucrats overall reluctance to categorise while also using categorical labels to describe groups was striking. This example points to the notion of an institutionalised culture in IT (Christensen et al. 2013): When a public organisation develops informal norms and culture it becomes "institutionalised".

Institutionalised elements and identities shape, and are shaped by, the members of the organisation and influence how they act. In the international branch of NAV, it appeared that the habit of applying labels, *and* the general resistance to categorise, and the overall openness towards transnationals, were institutionalised in the work culture. It struck me that this was part of the institutional "soul" (Christensen et al. 2013): it was a uniqueness shared among those working with transnational casework in NAV.

The organisational practice of categorising is, in Selznick's words, "infused with value beyond the technical requirements of the task at hand" (1957, 1). Tracing the institutional circuits of categories in NAV helped me see how the organisational values and norms were represented differently in texts and speech. While formal and informal categories and stereotypes were all institutionalised in NAV, formal categories were largely derived from authoritative texts, while some of the informal categories had spread from speech to texts, including authoritative texts, which then reinforced their use in spoken accounts. Some stereotypes were also institutionalised, but they were not apparent in the authoritative texts.

From this analysis, I concluded that the bureaucrats maintained an open approach to who transnationals were, though they used a large variety of labels to describe them. These contours of institutional soul urged me to look for traces of culture more generally in NAV by reading texts. I detected other institutional elements, particularly when talking with senior bureaucrats. I read decades-old institutional texts that described historical traits of the organisation. Building on this work, I mapped institutional circuits that lined up with the notion of "path-dependency", showed how traits of the institutional soul (e.g., the feeling of doing superior or special casework) had been kept and maintained through texts and actions. Indeed, this journey evolved to become the basis of ensuing analyses, focusing on bureaucratic dilemmas, entrepreneurial solutions, welfare state values, and organisational change.

Conclusions

In this chapter, I reviewed the intellectual path by which I became sensitive to IE and IT for my PhD project. While I initially entered these two fields by chance, the traits of each theory inspired me to explore and explain how they could be complementary and produce novel insights in an institutional analysis. Some may argue that IT and IE are diverging: IE offers a way to explore the actualities of the social in people's doings (Smith 2005) to avoid working at the level of abstraction often apparent in, for example, organisation studies. Critics may build on this point, arguing that combining IE and pre-set theories is inconsistent with the emancipatory nature of IE, since inquiry should be "given primacy over theory" (Smith 2006). But Smith does not rule out the use of theory. While social scientists should avoid replicating theoretical jargon and "reproduc[ing] what we already know" (Widerberg 2015, 14), Smith suggests research should work toward descriptions that can operate as precursors of concepts and theory – which can then be used to explain the observed.

As discussed in this chapter, IE and IT share relevant epistemological traits and focus on concepts and tools that can be used in complementary fashion. For me, the context and focus of my study was relevant to build on the specific traits of IE in the Nordics and IT in Scandinavia and I was encouraged by the call for interdisciplinarity within the two traditions. I cannot claim to have completed an institutional analysis fully in line with the ideals of either IE or IT, but my familiarity with the two approaches enabled me to deploy a large toolbox of methodological and theoretical concepts. I have been sensitive to elements from IE and IT in a need-based manner throughout the research, and for me, this turned out to be useful. The outcome of the analysis combining IE and IT will depend on the elements included: the context, the topic, the theoretical notions, and how they are mixed. Certainly, numerous pathways to connect these two research strands remain unmapped. Drawing on my own experiences, I believe further exploration of this field can yield fruitful insights for institutional ethnographers and organisational theorists alike.

Note

1 I use the connotation "institutional organisation theory" (IT) as an umbrella term to include elements from both "neo" and "old" institutional theory. It should be noted, however, that I also build on elements that originally stem from classic "instrumental" organisation theory.

References

Billo, E. and A. Mountz. 2016. "For Institutional Ethnography: Geographical Approaches to Institutions and the Everyday". *Progress in Human Geography* 40(2): 199–220.

Bogason, P. and E. Sørensen. 1998. *Samfundsforskning bottom-up: teori og metode.* [*Social Scientific Research Bottom-Up: Theory and Methods*] Roskilde: Roskilde Universitetsforlag.

Burrell, G. and G. Morgan. 1979. *Sociological Paradigms and Organizational Analysis.* Aldershot: Gower.

Christensen, T. 2012. "Organization Theory and Public Administration." 149–156, *The SAGE Handbook of Public Administration*, Peters B.G. and J. Pierre. Los Angeles, CA: Sage Publications.

Christensen, T., M. Lægreid, P. Roness, and K. A. Røvik. 2013. *Organisasjonsteori for offentlig sektor.* Oslo: Universitetsforlaget.

Collyer, M. and H. De Haas. 2012. "Developing Dynamic Categorisations of Transit Migration." *Population, Space and Place* 18(4): 468–481.

DiMaggio, P. J. and W. W. Powell. 1991. *The New Institutionalism in Organization Analysis.* Chicago, IL: University of Chicago Press.

Donaldson, L. 2005. "Organization Theory as a Positive Science." 39–62, *The Oxford Handbook of Organization Theory*, Knudsen, C. and H. Tsoukas. New York: Oxford University Press.

64   *Cathrine Talleraas*

Garud, R., C. Hardy, and S. Maguire. 2007. "Institutional Entrepreneurship as Embedded Agency: An Introduction to the Special Issue". *Organization Studies* 28(7): 957–969.

Lægreid, P. 2007. "Organization Theory – The Scandinavian Way." *Nordiske Organisasjonsstudier* 9(1): 77–82.

Lipsky, M. 2010. *Street-Level Bureaucracy: Dilemmas of the Individuals in Public Services*. 30th Anniversary Expanded Edition. New York: Russell Sage Foundation.

Lund, R. 2015. *Doing the Ideal Academic – Gender, Excellence and Changing Academia*. Doctoral thesis. Aalto University.

Lundberg, K. G. and H. L. Sataøen. 2014. "Institusjonell etnografi – Ei mogleg inspirasjonskjelde for den skandinaviske institusjonsteorien?" [Institutional Ethnography – An Inspiration for Scandinavian Institutional Theory?] *Nordiske organisasjonsstudier* 16(1): 30–50.

Meyer, J. W. and B. Rowan. 1977. "Institutionalized Organizations: Formal Structure as Myth and Ceremony". *American Journal of Sociology* 83(2): 340–363.

Pettigrew, A. M. 1985. *The Awakening Giant*. Oxford: Blackwell.

Roness, P. G. 1997. *Organisasjonsendringar: teoriar og strategiar for studiar av endringsprosessar.* [Oranizational Change: Theories and Strategies for Studies of Change]. Bergen: Fagbokforlaget.

Scott, R. W. 1995. *Institutions and Organizations*. Thousand Oaks, CA: Sage.

Selznick, P. 1949. *TVA and the Grass Roots*. Berkeley: University of California Press.

Selznick, P. 1957. *Leadership in Administration: A Sociological Interpretation*. Evanston, IL: Row Peterson.

Smith, D. 1987. *The Everyday World as Problematic: A Feminist Sociology*. Boston, MA: North Eastern University Press.

Smith, D. 2005. *Institutional Ethnography: A Sociology for People*. Oxford: AltaMira Press.

Smith, D. 2006. *Institutional Ethnography as Practice*. Oxford: Rowman & Littlefield Publishers Inc.

Smith, D. and S. M. Turner. 2014. *Incorporating Texts into Institutional Ethnographies*. Toronto: University of Toronto Press.

Steinmo, S., K. Thelen, F. Longstreth. 1992. *Structuring Policies: Historical Institutionalism in Comparative Analysis*. Cambridge: Cambridge University Press.

Talleraas, C. 2019. "Who are the Transnationals? Institutional Categories Beyond 'Migrants'." *Ethnic and Racial Studies*. doi:10.1080/01419870.2019.1599133.

Thoenig, J. C. 2007. "Some Lessons from the Nordic Way of Doing Science." *Nordiske Organisasjonsstudier* 9(1): 111–118.

Tsoukas, C. and H. Knudsen. 2005. "Introduction: The Need for Meta-theoretical Reflection in Organization Theory." 1–36, *The Oxford Handbook of Organization Theory*, Tsoukas, C. and H. Knudsen. Oxford: Oxford University Press Inc.

Widerberg, K. 2004. "Institutional Ethnography – Towards a Productive Sociology. An Interview with Dorothy E. Smith." *Sosiologisk Tidsskrift* 12(2): 179–184.

Widerberg, K. 2015. *I Hjertet av Velferdsstaten: En invitasjon til Institusjonell Etnografi. [At the Heart of the Welfare State: An Invitation to Institutional Ethnography]*. Oslo: Cappelen Damm Akademisk.

5 Actor network theory and institutional ethnography

Studying dilemmas in Nordic deinstitutionalization practices by combining a material focus with everyday experiences

*Ann-Torill Tørrisplass and
Janne Paulsen Breimo*

Introduction

The Nordic welfare model is known for its universalism, equality and comprehensive state intervention (Alestalo, Hort and Kuhnle 2009). This extensive role of the state has bred a developed care facility system where the state claims responsibility for a variety of groups of people. Housing is one of these responsibilities, and during the last decades, a prominent trend has been a downscaling of big institutions and replacing them by staffed individual or shared homes. The Nordic states adopted the normalization principle[1] earlier than other Western comparable countries, which led to deinstitutionalization and independent living legislation and policy (Rimmerman 2017). We have seen this in regard to the elderly, people with disabilities and children in care where institutions give way to individual or small group shared home facilities (Otnes 2015). Another group in need of housing is unaccompanied refugee minors. Unaccompanied refugee minors are children under 18 years of age, arriving without parents or other legal guardians (UDI 2019). Refugee minors are usually placed in group homes or residential care facilities with the intention of creating a home, but more often than not these housing arrangements are experienced as *institutions* (Eide, Kjelaas and Larsgaard 2017). These experiences are often related to how the houses are designed, i.e. the material aspect of them. Hence, in order to understand deinstitutionalization processes and policy we argue for a greater focus on *materiality* in welfare research. Still, the understanding of the individual experiences of these changes calls for an approach grounded in people's everyday experiences. The central argument in this chapter is that combining institutional ethnography (IE) and actor network theory[2] (ANT) is one way of accomplishing this. In the pages that follow we will illustrate how a combination of these two perspectives can be beneficial when studying the dilemmas and paradoxes of deinstitutionalization, putting a larger focus on the significance of the material, while still starting the investigations in people's experiences and everyday life. To illustrate, we will use an empirical example from a residential care facility for unaccompanied refugee minors and their own experiences of the residential care facility as both a home and an institution.

Background

In 2005, Dorothy E. Smith and Bruno Latour both published what are considered seminal books: "Institutional Ethnography – A Sociology for the People" (Smith 2005) and "Reassembling the Social – An Introduction to Actor-Network-Theory" (Latour 2005). IE and ANT both originated during the same period of time but on different continents – IE in North America and ANT in Europe (France). Much like IE, ANT has evolved from a critique of traditional social science (Corman and Barron 2017; Tummons 2010). Even though Smith and Latour seldom refer to one another, there are striking overlaps and similarities.

IE and ANT are both critical methodologies, and in their critique of positivist social science, both approaches draw on insights offered by Harold Garfinkel's (1967) ethnomethodology. As such, both IE and ANT can be regarded as anti-positivist approaches, rejecting the use of universalizing and subsuming concepts. Instead, they focus on using orienting concepts that direct the researcher to explore enactments (ANT) and the work that people do and how it is organized (IE). Moreover, both pay particular attention to objects – including texts (Thompson and Pinsent-Johnson 2011). Both focus on stepping away from the traditional micro–macro binary, ANT by keeping the social flat through localizing the global and connecting the sites (Latour 1999, 2005), and IE through emphasizing the investigation of trans-local relations through texts (Smith 1990, 2005, 2006).

IE and ANT as responses to the linguistic turn

Both IE and ANT can be regarded as reactions towards the witnessed "linguistic turn" in social sciences that moved the focus away from both "materiality" and "people", and their experiences, giving room for criticism towards the privileged role of language and discourse (Barad 2003; Svendsen 2010). Barad (2003, 801) claims that language has been given too much power, and that materiality "is turned into a matter of language or some other form of cultural representation". Smith argues that the linguistic turn has given "discourse" preference over human experience (Smith 2005).

In the wake of this, alternative traditions have flourished, of which IE and ANT are representatives. Commentators of the linguistic turn and its focus on language and discourse have directed their critique towards the disappearance of the human experience and people's own ability to reason and state agency (Hemmings 2005). For instance, Smith (1993) questions the massive focus on discourse and argues that the standpoint of the research needs to be found outside of discourse, not within it. She recognizes that discourse is out there but argues that it should not be the main and only focus and object of our inquiries, claiming that research should start in peoples' lives, not in discourse. Smith argues that text is a material form of discourse that mediates social organization. However, she insists that this kind of textual discourse can only be spotted and investigated through lived experience (Allan 2012, 373). Hence, for Smith, text is a material object that bridges the actual and the discursive. According to Allan (2012, 373) "the uniqueness of what Smith is arguing in light of the linguistic turn is that there is something other than text. Text isn't everything: There are embodied people who live their lives in actual situations that have real consequences". Smith defines texts as "material in a form that enables replication of what is written, drawn or otherwise reproduced" (2005, 228).

Both IE and ANT can be understood as responses to the linguistic turn and the subsequent increased focus on language and discourse. Smith is inspired by Foucault's (1970) notion of discourse and claims this to be an important dimension of the ruling relations, but she also argues that his conception of discourse displaces the knowledge in individual perception and locates it external to people's actual experiences (Smith 2005, 17–18). She argues that "there are experiences that a discourse will not speak" (ibid. p. 18). Smith's reaction to the linguistic turn is upholding the importance of starting the investigation in people's experiences, and from there moving towards the texts as material objects. Smith (2005) understands texts as mediators of discourse in shape of for example paper, video, picture or audio. For her texts are materially replicable words or images independent of particular local settings. Texts are the foundation of the generalized forms on which the ruling relations exists (ibid., 86). However, in order to understand how texts rule, you must start with the experience – not the text or discourse.

Smith (2005, 102) claims that one problem with introducing texts into ethnography is their ordinary inertia. A text produced 20 years ago (or more) could have a great impact on our present everyday life. We do not recognize them as being part of our everyday life because their ruling capacity is often not visible to us. She recognizes that texts both have a material status where it is visible in present time social organization, at the same time as it has the ability to coordinate activities through time and space. A text written many years back can still determine how people act and coordinate their actions, and at the same time a text written in a completely different setting can have the same effect in another place. In this way she is in line with ANT-inspired studies. For instance she recognizes Lindsay Prior's (2003) document studies (which are influenced by ANT), but states that the problem is that people disappear from the studies when documents as such are followed (ibid., 102).

On the other hand, Bruno Latour, a contributor to ANT, makes an even more dramatic turn away from the discursive focus, and claims that the social sciences separation of nature and society is based on the pre-Socratic opposition of *physis (nature, chaos)* and *nomos (law, order)* (Schinkel 2007). To Latour, the study of humans and non-humans interacting in networks is sociology in a nutshell, as he allots equal autonomous political weight to the objects as he does to humans (ibid.). ANT also emphasizes "the material" and its importance in research and empirical investigations. It originates from studies of science and technology (Bosco 2006, 136), and focusses on uncovering and tracing the many connections and relations among actors. These actors can be both human and non-human, material or discursive.

One major difference between the two orientations is the importance devoted to non-human actants. ANT creates an opening for regarding technologies as actants entwined in relation with other human or non-human actants. Within ANT, human and non-human actants are considered entangled in ways that make them difficult to separate. While ANT advocates for an interrelation between objects and subjects, IE is fundamentally people-oriented (Thompson and Pinsent-Johnson 2011).

Law (2009, 141), an influential contributor to ANT, states that ANT treats everything in the social and natural worlds as continuously generated effects of the webs of relations within which they are located. Research using the actor–network approach sets out to describe the heterogeneous relations that produce and reshuffle different kinds of actors, such as objects (artefacts), subjects, humans, animals, nature, machines, organizations, inequalities and so forth. Both people and objects can make people do things, carry meaning and intention, and travel across networks (Tummons 2010). Thus, within ANT, both people and objects are granted agency. This does not mean that objects necessarily have a sense of purpose, justice or intentional action. Rather, it means that they might authorize, allow, encourage, suggest, block, forbid and so on (Latour 2004, 226). In other words, non-human actors become "actors on their own".

Residential care facilities for unaccompanied refugee minors

To illustrate how IE and ANT can complement each other in an analysis, we will use empirical data from an ongoing project focussing on unaccompanied refugee minors who are resettled in Norwegian municipalities.[3] Minors under 15 years of age are cared for by the child welfare services, whilst the minors between 15 and 18 years of age are under the immigration authorities' care (Berg and Tronstad 2015). The UN Children Committee has repeatedly critiqued the Norwegian government for not providing the minors over 15 years of age equal care services as the ones under 15 years of age as well as other children under the care of the child welfare services (UDI 2018). Municipalities are responsible for providing care for unaccompanied refugee minors during resettlement in Norway (Eide, Kjelaas and Larsgaard 2017). The most common way of housing the unaccompanied refugees between the age of 15 and 18 is staffed residential care facilities (Garvik, Paulsen and Berg 2016). The fieldwork in this project was carried out in three different municipalities in Norway, which all have a long history of settling unaccompanied refugee minors. Seven unaccompanied refugee minor girls and 12 employees, working in different capacities with the unaccompanied refugee minors in the municipality, were interviewed. The data also consists of observations of two staffed residential care facilities.

The residential care facilities are similar in the sense that they are furnished and decorated like a home. The buildings look like a regular house from the outside and the living area has couches, a TV, curtains and pictures on the walls. The kitchen is like a kitchen in a private home. In the hallway, there is a place for shoes and coats, but you also find a set of pictures and names, presenting the staff members. A list on the wall tells you which one of the staff will be working when and where. There is also a door, in the living room or the hall (or some other place in the home), that leads to an office space. The children living there each have their own room, which serves as their private space.

This type of residential care living facility is juggling between being a home and an institution. Through the interviews, the unaccompanied refugee minors expressed how it affects them negatively when they feel like their home is an institution or "just work" for the employees. Previous research on this topic has underlined the different understandings of the unaccompanied refugee minors (Eide, Kjelaas and Larsgaard 2017). On the one hand, they are viewed as *children*, which calls for particular care measures. On the other hand, if integration is the goal, they are viewed as *immigrants* which calls for a different set of measures (Eide, Kjelaas and Larsgaard 2017).

To explicate the difference between IE and ANT we will discuss the empirical example, first through the lens of IE and then the lens of ANT, before we move on to combining them.

Through the institutional ethnographic lens

We originally explored the empirical example presented here, through an IE methodology. The interviews with the unaccompanied refugee minors provided the standpoint, and the problematic was derived from their accounts of how their daily life in the residential care facility went. Amaal, one of the unaccompanied minor girls, explained her experiences like this:

> Sometimes you feel like they are here to do a job, they show you they are just here to do their job. But we are human beings, of course, we don't have a family, and in a way the people working there are our family. [] It makes you feel like you are not living in your own home. I thought "Am I at a hospital, what are they doing?

Several of the unaccompanied refugee girls gave similar accounts, which made us curious to why they sometimes felt like they were living in an institution and other times not. Was it the way the employees acted, or was it the material surroundings, or maybe both? These reflections guided the following problematic to explore further *"how is it that the unaccompanied refugee minor girls sometimes experience the residential care facility like a home, and other times like an institution"*. The empirical example illustrates the importance of starting an investigation in the lived experiences of people (Smith 2005). Through the interviews with the girls, we found that the most important issue for them was how the different employees treated them. They liked it when the employees showed affection, socialized with them and gave them responsibilities, like in a family.

When asked about their relationship to the children in the residential care facility, the employees could reveal several reasons why the relationship was challenging. One of the women working there told us that she would never give out private information like her phone number or be friends with them on social media, because she needed to draw a line between her private and work life. She explained that she would give unaccompanied refugee minors her private phone number when they moved out of the residential care facility and into their own apartments. These were the self-imposed "rules" she had, and other employees had similar "rules". She told a story from a long weekend, where she and some other employees had brought the children on a mini-cruise. In the evening, she met some of the children in the staircase and they started talking. Then one of the refugee minors said to the others "I think we need to let her go, it's past her working hours and I don't think she wants to stay here and talk to us". She tried to convince them that it was ok, but felt awkward. This is an example of how difficult it can for the employees to balance the need for closeness, while at the same time keeping a professional distance.

The documents gave further insights into this problematic. Not just on the account of their content but also on the account of their presence in the residential care facility: Collages on the wall showing pictures of all the employees, lists showing the work schedule as well as to-do lists and lists covering house rules and responsibilities. IE studies often focus on texts as mediators of trans-local relations and discourses, whereas ANT studies often focus on texts (and other physical objects) as (material) actors in networks (Thompson and Pinsent-Johnson 2011). We will now analyse this example using ANT as a theoretical perspective and discuss how and in what way this research approach differs from an IE study.

Through the actor network theory lens

Going into a field like the residential care facility, using the ANT approach, the institution is viewed as a network of practices which are coordinated with each other. Just as in IE, the investigation might start in the position of the unaccompanied refugee minors (or some other position), but the researcher can leave the position and follow the network from one relation to the other, giving no position (standpoint in IE) prominence to another. The research problematic or question will be formulated in a way as to map out the network and each actors' relations to the others in the network, aiming at investigating and describing the relations between the different actors (Latour 2005). The question might be *"how are the relations between the different actors in the residential care facility coordinated and assembled?"* When using ANT all actors (human and non-human) are treated as knowers and are to be approached in their relation to other people or material artefacts. ANT differs from IE in this respect. While IE is fundamentally people-oriented, ANT is radically relational (Law 2017; Smith 2005). This means that the actor may be human or non-human, for instance a bike or a bird. There is no difference between human and non-human actors in an ANT study. Giving agency to objects might be controversial, but the reason is the assumption that we can't know what makes things happen or which elements will have crucial impact in a chain of events unless we integrate objects (Law 2017).

The question, *"how are the relations between the different actors in the residential care facility assembled?"* means that we can start investigation anywhere within the network of actors participating in the residential care facility. Tracing and emphasizing the relations between the unaccompanied refugee minors and the employees as well as the material facilities, such as the private versus common space, the door to the office, which is only for the employees, the rules, regulations, work schedule and so forth, provides the study with a new dimension: the material and its agency.

The door to the office space for the employees is a material example. What kind of barrier does this door represent? Can the children walk freely into this space in their home? Do they have to knock? Is it off limits? If you look at the door through the lens of ANT, the door can make people do something (Latour 2005). This means that both humans and non-human actors are granted agency within ANT. However, for non-human actors to be really effective, they need to be sponsored by people who can remind others of their importance. This implies that if the employees let the children know that they must knock before entering, or that the area behind the door is for employees only, they enhance the door's agency.

In ANT, concepts and categories of social relations and activities must not be used as discursive entities that lift the phenomena out of time and place. Rather, terms like social relations should direct our attention to people in their situated experience. Further, they should direct our attention to how these accounts and practices are coordinated with other sites. Here we find a common ground between IE and ANT. Latour, in his critique of traditional sociology, claims that social structures and categories are accentuated in a structuring way. By explaining the social *with* the social, the analysis becomes tautological (Latour 2005). He recommends a "flat ontology" – a starting point where the researcher does not make any assumptions regarding which structures that are "structuring" in a field. On the other hand, ANT's attention to a "flat ontology", also implies that an ANT study focusses its attention on different types and levels of relations, but not necessarily on the power relations that sets people apart. This is at the very core of any IE study – the structures of power that set people in different orders in relation to one another. In the next section we will give an example of how these research strategies can "talk" to each other.

Combining a material focus with everyday experiences

The increased interest of social researchers regarding how "social life" is influenced by "the material world" has been labelled "new materialism" by observers. What these researchers have in common is a shared commitment to the importance of materiality (Hein 2016). Still, various researchers define materiality in different ways, which means that materiality is often expressed and utilized differently. One relevant discussion is the relationship between the discursive and the material, and it can be argued that the exclusive focus on the discursive has led to a neglect of the material. Alaimo, Hekman and Hekman (2008, 3) claim that this trend of emphasizing the discursive before the material has been especially evident in feminist versions of postmodernism. ANT is one tradition that has reinvented the material focus in social research by juxtaposing human actors and non-human actors as units of analysis.

We argue that an emphasis on the material provides access to an important insight into our first problematic *"how is it that the unaccompanied refugee minor girls sometimes experience the residential care facility like a home, and other times like an institution?"* By remaining loyal to our question grounded in an IE study, we maintain the importance of starting in people's everyday experiences whilst implementing ANT's assumption that we cannot know what makes things happen or which elements have a crucial impact in the events we investigate.

One example is the work schedule hanging on the hallway wall. In IE, texts and rhetoric are understood as social activities that are influenced by ruling relations. Accordingly, relevant texts (text, audio, film or similar that is reproducible and independent of time and place) should be included as an obvious part of any IE study. IE conceptualizes texts as anything materially replicable and reproducible over time and space (Smith 2005). Texts are not granted agency within IE but need humans (with agency) to "sponsor" them in order to be activated. Furthermore, texts are understood as being "intertextual". This means that texts do not stand alone from other texts but that "higher level" texts interact, frame and control lower level texts. Consequently, focussing not only on the content of the text, and hence the coordinating effects of the text through the text-reader conversation (Smith 2005, 104), but also on how its very presence in the home, means and does something, provides a different angle for the analysis. For some of the children the text symbolizes the distinction between a home and an institution. A private home does not have a list showing the children which caregiver will be present. Latour's (2005) concept "action-at-a distance" sheds light on how a material object can influence decisions. A document produced in an organization can determine later actions, and as soon as it is written it "does something" and may produce other results than what was originally planned (Prior 2003). In this example the work schedule on the wall is intended to inform and regulate. It informs all the people in the residential care facility who is working when and regulates and controls that all hours are accounted for and that there will be adult caregivers present at all times. If you look at it through the lens of ANT, like a material object, the schedule also has some sort of agency. It *reminds* the unaccompanied refugee minors of the fact that for some people their home is a work place. It also *produces* other results than intended through its agency. Amaal, for instance, uses it to make decisions on whether she will eat her dinner in the common area or in her own private room.

ANT stresses that non-humans do not have agency by themselves because they *are never by themselves*. All these actors, the children, the employees, the living room, the lists, the office space, the pictures and so forth play a part in the experience the unaccompanied refugee minors convey. It has effects, it is connected and it coordinates not only the activity but also the experience that renders it a home and/or an institution. In an IE study, the researcher always keeps in mind that it is this subject position that is in focus. Still, the researcher also follows or traces people, relations and texts that are of importance in the mapping. But while ANT advocates for an interrelation between objects and subjects, IE starts with the experience of people and their everyday life experiences (Thompson and Pinsent-Johnson 2011).

Conclusions

This chapter has described both IE and ANT as reactions towards the linguistic turn in social sciences. Where ANT focusses on objects as actors in their own right, IE defines texts as a material bridge between the actual and the discursive. We argue that focusing on the material aspects of texts and other representatives of ruling relations is vital in order to investigate the current developments of the Nordic welfare states. Using the example of "home versus institution" for illustration, we portray how focussing on material aspects (not only the discursive) brings about other insights. Still, it is crucial to begin an investigation in the lived experiences and work knowledge of people.

The comparison shows that there are many common grounds between IE and ANT but also differences in their focus and solutions to problems. Their critique and solutions are strikingly similar but grounded in different fields of sociology. Their differences could be taken advantage of in order to map out the increasing complexity of the Nordic welfare model. Combining IE's people-centred approach with ANT's radical material understanding could provide us with tools to investigate how the Nordic model is changing and the effects this have on the people living and working within it.

74   *Ann-Torill Tørrisplass and Janne Paulsen Breimo*

Notes

1 I.e. making available patterns of life and conditions for everyday living which are as close as possible to regular circumstances and ways of life or society. Nirje, B. 1985. "The Basis and Logic of the Normalization Principle." *Australia and New Zealand Journal of Developmental Disabilities* 11 (2): 65–68.
2 We use the term "ANT" as a broad and simplified designation on the interdisciplinary Studies of Technology in Society (STS), with emphasis on the different contributors to ANT.
3 Our empirical example is not intended as a foundation for a full empirical analysis, but to be understood as an example we use in order to explain how a combination of IE and ANT can be fruitful.

References

Alaimo, S., S. Hekman, and S. J. Hekman. 2008. *Material Feminisms*. Bloomington & Indianapolis: Indiana University Press.
Alestalo, M., S. E. Hort, and S. Kuhnle. 2009. "The Nordic Model: Conditions, Origins, Outcomes, Lessons." *Working Paper Series of the Hertie School of Governance*.
Allan, K. 2012. *Contemporary Social and Sociological Theory: Visualizing Social Worlds*. Thousand Oaks: Sage.
Barad, K. 2003. "Posthumanist Performativity: Toward an Understanding of How Matter Comes to Matter." *Signs: Journal of Women in Culture and Society* 28 (3): 801–831. doi:10.1086/345321
Berg, B., and K. R. Tronstad. 2015. "Levekår for barn i asylsøkerfasen." [Living Conditions for Children in the Asylum Seeker Phase]. *NTNU Samfunnsforskning*.
Bosco, F. J. 2006. "Actor–Network Theory, Networks, and Relational Approaches in Human Geography." In *Approaches to Human Geography*, edited by S. C. Aitken, and G. Valentine, 136–146. London: Sage.
Corman, M. K., and G. R. Barron. 2017. "Institutional Ethnography and Actor-Network Theory: In Dialogue." In *Perspectives on and from Institutional Ethnography*, edited by J. Reid, and L. Russel, 49–70. Bingley: Emerald Publishing Limited.
Eide, K., I. Kjelaas, and A. K Larsgaard. 2017. "Hjem eller institusjon?" ["Home or Institution?"]. *Tidsskrift for velferdsforskning* 20 (4): 317–331. doi: 10.18261/issn.2464-3076-2017-04-05
Foucault, M. 1970. *The Order of Things: An Archaeology of the Human Sciences*. London: Tavistock/Routledge.
Garfinkel, H. 1967. *Studies in Ethnomethodology (1st ed.)*. Los Angeles: Polity.
Garvik, M., V. Paulsen, and B. Berg. 2016. *Barnevernets rolle i bosetting og oppfølging av enslige mindreårige flyktninger. [The Role of the Child Welfare Service in the Settlement and Follow-up of Unaccompanied Refugee Minors]*. ISBN 978-82-7570-461-8. Trondheim.
Hein, S. F. 2016. "The New Materialism in Qualitative Inquiry: How Compatible are the Philosophies of Barad and Deleuze?" *Cultural Studies – Critical Methodologies* 16 (2): 132–140. doi:10.1177/1532708616634732
Hemmings, C. 2005. "Invoking Affect: Cultural Theory and the Ontological Turn." *Cultural Studies* 19 (5): 548–567. doi:10.1080/09502380500365473
Latour, B. 1999. "On Recalling ANT." *The Sociological Review* 47 (S1): 15–25. doi:10.1111/j.1467-954X.1999.tb03480.x

Latour, B. 2004. *Politics of Nature: How to Bring the Sciences into Democracy.* Cambridge: Harvard University Press.

Latour, B. 2005. *Reassembling the Social: An Introduction to Actor–Network-Theory.* New York: Oxford University Press.

Law, J. 2009. "Actor Network Theory and Material Semiotics." In *The New Blackwell Companion to Social Theory,* edited by B. S. Turner, 141–158. West-Sussex: Wiley-Blackwell.

Law, J. 2017. "STS as Method." In *The Handbook of Science and Technology Studies,* edited by U. Felt, R. Fouché, C. A. Miller, and L. Smith-Doerr, 31–57. Cambridge: The MIT Press.

Nirje, B. 1985. "The Basis and Logic of the Normalization Principle." *Australia and New Zealand Journal of Developmental Disabilities* 11 (2): 65–68. doi:10.3109/13668258509008747

Otnes, B. 2015. "Utviklingen i pleie-og omsorgstjenestene 1994–2013." ["Development in Nursing and Care Services 1994–2013."] *Tidsskrift for omsorgsforskning* 1 (1): 48–61.

Prior, L. 2003. *Using Documents in Social Research.* London: Sage.

Rimmerman, A. 2017. *Disability and Community Living Policies.* Cambridge: Cambridge University Press.

Schinkel, W. 2007. "Sociological Discourse of the Relational: The Cases of Bourdieu & Latour." *The Sociological Review* 55 (4): 707–729. doi:10.1111/j.1467-954X.2007.00749.x

Smith, D. E. 1990. *Texts, Facts and Femininity: Exploring the Relations of Ruling.* London: Routledge.

Smith, D. E. 1993. "High Noon in Textland: A Critique of Clough." *The Sociological Quarterly* 34 (1): 183–192. doi:10.1111/j.1533-8525.1993.tb00137.x

Smith, D. E. 2005. *Institutional Ethnography: A Sociology for People.* Oxford: Rowman Altamira.

Smith, D. E. 2006. *Institutional Ethnography as Practice.* Oxford: Rowman & Littlefield.

Svendsen, S. H. B. 2010. "Vendinger etter poststrukturalismen." ["Post-Structuralism Turns"]. *Tidsskrift for kjønnsforskning* 34 (2): 164–168.

Thompson, T. L., and C. Pinsent-Johnson. 2011. "Institutional Ethnography and Actor Network Theory: The Possibilities and Challenges of Exploring the Relational in Adult Education Research." *Adult Education Research Conference.* Toronto, Canada.

Tummons, J. 2010. "Institutional Ethnography and Actor–Network Theory: A Framework for Researching the Assessment of Trainee Teachers." *Ethnography and Education* 5 (3): 345–357.

UDI. 2018. *Anbefalinger fra andre relevante aktører.* [Recommendations from Other Relevant Actors]. Retrieved on February 6th 2019: www.udi.no/globalassets/global/forskning-fou_i/asylmottak/samlet.pdf.

UDI. 2019. *Enslig mindrårig asylsøker.* [Unaccompanied Refugee Minor]. Retrieved on February 6th 2019: www.udi.no/ord-og-begreper/enslig-mindrearig-asylsoker/.

6 Institutional ethnography and feminist studies of technoscience

The politics of observing Nordic care[1]

Riikka Homanen

Introduction

This chapter is about doing politics in theory. Specifically, it is about how and what institutional ethnography (IE) and feminist studies of technoscience (FT) allow us to observe. I ask how one might conduct studies that explore normativity, not only in the researcher-author-subject relationship but also in the subject matter (cf. Mol and Mesman 1996). What kinds of (observed) realities might be viewed as politically acceptable?

I tackle these questions by combining IE as theorised by Dorothy E. Smith (1987, 2005) with FT as theorised by Donna Haraway (1996, 1997) and Annemarie Mol (2002, 2008a, 2008b) in an effort to discuss how the support provided by public Nordic maternity healthcare can be viewed as both controlling and enabling motherhood. I show that combining IE with certain insights from FT – which draws on science and technology studies, feminist research and actor network theory – offers a better grasp on why the subject of care, in the context of Nordic (maternity health) care services, cannot and ought not to be reduced to a disciplined product of idealised governmentality.

The Nordic welfare service model is simultaneously criticised as a mechanism of authoritarian control and admired as a guarantee of social support, care and equality (Homanen 2017a, 2017b; Nätkin 2006; Sulkunen 2009). In my study of maternal-foetal relations in maternity healthcare practices, I was interested in both these aspects (Homanen 2017a, 2017b). My theoretical and methodological starting point was IE, an excellent tool for explicating the institutional power relations enacted in nurses' work. However, IE does not provide many tools to look at the 'goodness' of Nordic care and its inherent (political) ontology of care: the social equality and support that provide people with agency. Care often both exceeds and collides with the logics of governance and valuation. To explore the 'goodness' of care I therefore employed an alternative ontology that was situational and unstable but allowed room for agency, and for subjects of institutional value beyond the dominant symbolic.

The politics inherent in IE and FT are widely applied by social scientists and feminist researchers studying institutions and/or science, technology and medicine. Drawing on ethnographic material including observations, video-recordings, interviews and documents from four maternity healthcare clinics in Finland,[2] this chapter demonstrates how IE and FT can be combined in a hybrid text in which the theoretical repertoires coexist, although not (always) simultaneously. I conceptualise IE and FT as two modes of ordering in the form of theoretical repertoires that relate to each other in many ways but cannot, and need not, be neatly synthesised or conflated if one wishes to apply them both. In my analyses there are simultaneous narratives from both orderings that are ultimately coordinated: they hang together, but not as one. As I show, irreducible differences in ontological commitments boil down to the (in)coherence of institutional agency and power: the political orders observed, and the alternatives arrived at, are different in nature. Before explicating this in more detail, I briefly introduce maternity healthcare in Finland.

Maternity healthcare in Finland

In Finland, maternity healthcare services are provided by public health nurses rather than doctors. The service is located in primary healthcare maternity clinics, rather than in hospitals. Pregnant women meet their appointed nurse approximately 10–13 times. The care is state-funded and offered by municipalities free of charge. It involves advice on matters such as healthy lifestyles and preparing for birth, and the monitoring of somatic changes experienced by the pregnant woman and baby-to-be. Attention is increasingly also paid to the psychological and home environment by encouraging future parents to consider parenting issues (e.g. Handbook of Maternity Healthcare 2007).[3] In addition to meeting pregnant women and their partners individually, nurses also give counselling classes for groups of parents-to-be, and they work in teams with other social care and child healthcare professionals. These teams meet regularly to assess and resolve families' problems.

Finland is different from many other Western countries, which offer more technologically oriented medical care provided by doctors (Benoit et al. 2005, 727–729). While researchers and activists elsewhere have identified the medicalisation of maternity healthcare as key to the history of care for pregnant women (Martin 1987; Oakley 1984), this pattern is not fully applicable to Finland (Kuronen 1999). Sweden and Denmark have similar systems: in Sweden, nurse-midwives provide antenatal care, while in Denmark it is nurses. In Norway, while general practitioners are responsible for care most women visit midwives/nurses.

Nurse-midwifery-centredness in maternity healthcare is not an exclusively Nordic phenomenon. For example, in the Netherlands and the UK care is provided by midwives and involves elements of demedicalisation, such as social support. It is not only in Nordic societies that nurses in maternity care offer a more personalised counterbalance to the medical profession, whether as performers of emotional labour, mediators between discourses of normality and risk, or intuitive and practice-oriented decision makers. However, I was empirically studying parental support in the practical context of its provision, not assuming it. 'Nordic-ness' was thus understood as produced in moment-to-moment everyday practices.

Historically, Finnish maternity healthcare has been a key institution for incorporating women into the nation to fulfil their responsibilities as mother-citizens in the name of pronatalism. All pregnant women have borne responsibility for attending healthcare institutions since the end of the 1940s, when maternity benefit was made conditional upon such attendance. In the early decades of organised maternity healthcare, motherhood was protected under a pronatalist population policy. The 1970s marked a turning point for the protection of motherhood, part of a more general shift in governance as an effect of cultural individualisation (Homanen 2017a; Sulkunen 2009). Welfare policy shed its pronatalist elements and placed a more gender-neutral and individual emphasis on parenthood. In this new model of the family, both parents participate in care (including maternity healthcare), and they procreate by choice rather than by obligation to the nation (Benoit et al. 2005, 728; Nätkin 2006). Despite the emerging emphasis on individual preferences, and even a tone of empowerment, attending maternity healthcare remains obligatory: women are required to visit a nurse or doctor before the 16th week of pregnancy in order to qualify for maternity benefit.

It is against this historical background that the particularities of Finnish care practices are realised as a subjectification into motherhood. I now move on to discuss the politics of exploring these practices through IE and FT.

From foetus to baby

IE is explicit about its politics. It usually takes people's subjugated experience-based knowledge as its methodological starting point (Smith 1987, 78–88, 2005, 7–25). The overall aim of IE is to explore social power relations as they organise the everyday practice of institutional work. IE research looks at how (unequal) power relations are realised in institutions, and it seeks their institutional 'function' or purpose. At the end of the research process, IE gives voice to experience-based knowledge that more often than not has been silenced by abstract, institutional, privileged representations and interpretations of things and actions (Smith 2005, 50, 62, 66). This is a profoundly political process, since many forms of social control rest on the erasure of various institutional actors, 'deleting their work from representations of the work' (Leigh Star 1991, 267).

To map out the ways in which institutional power relations operate in practice, the institutional ethnographer cumulatively orients herself to the other's interests, positions and knowledges, which transform, often unpredictably, across time and place (Homanen 2013; Smith 2005, 135). IE always avoids objectifying descriptions of peoples' lives. It does not produce nominalisations out of the commonalities found in participants' accounts or seen in observations, but rather puts them to test (Smith 1987, 135–142; 2005, 187–190).

At maternity clinics, I explored how the unborn foetus was allocated a place in the parents-to-be's mental images, households and kin relations. I asked the maternity nurses how they discussed the foetus during appointments with pregnant women, and whether their way of talking changed according to time and place. Many nurses reported that they purposely refrained from personalising the foetus during the early stages of pregnancy. This was a way to manage anxieties about screening results or miscarriage during early gestation. By talking about 'foetuses' and not 'babies', and focussing on the technical-medical aspects and 'facts' of screening technologies, nurses distanced pregnant women from the foetus on an emotional level. They told me that during later pregnancy they behaved differently, as that was the proper time to counsel parents-to-be about the transition to parenthood (see also e.g. Handbook of Maternity Healthcare 2007).

This temporal logic for enacting parental relations and the foetus was not entirely coherent, however. I noticed from my appointment video-recordings that even during the first appointment, nurses might talk about 'babies'. These babies were enacted with personal characteristics, identity and kin relations. For example, the ultrasound scan was promoted as a chance to 'see the baby' for the first time. How to explain this seeming contradiction between what was said and done, drawing on IE insights about how to study social relations that organise activities?

First of all, as IE suggests, my observations of activities and nurses' accounts made me look further into my research material and ask the nurses more questions about referencing the foetus at different sites and times of pre-natal care. That is, rather than making a generalising statement that nurses followed a certain temporal logic during care but unconsciously also broke that logic, I (also) used the accounts to point to the next step in a cumulative enquiry into the institutional process (Smith 1987, 2005). I discovered that during early pregnancy the nurses did indeed talk less about parenthood issues or in terms of babies than during late pregnancy. Further, they never talked in terms of babies in the discursive context of foetal screenings or miscarriage risks. They did not, then, really misrepresent their activities.

By reframing my analysis through both the nurses' insight and my own observations, I was able to see that the focus during early appointments might be on parenthood and life with a baby when the nurses were soliciting parental commitment to the baby-to-be and the pregnancy. This might take place, for example, when the partner's possible attendance at appointments was discussed. In sum, the nurses seemed to vary the ways of relating to the foetus according not just to gestational time but also to the context of the discussion.

Furthermore – and this brings me to my second point – talking about parenthood issues, and attempting to create parental emotional commitment to

the foetus even at the beginning of pregnancy, serves an institutional purpose. When actual parental counselling starts (at around 30 weeks' gestation), it is institutionally useful for there to exist some prior level of transition
to parenthood to build on. To conclude at a more abstract social-scientific
conceptual level, this is the everyday concrete nursing work that goes into
achieving the institutional agenda of subjectifying women into (good)
mother-citizens who take responsibility for their babies.

Using IE as a source of inspiration, we can see how (some) nurses' work
is hidden, and how it can serve the purpose of pushing pregnant women to
conform to the position of mother-citizen. This is the politics inherent in IE.
It makes silenced work (by nurses, in this case) audible, and brings the process of institutional subordination (the subjectification of pregnant women,
in this case) into view.

Agency for women, moral value for the foetus

Nurses' work often rests on experience-based knowledge gained through
direct personal encounters with clients over a long period. It is a historical,
local and intuitive practice. Pregnant women are not merely disciplined to
conform to specific institutional family values at the clinics. My research
showed that even when mothers-to-be were not seen as fit mothers, and
when there was intervention and judgement, women were not left alone with
their feeling of not fitting in, and their experience-based knowledges were
not negated. Rather, practical everyday solutions were sought by a team
(Homanen 2017a, 2017b). Different parenting values could be recognised, or
at least tolerated (Homanen 2017b, 365).

How to account for this kind of attentive and inventive care, which seemed
to exceed the interests of institutional governance and valuation? My answer
was to integrate analytical insights from the FT writers Donna Haraway
(1996, 1997) and Annemarie Mol (2002, 2008a, 2008b) on the performative
character of subjects, thereby widening the analytical IE perspective, particularly regarding the agency of both woman and foetus. This involved
perceiving the social world in terms of material semiotics, which, in turn,
considered social relations that institutionally existed not just between people but also with non-human or not-yet-human entities such as the foetus.

Material semiotic analysis – or material semiotics, as it is also called (Law
2008) – does not deny the foetus moral value or even individual status. However, it *also* allows a reproductive politics that takes into account women's
bodily integrity and rights. This is groundbreaking: within the humanist
traditions of thought shared by many people and institutions, the foetus as
a human life is portrayed as contending with the pregnant woman for individual agency. Concepts of individual agency tend to pit the interests of the
foetus against those of the pregnant woman. Her responsibilities towards
the foetus and her freedom of choice are placed in moral contradiction.
Depending on the emphasis – as also apparent in my research material – the

foetus is then represented either as an unborn child with social rights and autonomy or as a mere technically and clinically defined foetus. If and when the foetus is granted social rights, such as the right to be healthy, the pregnant woman's agency and bodily integrity are subject to limitations, as the foetus literally resides within her body. Material semiotics makes it possible to view a creature like a foetus in a way that avoids the political and theoretical burden of individual agency (or lack thereof).

Material semiotics perceives social worlds as constituted semiotically, on the basis of endless processes of reference and association (see Haraway 1997; Law 2008). In addition to language systems, it broadens semiotics to include all social 'sign systems': networks of symbolic and material entities that appear to matter in social processes and practices (Mol and Messman 1996, 428–429). The concepts of agency and agent are thus broadened: whatever 'works' can be an actor/agent. In this framework, the contradiction between foetus and pregnant woman as (partially) separate individuals disappears as all actorial elements take equal part in enacting the foetus and its relation to the pregnant woman. The individual status or agency of the foetus is not presumed but turned into an empirical question (Mol 2002, 1–29).

Material semiotics has been characterised as a broad analytic orientation (Law 2008) that is generally associated with Latour's (1987) actor network theory and its applications in science and technology studies. I am drawn to 'new' feminist material semiotics, particularly Donna Haraway's (1997; see also Haraway 1991b) political analyses. The 'newness' refers to the understanding of material semiotic enactment as performative. Networks of relations are viewed as unstable, context-specific, heterogeneous complexes in an ongoing enactment. Hence all entities enacted are also unstable, multiple and relational (Haraway 1997; Law 2004, 2008; Mol 2002, 2008a, 2008b).

Haraway (1996, 1997) focusses on movements and relations between the material/natural and the discursive/cultural. Through this orientation it is possible to enquire into how different power relations (historically) arrange people and things in asymmetrical positions in societal networks (Haraway 1997, 33–35). This is apparent when Haraway (1997, 35) criticises social science studies' blindness to certain asymmetrical historical relations: 'social science studies scholars, like Latour, [...] have mistaken other narratives of action about scientific knowledge production as functionalist accounts appealing in the tired old ways to performed categories of the social, such as gender, race, and class'.

Haraway does not presume categories but turns them into empirical questions.[4] The ever-changing relations between material, physical and symbolic entities and the sites of their enactment bear traces of (value) hierarchies that seek to sustain the authority of certain relations at the expense of others. To account for these traces of power, research must originate from the situated temporal and local characteristics of a given research field. These characteristics organise and are organised by historical social relations. Different hierarchies of value that tend to uphold the power and authority of some social relations instead of others organise the relations of different entities. For example, individualisation and neoconservative values have historical authority to reproduce the model where the relationship between foetus and pregnant woman is viewed as that between two individuals, rather than a model within which the foetus is part of the woman. This is also on the agenda of maternity healthcare institutions, as we saw above.

A Harawayan politics of the foetus is a politics that does not presume the essence of things or relations between things, but which can nonetheless point to when and why a particular perception of women's reproductive freedom and rights is the product of power and is open to question. Haraway's analyses typically also outline realities that are politically (more) acceptable (for example, the cyborg [Haraway 1991a] and companion species [Haraway 2008]).[5]

Let us return to the clinics to look at care realities. According to the material semiotic approach, the foetus is multiple, performed again and again during the care process. It does not necessarily have moral status in every situation. Enacted as a particular baby, it has a lot of moral value in most cases. Its enactment involves many material actors, who can be categorised as both human and non-human. Technological tests and devices, such as the ultrasound, have a special role as custodian apparatuses and are productive of social relations. The foetal figure they mediate is used to enact a foetus as kin and as an autonomous gendered individual, since routine use makes the intermediary role of the technology invisible.

The foetus, which is both produced through technology and based on women's experience-based knowledge, also 'enacts' itself and its relation to the pregnant woman, inside and outside the clinic. Its intrauterine activities define the ways in which relationships are formed. Nurses (and pregnant women), for example, interpret and translate these activities into the foetus' personal 'characteristics' and 'interests'. The activities are given meaning that derive not from the activities themselves, but from cultural and political preferences and agendas to make the foetus an active, autonomous and purposeful individual who 'wants' and 'needs', for example, nutrition or 'a smoke-free mummy'. Furthermore, nurses encourage pregnant women to interact with their foetuses.

Personalising the foetus by interacting with it, making choices about screenings and changing lifestyles and households are all certainly necessary during the transition to parenthood. However, it should be remembered that the personalisation process takes place in a specific (cultural) context. Not all foetuses end up as babies, or as babies that accord with (maternity healthcare) cultural preferences: an abortion may take place, or the mothers may not fit the institutional norm.

However, even though women are presented with many restrictions and responsibilities at the maternity healthcare clinics, there is also room for agency and choice. Annemarie Mol's (2008a) 'logic of care' is useful here. The logic of care is that care is an open-ended process with no clear boundaries:

if something does not work, nurses try something else to make things if not perfect, then as good as possible. Pregnant women's experiences are heard and their ideas respected in care decisions, making them more like 'team members' than 'care targets' (cf. Mol 2008a). Further, their experience is understood at the clinics as knowledge obtained in the process of experiencing and doing pregnancy. This logic of care is historical: long-term support, trusting professional relationships and listening to women's experiences have been the guiding principles of Finnish maternity healthcare since its establishment in the early 20th century (Wrede 2001).

The decentralisation of care across multiple partners and teams, and the shift towards more patient autonomy, has been interpreted as part of the emergence of a rationale in Nordic welfare services and governance techniques that insists on persuasion and encouragement rather than regulations and patronising sermons (Foucault 2007; Homanen 2017a; O'Connor, Orloff and Shaver 1999; Sulkunen 2009). This approach relies on people's rationality and capacity to come to know their own (family) life. Citizens' autonomy and privacy must be guaranteed and responsibility decentralised under the welfare state. Control is exercised, but it is indirect and does not rely on disciplinary techniques.

Rational (economic) parents are certainly enacted in care practices. The subject of care in maternity healthcare, however, cannot be reduced to a (successful or failed) neoliberal individual who is responsible for her own shortcomings. Not taking a strong stand on 'good' parenthood does not mean that nurses just leave parents-to-be and their communities to figure parenthood out by themselves. The care approach is *also*, and historically, about the transition to parenthood as a process of coming to know one's own parental identity through experiencing pregnancy supported by a long-term, trusting client-professional relationship. Nobody is left alone to reflect on the cultural competences of motherhood or their feelings of inadequacy. Thus institutional power does not have a totalising hold on practices and actors.

Semiotic analysis, then, reveals that encouraging women to interact with their foetuses and to come to know them slowly in the course of pregnancy can (also) be viewed as enabling subjectivities (maternal and foetal) and family life that result from contextualised reflection, interaction and the practicalities and materialities of everyday pregnant life. The institutional context of maternity healthcare can hence be viewed as both controlling and enabling motherhood.

Thus maternity healthcare protects the foetus through the woman and not in spite of her. When we do not make presumptions about agency, forms of being or institutional power, we can see how the foetus with its 'rights' and 'interests' is not (always) pitted against the pregnant woman. This is how a foetus can have moral status and value, without individual or personal integrity. This – very situated, partial and fragile – reality can be seen as a politically acceptable model for care in pregnancy.

Conclusions

In this chapter, I have unravelled the politics one performs when using one theory instead of another. The presumption on which I have worked is that methods make the normative order of the field under study. IE asks one to follow different people in institutions and to tease out their experience-based knowledge about their daily activities to account for the ways in which power relations and institutional agendas organise those activities. IE is a process that involves reframing the ongoing analysis through new, dialogically produced knowledge, with the aim not to make generalising statements about commonalities in participants' accounts, observations, video-recordings and so on but to put them to the test. IE opens up a space where the worlds of institutional (human) actors – in my case, nurses and pregnant women – are made audible. The erasure of these worlds is often the basis of the institutional control inflicted on actors in the networks of power relations that organise the institutional practice. IE is on the side of the weak.

FT and material semiotics are also concerned with actors, but not just people. It regards people and non-human entities as signs that co-constitute each other in an endless open-ended network or logic, 'an Order of Things' (Mol and Mesman 1996). The Order of Things which is in the interest of FT approaches is concerned with signs and entities that are not incorporated into the Order, rather than silenced or erased people. Material semiotics reveals the effort it takes to constantly keep certain entities – be they values, people, technology, not-yet-humans or whatever – out of the Order. It also illustrates how fragile the established Order is, and how it requires constant upkeep. Material semiotics also demonstrates that the Order is not one but multiple. What is kept out of one Order is incorporated into another. Life can be different; different logics coexist. This is where its politics lies: it exposes orderings and excavates alternatives (which may have been hidden in the existing world all along).

In the care practices in my research, there are coexisting logics for enacting the foetus (in relation to its mother). There is the institutional agenda of subjectifying women into mother-citizens who take responsibility for their babies, which is actualised through temporal and site-specific parental counselling. In the process, the foetus is rendered into a kin person-individual with rights, needs and interests. The counselling work in many ways rests on experience-based knowledge that is historical, local, intuitive and to some extent hidden. This is what we learn with IE.

FT semiotic analysis shows us that this one institutional reality is not the only one, although perhaps it is the one that is culturally enforced. Nor is it stable. The logic of Nordic maternity care work is to listen to pregnant women's experience-based knowledges, to work with them in a team on a consistent long-term basis, and to look for practical everyday solutions to improve the lives of all participants. The foetus is not a (semi-)individual pitted against the pregnant woman in this reality of care. Rather, it is part of the woman. Yet it may still have moral value, and women may have freedom of choice and agency. This is politically acceptable.

It is also a (fragile and partial) political reality that is specific to this Nordic welfare service-in-the-making. In order to observe it and its coexistence with disciplinary and subtler ways of subjectifying women into responsible mother-citizens, I needed this particular form of exploration that combined IE with FT.

The great difference in ontological commitment between IE and FT boils down to the fact that the institutional power relations and hierarchies scrutinised by IE are productive of only one alternative – which FT sees as a situated and unstable reality. Furthermore, in IE social orders exist only between people enacted as subjects, whereas in FT humanity loses its special status. Non-humans and not-yet-humans may be acting subjects too. These different commitments result in different politics.

The difference is not, however, a conflict that needs to or can be resolved. Neither can or need IE and FT be fused into some smooth theory. To use them both is to use a hybrid method and tell simultaneous stories – like those told above – that hang together, but not as one.

Notes

1 This research was funded by Academy of Finland Postdoctoral Researcher's Project Marketisation and Social Inequities in Reproductive Healthcare (project number 274867) and Academy of Finland Project Valuating Lives through Infertility and Dementia: Science, Law and Patient Activism (VALDA) (project number 308159).
2 The data was collected during 2006–2008 and consisted of video tapes (68 appointments, 18 team meetings); observations from maternity healthcare appointments, professional team planning meetings (19), training sessions for nurses and family counselling classes at four maternity healthcare units; seven interviews with pregnant women, and seven with public health nurses; and documentary material used by the nurses in their work.
3 *The Handbook of Maternity Healthcare (Äitiysneuvolan käsikirja)* was a document published on the municipal healthcare service's intranet in 2007.
4 Smith does not presume them, either. Indeed, she explicitly questions them (see e.g. Smith 2009), but the way in which social organisation is realised in her theory does not include simultaneously looking for different orderings at the interface of the material and symbolic.
5 The cyborg and the companion species can be viewed as subjectivities that question the dichotomies human/animal and human/machine. As concepts, they show how humans, machines and animals co-produce each other in dialogue. These value-laden dichotomies are products of power, and anything but 'natural'.

References

Benoit, C., S. Wrede, I. Bourgeault, J. Sandall, R. De Vries and E. R. van Teijlingen. 2005. "Understanding the social organisation of maternity care systems: midwifery as a touchstone." *Sociology of Health and Illness* 27:6, 722–737.

Foucault, M. 2007. *Security, Territory, Population: Lectures at the Collège de France 1977–1978*. Basingstoke: Palgrave Macmillan.

Handbook of Maternity Healthcare (Äitiysneuvolan käsikirja) 2007. [www document in the city healthcare intranet] (received 8.4.2007).

Haraway, D. 1991a. "A cyborg manifesto: science, technology, and socialist-feminist in the late twentieth century." 149–181, *Simians, Cyborgs, and Women: The Reinvention of Nature*. New York and London: Routledge.

Haraway, D. 1991b. "Situated knowledges: the science question in feminism and the privilege of partial perspective." 183–201, *Simians, Cyborgs, and Women: The Reinvention of Nature*. New York and London: Routledge.

Haraway, D. 1996. "Feminist diffractions in science studies." 428–442, *The Disunity of the Sciences: Boundaries, Contexts, and Power*, edited by P. Galison and D. J. Stump. Stanford, CA: Stanford University Press.

Haraway, D. 1997. *Modest_Witness@Second_Millenium.FemaleMan©_Meets_ OncoMouse™: Feminism and Technoscience*. New York and London: Routledge.

Haraway, D. 2008. *When Species Meet*. Minneapolis & London: University of Minnesota Press.

Homanen, R. 2013. "Reflecting on work practices: possibilities for dialogue and collaborative knowledge production in institutional ethnography." 213–235, *Knowledge and Power in Collaborative Research: A Reflexive Approach*, edited by L. Phillips, M. Kristiansen, M. Vehviläinen and E. Gunnarsson. New York and London: Routledge.

Homanen, R. 2017a. "Enabling and controlling parenthood in publicly provided maternity healthcare: becoming a parent in Finland." *Sociology of Health and Illness* 29:3, 443–457.

Homanen, R. 2017b. "Making valuable mothers in Finland: assessing parenthood in publicly provided maternity healthcare." *Sociological Review* 65:2, 353–368.

Kuronen, M. 1999. *The social organisation of motherhood: advice giving in maternity and child healthcare in Scotland and Finland*. Doctoral thesis. University of Stirling, UK.

Latour, B. 1987. *Science in Action: How to Follow Scientists and Engineers Through Society*. Cambridge, MA: Harvard University Press..

Law, J. 2004. *After Method: Mess in Social Science Research*. Abingdon and New York: Routledge.

Law, J. 2008. "On sociology and STS." *Sociological Review* 56:4, 623–649.

Leigh Star, S. 1991. "The sociology of the invisible: the primacy of work in the writings of Anselm Strauss." 265–283, *Social Organisation and Social Processes: Essays in Honor of Anselm L. Strauss*, edited by D. Maines. Hawthorne, CA: Aldine de Gruyter.

Martin, E. 1987. *The Woman in the Body: A Cultural Analysis of Reproduction*. Boston, MA: Beacon Press.

Mol, A. 2002. *The Body Multiple: Ontology in Medical Practice*. Durham, NC: Duke University Press.

Mol, A. 2008a. "I eat an apple: on theorizing subjectivities." *Subjectivity* 22:1, 28–37.

Mol, A. 2008b. *The Logic of Care: Health and the Problem of Patient Choice*. London and New York: Routledge.

Mol, A., and J. Mesman. 1996. "Neonatal food and the politics of theory: some questions of method." *Social Studies of Science* 26:2, 419–444.

Nätkin, R. 2006. "Contradiction between gender equality and protection of motherhood: reproduction policy in Finland." 25–40, *The Policies of Reproduction at the Turn of the 21st Century*, edited by M. Mesner and G. Wolfgruber. Innsbruck: Studien Verlag.

Oakley, A. 1984. *The Captured Womb: A History of Medical Care of Pregnant Women*. Oxford: Blackwell.

O'Connor, J. S., A. S. Orloff and S. Shaver. 1999. *States, Markets, Families*. Cambridge: Cambridge University Press.

Smith, D. E. 1987. *The Everyday World as Problematic: A Feminist Sociology*. Toronto: University of Toronto Press.

Smith, D. E. 2005. *Institutional Ethnography: A Sociology for People*. Lanham, MD: AltaMira Press.

Smith, D. E. 2009. "Categories are not enough." *Gender & Society* 23:1, 76–80.

Sulkunen, P. 2009. *The Saturated Society: Governing Risk and Lifestyles in Consumer Culture*. Los Angeles, CA: Sage.

Wrede, S. 2001. *Decentering Care for Mothers: The Politics of Midwifery and the Design of Finnish Maternity Services*. Åbo: Åbo Akademi University Press.

7   Making sense of normalcy
Bridging the gap between Foucault and Goffman

Ann Christin E. Nilsen

Introduction

What is normalcy? How do our perceptions of normalcy come about? What kinds of ruling relations are they embedded in? These were some of the questions that were triggered by my research on how staff in Norwegian kindergartens deal with the ideology of early childhood intervention. Acknowledging that these are core questions in sociology, and particularly within the sociology of deviance, I reacquainted myself with the work of some of the most influential scholars of contemporary sociology: Michel Foucault and Erving Goffman. Both have contributed with important insights into the social construction of normalcy, yet their approaches differ; Foucault is known for his discourse analytical approach, and Goffman for his interactional approach. In an article published in *Economy and Society* in 2004, Ian Hacking (2004) argues that these two scholars should not be perceived as opposites, but as complementary. In this chapter I propose that institutional ethnography (IE) provides a suitable framework of inquiry to bridge the gap between them in empirical research. By revisiting the concepts of work/work knowledge and ruling relations, I argue that IE offers an opportunity to realise the complementarity between Foucault and Goffman in their approaches to normalcy and deviance.

Background

My interest in understanding how perceptions of normalcy come about grew out of my research on early childhood intervention in Norwegian kindergartens. Early intervention is an ideal that has become pivotal not only in Norwegian kindergartens but also globally and across different sectors, fuelled by an international social investment paradigm which is rooted in socio-economic and developmental psychological arguments (Esping-Andersen 2002; Heckmann 2006).[1] Intended to promote a safe and healthy development and life situation for all children, the ambition of early intervention is to identify children who are "at risk" or have "special needs" in order to initiate some kind of compensatory or overreaching action.

Implicitly, judgements as to what may be perceived as normal and deviant behaviours, either in the child or in his or her family, have to be made.

In Norway, as in the other Nordic welfare states where the public sector is comprehensive, professionals are an extended arm of the state, responsible for putting state policy into practice and for guaranteeing the authority of the state vis-à-vis its citizens. The ambition of early intervention renders professionals working with children accountable; it is their obligation to identify "children at risk" or "children with special needs" and to initiate interventions as early as possible. I will refer to the professionals' work promoting early intervention as *concern work*, and the children identified as *concern children*. Exactly how state-initiated moral ambitions are transformed into practical action on the frontline is a concern raised by several scholars (e.g. Lipsky 1980; Bourdieu 1999; Evetts 2009). Building on that legacy, my primary research interest was to explore the concern work of kindergarten staff; How do they *do* concern work? As the research process evolved, my curiosity also turned towards how this work is *socially organised* and, not least, what concern work and early intervention *does*.

Prior to embarking on IE, I considered other research approaches. I was inspired by previous research informed by insights associated with post-structuralism, notably Foucault and his concepts of *regimes of truth, discipline* and *governmentality*. Several empirical studies on professional work with children on the frontline of the Norwegian welfare state have used discourse analysis informed by Foucault (e.g. Neumann 2009; Franck 2014; Ulla 2014). Foucault is arguably one of the most referenced scholars in Nordic social research on professions and professionals (Christoffersen 2011). In addition, some of the most important theories of the emergence of our current understanding of child care in the intersection between the private and the professional domains build on a Foucauldian legacy (Donzelot 1979; Rose 1999; Turmel 2008). Foucault's work on knowledge and power has been foundational for current understandings of how notions of normalcy and deviance emerge and are maintained within the disciplinary power of the state and the state professions (e.g. Foucault 1977, 2001). In other words, I could not avoid paying attention to Foucault. Yet, despite acknowledging the disciplinary role of discourses and the value of archeologically tracing how these discourses have come about, I deliberately chose not to conduct a discourse analysis. My intention was to focus on the actions and activities of the kindergarten staff, aiming at exploring the relations within which this work is concerted.

Phenomenological and interactionist approaches were therefore another possibility I considered. Since my research was to focus on normalcy and deviance, I found Erving Goffman's work on *Stigma* (1963) and *Asylums* (1961) particularly inspirational, as were his concepts of *impression management* and *interaction rituals*. Whilst Foucault is associated with the analysis of how perceptions of normalcy and deviance are embedded in discourses that affect and regulate who we are and how we think, Goffman was dedicated to exploring normalcy and deviance as effects of labelling processes involving social interaction. The two were contemporaries; Goffman's *Asylums* and Foucault's *Histoire de la Folie* were both published in 1961.

It was when I came across an article by Ian Hacking, in which he argues that Foucault and Goffman should be perceived as complementary thinkers (Hacking 2004), that I discovered my research might benefit from taking both scholars into account. In his own research on interactions between classifications of people and the people being classified, published in the essay "Making up people" (2002), Hacking finds inspiration from both scholars. He does not, however, propose *how* their approaches should be used complementarily in empirical investigations. Picking up Hacking's discussion, the argument in this chapter is that IE provides an opportunity to bridge their approaches in empirical research, as it offers concepts and tools for exploring how people's everyday work is coordinated in trans-locally operating institutional relations. I will start with an outline of Hacking's argument. Then I will turn to IE and discuss its bridging potential, followed by an empirical example which aims to illustrate my point.

Hacking's argument: bringing together top-down and bottom-up analyses

Ian Hacking is a Canadian philosopher who is known, among other things, for his contribution to the understanding of the concept of probability and for drawing attention to the importance of historical ontology, i.e. tracing the historical emergence of concepts and objects. His work is exceptional in bringing attention to how statistics and the theory of probability shapes society and how people are constituted by the descriptions of acts available to them. In particular, he has studied the interaction between systems of classification and people who are being classified. He argues that classifications do not only modify and alter the way people behave but also the classification systems themselves. Classification thus has looping effects. He called the approach he developed *dynamic nominalism*, i.e. "a nominalism in action, directed at new or changing classifications of people" (Hacking 2004, 279). It has also been referred to as *dialectic realism*, a term Hacking favours because

> classes of individuals that come into being are real enough (...) They come into being by a dialectic between classification and who is classified. Naming has real effect on people, and changes in people have real effects on subsequent classifications.
>
> (ibid.)

My first acquaintance with Hacking's work was through the essay "Making up people" (2002). In this essay Hacking explains how discursive features of a phenomenon are taken up and reproduced by social interaction, yet also come to shape that social interaction and our potential for action. This argument anticipates well the potential he sees in combining the discourse perspective of Foucault with the interactionist perspective of Goffman.

According to Hacking, Foucault proposed ideas of a structure that determines discourse and action from the top down, whereas Goffman paid attention to the local incidents and peculiarities that lead us from the bottom up (Hacking 2004, 288). This top-down and bottom-up dichotomy is, of course, a simplification. Both Foucault and Goffman recognised the dynamics between discourse and everyday actions, structure and agency or macro and micro as constitutive of social life. For instance, in *Frame Analysis* (1974), Goffman proposed an analysis of how the organisational and normative framing of situations is constitutive of the subjective meaning allocated to social events. Whether a situation is collectively framed as, for instance, entertainment or professional practice has an impact on how the situation is made sense of subjectively. Furthermore, his concept of total institutions, which I will return to below, is intended to capture the institutional conditions of social interaction. In Foucault's studies, it is particularly the notion of technologies of self that takes up how objectifying power dynamics enter into people's everyday lives, epitomising how human beings turn themselves into subjects. Despite these nuances, Hacking's distinction between Foucault and Goffman does arguably identify what constitutes their main contributions to the legacy of the study of normalcy and deviance.

Goffman is known for his studies of face-to-face interaction, and his commitment to scrupulously taking notes of all verbal and bodily exchanges between individuals. His project was to understand the social processes through which people are constituted, define themselves and are understood by others. His work on everyday interaction rituals has become legendary, as has his dramaturgical analogy with concepts such as backstage and frontstage (Goffman 1959). In *Asylums* (1961), he introduced the concept of total institutions. These are institutions such as prisons, boarding schools or psychiatric hospitals where people – both residents and staff – are cut-off from the wider society for a duration of time. Goffman depicts how such institutions are places of coercion that change people, yet not necessarily as intended. The changes are not brought about from systems of control, but rather from social interaction, i.e. in behaviour (words, glances, gestures etc.) and rituals inserted into the situation by people in different roles. Goffman's subsequent analysis of the social processes that lead to stigma and subtle oppression reveals how people, in Hacking's terminology, are "made up" as certain types, i.e. how people are understood by others and accordingly understand themselves (Goffman 1963). Hacking's own theory of how people are "made up" has consequently been criticised for re-inventing the wheel – a critique Hacking welcomes (2004, 280). However, Hacking is not only concerned about how socially constructed categories have labelling effects on an individual level but also argues that these processes happen at an institutional level and are maintained through the very institutions they are a part of. Indeed, Goffman studied how patterns of normalcy and deviance are constituted and maintained through face-to-face encounters within institutional settings. However, he did not pay much attention to the historical conditions of the social interaction and practices that are constitutive of institutions. Foucault's archaeologies and genealogies, tracing how systems of thought have come about, mark a striking contrast. Bringing attention to what Hacking refers to as abstracted discourses, detached from the people who are a part of them, his project was "the pure description of discursive events" (Foucault 1969, cited in Hacking 2004, 278). Hacking argues that what is missing from Foucault's analysis is an understanding of how discourses become a part of people's everyday lives, how they become institutionalised and a part of institutions at work. What is missing from Goffman's analysis, on the other hand, is an understanding of how institutions come into being and their formative structures (Hacking 2004, 278).

Hacking deliberately avoids proposing a doctrine of method that lies between those of Foucault and Goffman (Hacking 2004, 278). As a framework of inquiry, IE is well suited to bridging their different perspectives on how perceptions of normalcy and deviance come into being. In particular, the entanglement of discourses that may appear abstracted from people, and the activities of people in their everyday lives, are apprehended within the concepts of "ruling relations" and "work/work knowledge".

Before I unpack these concepts, it is worth mentioning that I am not bringing an entirely new idea to the table. Indeed, in the role of her thesis-supervisor, Goffman has without doubt had an impact on Dorothy Smith's work, especially in rendering the everyday world visible to sociology (Campbell 2003). From Foucault, Smith finds inspiration in the conception of discourse (Smith 2005, 17, 2012c), albeit insisting on exploring how the subject is located within, and not as it is subdued by, discourse. Moreover, in the article upon which I am building my argument, Hacking accounts how he asked Smith for advice to come up with a social and human concept that would be worth studying "in action", i.e. as it is changing (Hacking 2004, 280). Smith suggested child abuse, which was a suggestion Hacking took up in a later article (Hacking 1991). Bringing the perspectives of these scholars together is, in other words, not a straw man's argument, but neither is it very innovative. Nevertheless, it is within this context it becomes relevant to display *how* their perspectives are complementary in empirical research.

The bridging potential of institutional ethnography

First, let us recapture two fundamental understandings of people in IE. First, people are perceived as essentially social and thus all our activities are socially organised. The "social" refers to the coordination of consciousnesses, transcending time and space. Whether we read the newspaper, find our way at an airport, do the dishes or attend a meeting, these activities are directly or indirectly linked to actions performed by other people. Second, and building on an ethnomethodological legacy, people are perceived as "knowers". We reflect on what we do, we make choices, prioritise, and we have opinions and make compromises, although we may often be unaware of it. This stance is clearly in opposition to what Smith refers to as mainstream sociology, which she claims objectifies people (Smith 2005, 2012b). She argues that the inclination of sociologists towards grand narratives involves removing people from the analysis and substituting them with a category or discursively prescribed characteristics, such as "middleclass woman", "black man" or "vulnerable child". Smith claims that in doing so, sociologists tend to reintroduce the individual into the analysis not as a subject but as a category or figment of a discourse (Smith 2012b).

In contrast, institutional ethnographers focus on people's doings, thoughts and their interaction with other people as they participate in institutional processes, i.e. their *work* and *work knowledge*. The ambition is to make visible the complex coordination of consciousnesses that constitute institutions. Institutional arrangements often appear as objectifying and ruling structures, devoid of people's agency, yet they are brought forward by the concerted activities of people who are located at different places and at different times within a functional complex. Studying what people do and how they reflect on what they do, i.e. their work/work knowledge, opens a window into discovering the trans-local and ruling relations they are a part of. For instance, how do people interact with other people, texts, categories, codes and concepts? *Ruling relations* can be described as objectified systems of knowledge that are produced by people's concerted activities, yet they are independent of particular individuals (Smith 2012a, 2005). Ruling is an integral part of social relations and can only be regarded as a part of social activity. How ruling occurs can therefore best be understood by studying how institutional arrangements are incorporated into the daily activities and interaction of the people that are a part of the institutional complex. In other words, in order to discover ruling relations, we need to explore people's work to relate to (text-mediated) institutional discourses, concepts and codes, while acknowledging that people take part in ruling relations, both as objects and producers of ruling. Studying the discourses in themselves gets us only half-way. In order to discover how discourses coordinate actions, we need to explore how people activate, negotiate and navigate between different abstracted, yet often textually mediated, discourses in their everyday lives. As a framework of inquiry, IE provides methodological and conceptual tools that render these connections empirically accessible.

Hacking (1999) reminds us that categories are socially constructed ideas and understandings, and not individuals or specimens. These ideas and understandings do not exist on their own, but are incorporated into, and can only function as a part of, a matrix. Categories are woven into a complexity of institutions, procedures, media, stakeholders, infrastructure etc. When we use categories it is the idea, and the matrix it is a part of, we refer to, and not an embodied or material subject. Categories are, as such, discursive. Similarly, Smith insists on starting a social inquiry in people's actual experience and rejects treating people's experiences as an expression of categorically ascribed characteristics. Drawing on the epistemology of Marx, she points out how descriptive categories and concepts are theoretical primitives which carry specific historical and ideological meanings that are reinforced by our usage of them (Smith 2004; Lund and Magnussen 2018). However, when people are categorised as certain "types" the discursive features of the category are combined with empirical observations. This is also a crucial point in IE, as exemplified by Smith in the article "'K is mentally ill'. The anatomy of a factual account" (Smith 1978). In this article, Smith shows how a person (K) is constructed as a mentally ill person since people make connections between rules of behaviour and definitions of situations (what is "normal"), on the one hand, and descriptions of empirical observations of K's behaviour, on the other hand. Smith refers to this as a "cutting-out" procedure: By focussing on specific actions and incidents (empirically) in specific ways (discursively) an account is made in which K is acknowledged as a mentally ill person by the people who share the same cultural references. It is how the behaviour is described and combined with discursive categories that shape the account of K as a mentally ill kind of person.

Concern work – an institutional ethnography of interaction and discourse

In my project on early childhood intervention, I studied kindergarten teachers' concerns, i.e. their work to identify "children at risk" or "children with special needs" and to initiate some kind of intervention. The data material consisted of interviews and observation in kindergartens as well as interviews with other welfare service providers working with children under school age. As a part of my fieldwork I attended a meeting between professionals employed within different municipal services: a public nurse, an education specialist, a child welfare agent, a physiotherapist, two members of the kindergarten staff and the head of the kindergarten, who was leading the meeting. Prior to the meeting, the professionals from the other services had systematically observed the children in the kindergarten. The purpose of the meeting was to discuss their observations, with the overall aim to identify "children at risk".

During the meeting the professionals discussed the well-being of several children. Some of the concerns raised about specific children were, for instance, difficulties making friends, frequent crying, a lack of interest in outdoor play, constant running and shouting, bad teeth, messy hair and over-sized clothes. As these empirical observations of children were launched, the professionals would also propose or hint at an appropriate diagnosis, such as poor social skills, poor motor skills, depression, poor

attachment to parents or adverse family characteristics. These two examples can illustrate:

> The nurse is concerned about three year old "Lisa". She describes Lisa
> as a demanding child in terms of need for care. Lisa cries a lot, is passive
> and sad. Despite her age, she still has to be fed by one of the kindergar-
> ten teachers, or else she doesn't eat. The nurse adds that Lisa recently
> moved from another country and has a "new" dad, so there are a lot of
> changes going on in her life at the moment. According to the nurse, Lisa
> seems depressed, but she underlines that she does not want to give Lisa
> a diagnosis.
>
> The child welfare agent mentions "John", who is in foster care. None
> of the professionals are particularly worried about John at the moment,
> as he is progressing well, but the child welfare agent says that John's
> grandmother has raised some concerns by reporting that there are peo-
> ple with ADHD in the family. One of the kindergarten teachers says
> that John has indeed been quite active and unfocused. There is nodding
> around the table. Then the education specialist says that they need to
> pay attention to this. The nurse agrees, and adds that it is probably no
> secret that there are drugs and violence involved.

These examples bear witness to the ways in which empirical observations
are combined with discursive features that imply some kind of causality.
Passivity and sadness are linked to depression, which is again linked to
transitions. The Attention Deficit Hyperactivity Disorder (ADHD) diagnosis is assumed to be an underlying cause for John's activity level and lack of
focus and is presumptively linked to drugs and violence. Importantly, the
construction of Lisa and John as specific "types" of children is needed in
order to enable professional intervention.

Let's take a moment to consider what is at stake for the people at the
meeting. They have all been appointed to attend a municipally initiated programme intended to enhance early intervention, of which the meeting and
prior observation is a part. Rooted in a social investment paradigm and
immersed in good intentions, the local politicians – on the county direc-
tor's initiative – have launched a strategy aimed at improving negative statistics in the municipality; high unemployment rates, poor living conditions
and a high proportion of child welfare support recipients. Early childhood
intervention has been launched as the "medicine", fuelled by the substantive amount of research that has been used to advocate for investment in
children, both in Norway and internationally (e.g. Esping-Andersen 2002;
Heckmann 2006; Havnes and Mogstad 2011). In other words, the role of
the professionals is to realise the political and moral obligation of identifying children at risk and to initiate a suitable intervention. Faced with each
other, it is presumably in the interest of the professionals to show that they
do their job and that they are accountable. Their *frontstage* behaviour is

consequently to be concerned, to show each other that they have made observations that are worrying, that they "see" the risk factors and that they have evaluated their severity. In Goffman's terms, we can interpret it as a case of impression management. In Smith's terminology, it is a part of their work knowledge, i.e. *doing concern work*.

To justify their empirical observations of the children the professionals referred to a list of risk factors. This list is taken from one of the most cited professional books in Norwegian on children at risk, which builds on a scientific rationale associated with developmental psychology (Kvello 2011). Implicit in this rationale is the assumption that children's brain structure develops during the pre-natal and first years of life – through the interactive influences of genes and experience – and that this development is fundamental to the child's later ability to learn. This rationale is reflected in a wide selection of boss texts, also underlining the socio-economic benefits of early intervention (Nilsen 2017). The author of the list claims that it contains complex knowledge that can be used as a starting point for discretionary judgement, and that the "checklist does not get better than the competence of the people using it" (Kvello 2011, 166, my translation). Nevertheless, the list has obtained an authoritative status and is, as such, a manifestation of what Foucault calls a regime of truth and the implicit discursive features that constitute children at risk. Combining their empirical observations with the discursive features provided by the list, the professionals successfully "cut out" accounts of children who can be classified as concern children.

Interestingly, in the individual interviews with the kindergarten staff after the meeting, several of the interviewees told me that they did not necessarily agree with the visiting professionals. Quite often, they had knowledge of the children and families in question that made them see things differently, for instance that "Jasmin", whose family characteristics signal adversity according to the checklist (immigrant, unemployed, low-income), had parents who would engage actively in the activities of the kindergarten and the well-being of their children, or that "William", whose parents were considered resourceful (white ethnic Norwegian, higher education, high-income, stable jobs) and who did not acknowledge the concerns of the kindergarten staff, was unable to communicate with his peers. In such cases, the ascribed categories did not fit with the everyday observations of the kindergarten staff. However, the presence of the professionals from other services, and the implicit obligation to identify children at risk, made them reluctant to overtly disagree. In other words, *backstage*, the kindergarten teachers' concern work appeared different from what happened frontstage. Moreover, the kindergarten staff sometimes mobilised other institutional discourses to "make up" a different type of child. For instance, I discovered two different, and sometimes conflicting, institutional discourses that were textually mediated in boss texts, such as the authoritative national *Framework Plan for Kindergartens*: a discourse of early intervention and a discourse of diversity

(Nilsen 2016). Whereas the former is brought forward by the social investment paradigm and calls for an alertness to the negative implications of deviation, the latter is brought forward by an ideology of tolerance and calls for a positive appraisal of behaviours that differ from the majority norm. Hence, these discourses could justify different actions. In what different ways they are taken up as prescriptive of certain actions can only be deduced by studying the everyday work and interaction of the people involved.

The examples reveal how the institutional discourses of early intervention and diversity are reflected in the professionals' work knowledge and enter into their everyday concern work in ways that form institutional practices. When Lisa and John are made into concern children, institutionally convincing arguments are brought forward and negotiated by combining empirical observations with discursive categories (e.g. diagnoses). These are the ruling relations of concern work. The construction of Lisa and John as concern children is thus incorporated into the institutional language and practice, maintained – and negotiated – in the interaction between professionals and the functional complexes they are a part of. What the professionals think, say, and do, cannot be disentangled from the institutional discourses. Simultaneously, the institutional discourses only become effective when they are taken up by people in their local, everyday work. What Goffman refers to as interaction rituals thus imply a reliance on certain knowledge systems, or regimes of truth, to use a concept from Foucault. It is in this intersection that concern work is carried out, as professionals partake in the ruling relations of concern.

Conclusion

The understandings of normalcy and deviance developed by Goffman and Foucault have been instructional for many strands of sociological inquiry – and for good reasons. Goffman and Foucault's contributions to sociology have brought about different legacies that tend to be separated. However, as Hacking argues, it makes sense to see them as complementary in their attempts to understand how perceptions of normalcy and deviance come about, and I argue that IE may provide a way to bridge them in empirical research. Acknowledging that normalcy and deviance are socially and discursively constructed is indeed a prerequisite for carrying out an IE. The question of interest is *how* these perceptions come about within specific institutional settings. This is an empirical – not a theoretical – question. I argue that the concepts of *work/work knowledge* and *ruling relations* are particularly useful to empirically trace connections between the coordination of people's everyday doings and the discursively organised institutions they are a part of. The strength of IE is its suitability to render institutions – understood as functional complexes in motion – empirically accessible.

It has to be noted that my argument is not that we necessarily *need to* frame IE within or through these theories. Rather, I am arguing that it makes sense for IE to "talk" with these theories. First, because it enriches the analysis and broadens the scope of theoretical contribution from IE studies to sociology at large. IE is not a sociology of its own – at least not in the Nordic countries – but has potential to both enrich and be informed by other sociological theories and methodologies. Smith's epistemological work is indeed an example of that. Second, because it invites us to revisit and challenge some of the concepts and understandings embedded in IE, thus avoiding the uncritical reproduction of an IE jargon that can end up being institutionally capturing.

Note

1 Investing in early childhood, e.g. through early childhood education and care (ECEC), has been proposed as one of the best investments a society can make by international proponents such as UNICEF and the World Bank. In Norway, this view is reflected in a massive expansion of the kindergarten sector in recent decades. More than 97% of Norwegian 3–5 years old children attend kindergarten, and roughly 82% of children aged 1–2 years old. The kindergartens are not free of charge but are strongly subsidised by the state. Accordingly, other initiatives to promote early childhood intervention have also been promoted, aimed at reducing social marginalisation and exclusion in society at large. The public Child Welfare Services (CWS) is important in this respect; their statutory obligation is to ensure that children and youth in detrimental life situations receive assistance and care. Roughly 3% of all children in Norway receive support from the CWS. Following reports in international media, starting in April 2016 (notably the BBC documentary *Parents Against the State*), the Norwegian state has been accused of overreach in its efforts to protect children from potentially abusive situations, giving rise to a warning regarding human rights violations issued by the European Court of Human Rights (ECHR) in Strasbourg. The critique of the CWS, both nationally and internationally, has inspired a debate about whether good intentions, i.e. to protect children from harm, may also, potentially, have harmful effects.

References

Bourdieu, P. 1999. "An Impossible Mission." In *The Weight of the World: Social Suffering in Contemporary Society*, edited by P. Bourdieu, A. Aracardo and P. Ferguson, 189–202. Cambridge: Polity Press.

Campbell, M. 2003. "Dorothy Smith and Knowing the World We Live In." *The Journal of Sociology and Social Welfare* 30 (1): 3. article 2.

Christoffersen, S. A. 2011. "Profesjoner og profesjonsetikk: hva er det?" [Professions and Professional Ethics: What is That?]. In *Profesjonsetikk*, edited by S. A. Christoffersen, 18–43. Oslo: Universitetsforlaget.

Donzelot, J. 1979. *The Policing of Families*. New York: Pantheon Books.

Esping-Andersen, G. 2002. "A Child-Centered Investment Strategy." In *Why We Need a New Welfare State*, edited by G. Esping-Andersen, D. Gallie, A. Hemerijck and J. Myles, 26–67. Oxford: Oxford University Press.

Evetts, J. 2009. "New Professionalism and New Public Management: Changes, Continuities and Consequences." *Comparative Sociology* 8 (2): 247–266. doi: 10.1163/156913309X421655

Foucault, M. 1969. L'Archéologie du savoir. Paris: Éditions Gallimard.

Foucault, M. 1977. *Discipline and Punish: The Birth of the Prison.* New York: Pantheon Books.

Foucault, M. 2001. *Madness and Civilization: A History of Insanity in the Age of Reason.* London: Routledge.

Franck, K. 2014. "Constructions of Children in-between Normalcy and Deviance in Norwegian Day-Care Centres." PhD diss., Norwegian University of Science and Technology.

Goffman, E. 1959. *The Presentation of Self in Everyday Life.* New York: Random House.

Goffman, E. 1961. *Asylums.* New York: Doubleday.

Goffman, E. 1963. *Stigma: Notes on the Management of Spoiled Identity.* Englewood Cliffs, NJ: Prentice-Hall.

Goffman, E. 1974. *Frame Analysis: An Essay on the Organization of Experience.* New York: Harper & Row.

Hacking, I. 1991. "The Making and Molding of Child Abuse." *Critical Inquiry* 17 (2): 253–288. doi: 10.1086/448583

Hacking, I. 1999. *The Social Construction of What?* Harvard, MA: Harvard University Press.

Hacking, I. 2002. "Making Up People" Chap. 6 in *Historical Ontology,* edited by I. Hacking, 99–114. Cambridge, MA: Harvard University Press.

Hacking, I. 2004. "Between Michel Foucault and Erving Goffman: Between Discourse in the Abstract and Face-to-Face Interaction." *Economy and Society* 33 (3): 277–302. doi: 10.1080/0308514042000225671

Havnes, T. and M. Mogstad. 2011. "No Child Left Behind: Subsidized Childcare and Children's Long-Run Outcomes." *American Economic Journal: Economic Policy* 3 (2): 97–129. doi: 10.1257/pol.3.2.97

Heckman, J. J. 2006. "Skill Formation and the Economics of Investing in Disadvantaged Children." *Science* 312 (5782): 1900–1902. doi: 10.1126/science.1128898

Kvello, Ø. 2011. *Barn i risiko: Skadelige omsorgssituasjoner [Children At Risk: Harmful Conditions of Care].* Oslo: Gyldendal Norsk Forlag.

Lipsky, M. 1980. *Street-Level Bureaucracy: Dilemmas of the Individual in Public Services.* New York: Russell Sage Publications.

Lund, R. and M. L. Magnussen. 2018. "Intersektionalitet, virksomhedskundskab og styringsrelationer: Institutionel Etnografi og hverdagens sociale organisering." [Intersectionality, Work Knowledge and Ruling Relations: Institutional Ethnography and the Social Organization of Everyday Life]. *Tidsskrift for Kjønnsforskning* 42 (4): 268–283.

Neumann, C. B. 2009. *Det bekymrede blikket: En studie av helsesøstres handlingsbetingelser. [The Concerned Gaze: A Study of Public Nurses Conditions for Action].* Oslo: Novus Forlag.

Nilsen, A. C. E. 2016. "In-Between Discourses: Early Intervention and Diversity in the Norwegian Kindergarten Sector." *Journal of Comparative Social Work* 11 (1): 1–22.

Nilsen, A. C. E. 2017. "The Expansion of Early Childhood Development Services and the Need to Reconceptualize Evidence." *Contemporary Issues in Early Childhood* 18 (3): 269–280. doi: 10.1177/1463949117731021

Rose, N. 1999. *Governing the Soul: The Shaping of the Private Self.* 2nd ed. London: Free Association Books.

Smith, D. E. 1978. "'K is Mentally Ill': The Anatomy of a Factual Account." *Sociology* 12 (1): 23–53. doi: 10.1177/003803857801200103

Smith, D. E. 2004. "Ideology, Science and Social Relations a Reinterpretation of Marx's Epistemology." *European Journal of Social Theory* 7 (4): 445–462. doi: 10.1177/1368431004046702

Smith D. E. 2005. *Institutional Ethnography: A Sociology for People.* Lanham, MD: AltaMira.

Smith, D. E. 2012a. "Ruling Relations." Chap. 5 in *Writing the Social: Critique, Theory and Investigations.* Toronto: University of Toronto Press.

Smith, D. E. 2012b. "Sociological Theory: Methods of Writing Patriarchy into Feminist Texts." Chap. 7 in *Writing the Social: Critique, Theory and Investigations.* Toronto: University of Toronto Press.

Smith, D. E. 2012c. "Telling the Truth after Postmodernism." Chap. 6 in *Writing the Social: Critique, Theory and Investigations.* Toronto: University of Toronto Press.

Turmel, A. 2008. *A Historical Sociology of Childhood: Developmental Thinking, Categorization and Graphic Visualization.* New York: Cambridge University Press.

Ulla, B. 2014. "Auget som arrangement: Om blikk, makt og skjønn i profesjonsutøvinga til barnehagelæraren." [The Eye as Arrangement: On Gaze, Power and Discretion in the Professional Practice of the Kindergarten Teacher]. *Nordisk Barnehageforskning* 8 (5): 1–16. doi: 10.7577/nbf.774

8 Exploring "whiteness" as ideology and work knowledge

Thinking with institutional ethnography

Rebecca W. B. Lund[1]

Introduction

Historically, Nordic welfare states and their social policies have, with vary-ing degrees of success, taken into account stratifications of class and gender in an effort to map, understand, and respond to different forms of inequal-ity and their social reproduction (see e.g. Thideman-Faber et al. 2012). How-ever, those same institutions and policies have tended to be blind to issues of race. Indeed, whilst specific Nordic anti-racist, anti-imperialist movements and academics have engaged critically with issues of race, ethnicity, and colonialism, Nordic countries themselves, in a wider context, retain an in-ward (and project an outward) image of themselves as untouched by colo-nialism and racism (see Keskinen et al. 2016).[2] Indeed, in such countries the welfare state has to a large degree been founded on a particular his-torical construction of cultural, religious, and racial homogeneity (see e.g. Danbolt and Myong 2019; Markkola 2000, 2001; Markkola and Naumann 2014; Mulinari et al. 2016). In terms of race, it is perhaps more accurate to say that Nordic people, a majority of whom can be characterised as "white," simply do not perceive themselves as raced (Frankenberg 1993). Rather, in the Nordic context, race is something ascribed to a minority Other and to minority experience, and in research on race the members of minorities, as in North America, are often "expected to do far more than their fair share of explaining to others" (DeVault 2016, 271). Further, racism has generally not been accepted as rooted in ideology and institutions but is usually in-dividualised and perceived either as a case of "extremely bad and impolite behaviour towards guests" or as being perpetrated by a few "rotten apples" (Palmberg 2016, 36; see also Keskinen et al. 2016). This is despite the fact that Nordic peoples have historically constructed each other through hier-archies of "whiteness" whilst engaging in the Othering and subordinated inclusion of "non-white" and racialised Sami, Inuit, and Roma peoples and cultures as well as immigrant populations (see Kuokkanen 2007; Loftsdottír and Jensen 2012; Mulinari and Neergaard 2004).

In all Nordic countries, formal citizenship rights continue to go hand in hand with reported experiences of social, political, ethnic discrimination

(Keskinen et al. 2016, 5). In Denmark, for instance, the granting of citizenship rights depends on passing a Danish language test, a comprehensive test in Danish history and politics, as well as a test that establishes whether you are sufficiently committed and connected to Denmark. Once citizen status has been granted, there is a formal ritual in which the new citizen *must* shake hands with a city official. This has been justified politically on the basis that, as a Nordic tradition going back to the Vikings, hand shaking serves as a sign of putting aside weapons. However, this ritual also forces Muslim men and women to put aside their cultural commitments in favour of Danish tradition. The ritual, as such, symbolises that citizenship is granted on the basis of accepting cultural assimilation. Moreover, statistics from each of the Nordic countries show that employment segregation, both vertically and horizontally, is a major issue. It is incredibly difficult even for well-educated non-Western immigrants to find employment, and even if they do so, such employment tends to be so-called low status jobs, such as bus driver, taxi driver, or care worker. Here studies from Finland have shown that the most common reasons given for unemployment of non-Western immigrants are "lack of education," "degrees and prior work experience not recognized," "weak Finnish language proficiency," "deficient cultural competence of the host society," "distrust towards non-national workers by employees and clients," "lack of social networks," "bullying," and "discrimination" (see e.g. Heponiemi and Silvan 2017). Finally, in Nordic media and political discourse, ideas of "nationhood and belonging" and "gender equality" are often linked to stories of "bad patriarchies," the "homogenisation" of immigrant women, and the "criminalisation of racialised men." Collectively, all of the above narratives has been perceived as part of *welfare state nationalism*—a term coined by Nordic post-colonial feminists (Keskinen et al. 2016, 5).

Whilst claims of race blindness, race neutrality, and the denial of racism do not always stem from bad intentions, a significant body of research shows how blindness, neutrality, and denial are often implicated in the (re)production of racial inequity and injustice, and the maintenance of white privilege (Ahmed 2012; Andreassen and Myong 2017; Berg 2008; Danbolt and Myong 2019; Frankenberg 1993; Keskinen et al. 2016).

In this chapter, I will think with the method of institutional ethnography (IE) and Dorothy Smith to examine whiteness in the Nordic context. This chapter will consist of three sections. First, I introduce some excerpts from life story interviews with Finnish feminist scholars, which I conducted as part of my research project "Epistemic Injustice in Feminist Knowledge Production"—interviews in which many of my participants took up the theme of "whiteness," even though it was neither something I had asked for, nor a subject in which I had a predefined interest. In this first section I also provide brief contextualisations and interpretations of the interviews, explicating what I perceive to be a central contradiction surrounding the "race question" in contemporary feminist studies, at least in Finland—namely that scholars on the one hand are increasingly sensitive to questions of race, but on the other hand often fail to perceive themselves as raced. I conclude the section by collating the questions raised by the excerpts. Second, I draw on the conceptual resources of IE, particularly *work knowledge* and *standpoint*, to think about whiteness as a practice and activity that can be discovered in accounts of everyday life (DeVault 1995, 2016). I return to and re-engage critically with the interview excerpts, drawing on the conceptual resources of IE in order to examine, with hindsight, the questions I might have put to my participants. Third, connected to the previous section, I point towards the white body as an *ideological code*—one that, (often) unknowingly, mediates and coordinates discourse. Fourth and finally, I conclude this chapter and suggest how I might have used IE to design a study on whiteness in the Nordics.

Gender studies in the Nordics: a contradictory relationship to "race" and "whiteness"

My current research project, "Epistemic Injustice in Feminist Knowledge Production," is based on life story interviews conducted with Finnish feminist academics between 2017 and 2019. The research project focusses on how feminist knowledge production is shaped in relations of class and gender/sexuality, and examines the contribution of Gender Studies to the reproduction of inequity in academia and beyond. My research participants occupy various positions within academia regarding, for example, employment security and their position within the institutional hierarchy. Whilst all my participants are ethnically Finnish and white, they differ with regard to their class, sex, and gender identity. Although whiteness and race were not the focus of my research, they were both themes that many of my research participants took up. Indeed, without ever being asked explicitly, most of my participants brought up the subject of "whiteness" in some way. Below I introduce some excerpts from my interviews, giving a sense of how the topics where brought up:

REBECCA: You mentioned before that you grew up in a very white neighbourhood. What do you mean by that?

LUKE: Well *obviously,* I didn't know anything about racism. I wasn't aware of those issues at all. I know now, looking at it through a gender studies lens, that the unawareness was made possible, by growing up in a white middle-class neighbourhood ... I think that's still one of the most important things in feminist studies ... you can't do just equality work, you can't just teach people about gender equality between white women and men. I try to be quite careful that we discuss for example racism and learn to look at gender studies not as a kind of study about women and men but also from an intersectional perspective.

REBECCA: Before we end for today, I was just wondering whether you have ever thought about the community, but also the universities you've been in. Have they been multicultural in any way or have they been very Finnish?

LAURA: Of course! I think the schools were quite Finnish, we didn't even have Roma, or any ... I don't know about people of Sami background. But then at Oulu University, you can study Sami culture and languages and some of my closest colleagues were from Sami studies, so there was some ethnic diversity. It has generally been very white Finnish communities I've been working in. Also, when I was working at Helsinki University, there were two non-Finns, but still they were white. And then in the [X] project it has been actually interesting to see ... we had [X], who is from Uganda, but she left the project and now we have [X] who is from Iran. Both are based in Norwegian universities. So yeah, generally it's been really white Finnish communities. And also, I think in Finnish Universities, I think it's changing a bit now, but there's this very strong stability in career paths. You do your Masters and your PhD in one university, your post-doc in the same university and then you get a permanent position in that university too. There has not traditionally been people coming and going and there hasn't been people coming in from other places ... And if there have been such people, they haven't been my collaborators.

INGRID: There were many frustrating experiences at those research seminars. "Why do you write about Wittgenstein, this dead white old man?" and I'm like, isn't, Deleuze and Foucault also dead white men [laughs]. And then people ask me, yeah but "why do you only cite a white archive of scholars" ... but then I actually write about Derrida and he's suddenly turned into this white scholar, it's just weird, yeah.[3]

ELIZA: So far, all the people I've interviewed have been white. And also, well, not everybody, but almost all of them have an academic education, they are white ... they are middle class. I wonder what that actually does to the outcomes. And how I could actually address that critically. But the whole history of race and racism in Finland is quite different from the US, and a lot of people are actually struggling a bit to make US texts about race relevant in Finland ... The feeling I have is that there's a lot of research about immigrants and asylum seekers, but that seems to make whiteness invisible again.

IKE: The research is about launching queer indigenous studies, in Finland and in Nordic countries where it hasn't really happened yet. But it is happening, very much so, in North America and in Australia and New

Zealand ... If I come back here, I wanna build this department to be less white [laughs]. I see that there is a development taking place with my support, but I think it will also happen without my support.

REBECCA: You think so?

IKE: Yes.

REBECCA: Why? Do you see that as a natural development or what is it that makes you say that?

IKE: No not necessarily. I hope that it will be. It's rather that gender studies has mainstreamed the value of racial ethnic diversity, for better or for worse, to a certain degree. And yet decolonising curricula has not happened at all, in Finland at least. A bit more so in Sweden. This is something that we need to do within gender studies and outside of gender studies. It cannot continue, this centrality of whiteness.

As the excerpts above illustrate, issues of whiteness, race, and/or ethnicity arose when participants spoke about the neighbourhoods, villages, or school systems in which they grew up and were occasionally brought up in connection to their current workplace or scholarly interests. However, only in a few cases (out of my approximately 20 interviews) did people mention their own racial position. The "unmarked, unnamed status is itself an effect of its dominance ... their seeming normativity, their structured invisibility" (Frankenberg 1993, 6). The quotes stand testament to "the social geography of race"—a term coined by Ruth Frankenberg (1993, 43). Finland remains undeniably very white, yet there has been increased immigration to Finland from the Global South over the past 19 years (Statistics Finland 2017). Additionally, the Finnish population is comprised of a considerable minority of Sami and Roma peoples (Grönfors 2012; United Nations 2016). The interviews bear the marks of current debates in Nordic feminist scholarship, student activism and beyond, in which critical race studies and intersectionality (imported from US scholarship) are increasingly translated and adapted to a Nordic context. However, these narratives still sit somewhat awkwardly within a Finnish context, being mostly taken up as something to be remarked upon and shown concern for—almost in a habitual manner. However, this form of engagement does not necessarily result in a reflexively challenging of, or promoting change in, people's (own) practices. As such white privilege is reproduced. The interviews, however, also bear the marks of a wider political climate in the Nordics and Finland where hostility towards immigration, so central in right-wing populist political rhetoric, has now become increasingly mainstream—something that, either implicitly or explicitly, *all* of my participants defined themselves as opposed to. Finally, the quotes bear the marks of my participants' *and* my own "color- and power-evasive repertoire" (Frankenberg 1993, 32)—that which is said, unsaid, or left unquestioned. Despite feminist scholars' awareness of racism and white privilege as structural phenomena, the subject is also deeply personal and difficult to talk about. The accounts of my participants, in other words, carried the signs of contradiction. On the one hand, their theoretical insights into intersectionality and critical race studies have provided them the resources to identify whiteness as a position of privilege rooted in historical processes, arguing that this should be addressed in feminist research and activism. Yet, on the other hand, they more often than not (re) produced their own personal whiteness as a race neutral position, through its non-naming when speaking about their work, their colleagues, their international experience, their class and sexuality, thus activating the dominant Nordic discourse of race blindness.

Going over my interview transcripts, I began to question how we can remain empirically open to, and thus able to discover the relevance of, whiteness in overwhelmingly white environments. In the Nordic countries, many parts of the public sector, including higher education, are still predominantly white. Whilst there may be good reason to focus on other social relations, such as gender and class, being sensitive and aware of the role of race and whiteness is also crucially important. So, how does a white scholar sensitise him- or herself to see that which might otherwise be taken for granted? Which role should the category of whiteness play, when should it "enter" analysis, and how? I argue here that Dorothy Smith and IE offer tools via which the above can be explored in ways that take into account historical processes and actual experience, simultaneously explicating that which is downplayed and not readily available to the researcher.

Whiteness as work knowledge

How is whiteness enacted and played out on an everyday basis? Where does it play out and by whom? How might it be discovered using the concept of work knowledge? In IE we are interested in "work knowledge" and the embodied activities people engage in from when they wake up until they go to bed. We then seek to identify the social relations and the forms of social coordination to which these activities connect people. We are hooked into, or embedded in, translocal ruling relations that shape our lives—sometimes in ways that we are unaware of. Thus, the focus is not on the individual experience *per se*, but rather on the social organisation of everyday life, albeit remaining conscious of individual experience. Non-white bodies can also *do* whiteness, although it will be more difficult to "pass" because of the ideological markers attached to skin. Whilst for the non-white population, doing whiteness involves the work of "fitting in" to, or attempting to find "comfort with" the racial norm, what does it mean for a white person to do whiteness? How might one even begin to discover and explicate this? Sociologist Marjorie DeVault (1995, 2016), in her IE of female African American and European American food and nutrition professionals in North America, discovered gender, race, and ethnicity as forms of *work knowledge*. She showed the ways in which—via interactionist ethnomethodologically inspired "active listening and analysis," as opposed to "passive listening and recording" (DeVault 2016, 268)—she was able to see those social and ruling relations that may be present yet unacknowledged. Following DeVault's example, I will re-examine some of the excerpts from the dialogical interviews through the lens of *work knowledge*—not only the work knowledge of my participants but also my own work knowledge.

Luke, one of the research participants introduced earlier, did not have a "conscious conception of cultural and race difference," but she did have "an experience of a racially structured environment" (see Frankenberg 1993). Here I might have followed up by asking: "Why would you not know about racism just because you had grown up in a white middle-class neighbourhood?" One possibility is that Luke may not have experienced racism enacted upon her own body or personally known anyone who had. Yet did no one ever talk about race or racism in her family, on TV, in school, or in the neighbourhood and if not, what might the reasons be for this silence? One might question if it points towards endemic narratives of avoidance, blindness, neutrality, or otherwise. I might have asked if it was when entering gender studies (in her twenties) that she first encountered or considered questions of race and racism. Additionally, I might have asked how these questions were introduced and what they came to mean for her work, for the evaluation of her "previous" self, as well as her gender studies colleagues? My quiet acceptance of her explanation would suggest that I did not find it remarkable that race had been a non-topic in her earlier life. It is a form of institutional capture, but it seems to me that the capture itself is interesting when unpacked—we both accepted race and racism as a non-topic. This is one way in which whiteness is done.

Laura exclaims that she has "of course!" reflected on the diversity, or lack of it, in her schooling and work environments. She thus seems to show an alertness towards racial/ethnic diversity—a diversity that Ike claims is becoming "mainstream within gender studies." Laura explains what she recalls as a predominantly Finnish and white environment and, once again, I quietly accepted her explanation. However, I could have asked a number of questions that might have explicated the underlying work, assumptions, discourses, and ideologies shaping this account, *if* I had listened and analysed actively. For example, I could have asked: "Do you not remember whether there where Sami and Roma people in your childhood school? If so, why not?" What we remember and do not remember about our childhood is not about closing in on a more "truthful" account, but rather concerns understanding, with the benefit of hindsight, who and what are ascribed significance. Moving forward in Laura's life story, I might have asked whether *all* Sami people at Oulu University, to her knowledge, studied and worked in Sami studies, or whether they were also present in other disciplines. It is not unthinkable that Sami would have made themselves "invisible" outside Sami studies. Indigenous students and scholars, as well as indigenous experience and knowledge, often struggle to pass as having legitimacy and epistemic status in white Western universities (see e.g. Kuokkanen 2007; Tuhiwai Smith 1999, 1). What might that tell me about the social geography of race and ethnicity in a Finnish university? What might it have told me about knowledge production and epistemic habits that reproduce the Finnish perspective as dominant and the indigenous Sami as Other (see e.g. Kuokkanen 2007)? Indeed, would it have told me that at all? I might have continued by asking: "What did your collaboration with Sami scholars involve? How did you work together? Was there ever an awareness of 'difference' in your ways of working or socialising? If so, then how? How did that make you feel and act?" It would have been interesting to know whether and how collegiality was practised—whether it involved the (re)production of certain markers of difference, or rather, subverted them. Finally, when Laura speaks of the history and change in Finnish universities from a place of "stability" to a place of "less stable" career paths with competition from "the outside" and lots of moving around, I might have followed up and asked: "How and where do you see that there is an increase in the amount of non-Finns and non-white people?" "What are the reasons for the shifts as you see it?" "How does that make you feel and why do you think it is less stable?" It would have been interesting to hear how this change would be experienced from the perspective of a white woman still precariously positioned in academia and furthermore, which texts and discourses she would enact in telling me about it.

The quote from my interview with Ingrid tells us about some curiously contradictory practices within her scholarly community. On the one hand, Ingrid's colleagues show sensitivity and alertness towards the tendency of Western scholars to reproduce the ruling position of Western white male scholarly contributions, with all the consequences that follow from that scholarly practice (see e.g. Connell 2007). They do the work of questioning her scholarly citation practice. On the other hand, they only seem to problematise this scholarly practice when it comes to certain white men and then also assume that a famous philosopher, such as Jacques Derrida, must be white. Here it would have been interesting to explore how thinkers are differently positioned in terms of the value they can draw from their ascribed race, class, sexuality, and gender position—and how this positioning had taken place and how it was enacted by gender studies scholars. Another question I should have asked Ingrid concerned the defensive strategy of answering critical questions with a critical question. This could be seen as (re)producing her own personal whiteness and citation practice as race neutral or, at the very least, unproblematic. However, this seemed a difficult question to ask at the time. I chose to avoid the discomfort of asking such a question. This is an example of "color- and power-evasive repertoires" (Frankenberg 1993, 32–33), which can be seen as another way of doing whiteness.

The universal ramifications of colonialism: whiteness as ideological code?

In the words of Dorothy Smith, ideological codes

> orders and organizes texts across discursive sites, concerting discourse focused on divergent topics and sites, often having divergent audiences, and variously hooked into policy and political practice. This ordering and organizing of texts is integral to the coordination and concerting of the complex of evolving T-discourses[4] ... it is a constant generator of procedures for selecting syntax, categories, and vocabulary in the writing of texts and the production of talk and for interpreting sentences, written or spoken, or ordered by it. An ideological code can generate the same order in widely different settings of talk or writing— in legislative, social scientific, and administrative settings, in popular writing, television advertising, or wherever.
>
> (Smith 2004, 158–159)

I would argue that whiteness, and perhaps, in particular, whiteness as it is carried and enacted by the white, male, middle-class body (I write *perhaps* because that would have to be discovered empirically), can be said to be an ideological code in the way Smith describes above. Loftsdottír and Jensen (2012) and Ahmed (2012) tell us that the white body and whiteness usually manifest themselves in the privilege of being allowed to forget about one's skin colour—a privileged affordance linked to other historical markers of inferiority and superiority (see also Andreassen and Myong 2017; Danbolt and Myong 2019). The power of whiteness to organise discourses across varying contexts becomes, I suggest, particularly strong when whiteness is not assigned a place in the social relations of race. This depoliticises and individualises racism.

Colonialism is not a universal narrative, but it is "a narrative with universal ramifications," playing out historically and contemporarily in various contexts and regions, including the Nordics (Loftsdottír and Jensen 2012, 1). Indeed, so Loftsdottír and Jensen (2012) remind us, whilst the Nordics were "peripheral to the major metropolitan cultures, they generally participated actively in the production of Europe as the global centre and profited from this experience." This has shaped racial, gendered, and national relations of the contemporary Nordic region, and colonial perceptions of the world and "other cultures" continue to be reproduced in this context (Loftsdottír and Jensen 2012, 1–5). An example of historical manifestations of "colonial complicity" (Keskinen et al. 2016) in the Nordics can be identified by looking at highly influential texts, including academic texts, fiction, popular culture, advertising, policies, and policy discourse. One such example is the work of the Danish author Karen Blixen, who shaped generations of Nordic people's view on people from sub-Saharan Africa with her book *Out of Africa* (1937).

Another example is the work of the Swedish Carl von Linné, the father of modern taxonomy, whose book *Systema Naturae* (1735) provided a strongly ethnocentric racist classification of the human species in five "varieties" (see discussion Banton 1987, 4). Further examples of colonial complicity can be found in the beloved Swedish children's stories about *Pippi Longstocking* and her father the "negro king" by Astrid Lindgren (1945–1948). Yet colonial complicity also plays out via the power relations amongst Nordic peoples and between nations themselves (where e.g. the Finns were considered "less white" and backwards compared to the Swedes): a dynamic particularly manifest today in the position of Greenlander/Inuit, Sami, and Tornedalien peoples (see e.g. Jensen 2012; Petterson 2012). A recent example of the way in which Roma peoples are positioned today can be seen in Jenni Helakorpi's et al. (2018, 2019) studies of the discursive construction of Roma people in contemporary Nordic education policy documents and practice. Whilst policies aimed specifically at the Roma and the educational practices developed with the intention to ensure the children of Roma educational success have been developed with the best of intentions—to ensure social mobility and societal inclusion, and also to show sensitivity towards cultural specificities—they do, however, go hand-in-hand with particular forms of ethnic categorisation, discrimination, racialisation, and stereotyping. The Roma have to become tolerable and "fit in" to the educational institution. However, one may ask, tolerable to whom? The white majority? The middle-class value of social mobility? These policy texts, I suggest, speak from the (hidden) standpoint of the white middle-class majority.

The Nordics, from the standpoint of the non-white population, would appear to represent, in the words of Sarah Ahmed (2012), "[a] sea of whiteness." Unless you live in specific immigrant dense suburbs and do not leave, you encounter more white people (statistically speaking) than you will meet non-white people. Non-white people have a tendency to become either "invisible" or "hyper-visible" in the crowd. They either pass and fade into the background, or they do not (Ahmed 2012). Contrasting connotations are equally ascribed to the non-white population: they are often framed as a risk category, that due to a vulnerable social position may end up marginalised in society, but also a potential resource for an ageing society or for their "presumed" culturally diverse skills (e.g. Nilsen 2016). In both instances, they are Othered, either by being reduced to an institutional risk category; by having their experience and particularity reduced to stereotypes; or by someone else (usually a white person) speaking *about*, rather than *with* or *for* them. The skin, through a complex system of historical and textual processes, has become an ideological marker. The white skin is an ideological code rooted in historical processes of colonialism and racial hierarchies, in which whiteness is constructed not only as the norm but also as superior. Around this code we must discover how textually mediated discourses of difference and race become organised and play out. As Dorothy Smith (2009) argues:

inequalities identified as racial have to be discovered in historical continuities of disadvantage that are marked ideologically as genetic difference. There are, of course, genetic bases for ideological markers such as
skin colour, but not for the boundaries of difference identified with race.

(78)

Conclusion and another time

With this chapter, I have been thinking about whiteness through the lens of
IE. I have explored the data I produced for a project where the focus was *not*
on whiteness, but my participants nonetheless brought up whiteness when
we spoke about their life stories. I have critically scrutinised what I would
have done differently, had it been a project about whiteness and had I actively sought to open up racial relations. The work of my participants as well
as my own work may be producing, reproducing, or challenging racial ideologies, discourses, and practices that enforce difference or claim neutrality.
This chapter has hopefully provided some insights into the role of race and
whiteness in the Nordics. This theorising is central to understanding the
societal and contextual particularities of my interviews. This chapter, however, also makes visible that without starting investigation from actual experience and everyday work knowledge, it is difficult to produce new insights
about how racial relations and whiteness play out in diverging contexts. It
is too easy to reproduce established narratives about the workings of racial
relations, racism, and race blindness. If I was to do this study all over again,
with a focus on race and whiteness in Finnish academia and gender studies,
I would have taken the following steps:

1   Identify standpoint, from which I could learn something about taken
     for granted institutional orders and racial relations in academia. This
     could be based on statistics, interviews, and/or spontaneously occur-
     ring encounters with a student or a staff member—either of colour or
     white. The choice of standpoint would be empirically and contextually
     justified based on whether their experience would help open up institu-
     tional orders in a new way.
2   On that basis, I would initiate interviews with members of staff and
     students in order to learn from them about their life story and every-
     day work knowledge: what they do, how they engage with peers and
     colleagues, and how they learned to do what they do. I would perhaps
     complement this approach with participant observation of research
     seminars, department meetings, curriculum planning, teaching sessions
     or otherwise, at a particular department, in order to learn about every-
     day practices and work knowledge, and look for textual clues. I would
     look and listen carefully for racial knowledge or vocabulary.
3   The textual clues would point me towards directly or indirectly organ-
     ising texts coordinating everyday life and relations at the university and

beyond, such as particular theories, university policies, EU policies, national policies, welfare regulations, or particular practices within the department. These may, in turn, include references to racial ethnic stereotypes, categories, and ways of knowing, or they may reference ways in which racial ethnic difference and inequality is downplayed and glossed over.

4   Having identified immediately relevant texts, I would place them within a wider intertextual hierarchy and the historical processes out of which they have grown. These may point towards racialised and colonial processes and ideologies, and they may also point elsewhere. It will have to be discovered.

5   Finally, I would return to standpoint and explicate how these shape experiences and hold people accountable to certain ways of doing work, and particular "ruling" standpoints.

Notes

1 This research was funded by the Academy of Finland, postdoctoral research project: *Epistemic Injustice in Academia: Class and Gender in Feminist Knowledge Production*. Project number: 310795.
2 More recently, it should be mentioned that Danish colonialism (Danish West Indies, Greenland, Faroe Islands) and their involvement in the slave trade (Danish Gold Coast)—particularly in connection to the recent centenary of Denmark's sale of the Danish West Indies to the United States in 1917—has been the subject of much attention, as seen in numerous academic and popular history books, TV documentaries, films, and exhibitions.
3 The philosopher Jacques Derrida was Algerian but lived and worked in France.
4 "T-discourses" to indicate that it is discourse, mediated and organised by material and replicable text.

References

Ahmed, S. 2012. *On Being Included: Racism and Diversity in Institutional Life*. Durham: Duke University Press.

Andreassen, R., and L. Myong. 2017. "Race, Gender and Researcher Positionality Analysed through Memory Work." *Nordic Journal of Migration Research* 7 (2): 97–104.

Banton, M. 1987. *Racial Theories*. Cambridge, UK: Cambridge University Press.

Berg, A. J. 2008. "Silence and Articulation: Whiteness, Racialization and Feminist Memory Work." *NORA: Nordic Journal of Feminist and Gender Research* 16 (4): 213–227.

Blixen, K. 1937 [2001]. *Out of Africa*. London: Penguin UK.

Connell, R. 2007. *Southern Theory: Social Science and the Global Dynamics of Knowledge*. Cambridge: Polity Press.

Danbolt, M., and L. Myong. 2019. "Racial Turns and Returns: Recalibrations of Racial Exceptionalism in Danish Public Debates on Racism." In *Racialization, Racism and Anti-Racism in the Nordic Countries*, edited by P. Hervik, 39–61. London: Palgrave Macmillian.

DeVault, M. 1995. "Ethnicity and Expertise: Racial-Ethnic Knowledge in Sociological Research." *Gender and Society* 9 (5): 612–631.

DeVault, M. 2016. "Ethnicity and Expertise: Racial-Ethnic Knowledge in Sociological Research." In *Introduction to Qualitative Research Methods: A Guidebook and Resource*, 4th Edition, edited by in S. Taylor, R. Bogdan and M. DeVault, 267–282. Hoboken: Wiley.

Frankenberg, R. 1993. *The Social Construction of Whiteness: White Women, Race Matters*. London: Routledge.

Grönfors, J. 2012. Roma in Finland. Brussels: European Roma Rights Centre. Retrieved on April 14th 2019 from: www.errc.org/roma-rights-journal/roma-in-finland

Helakorpi, J., S. Lappalainen and R. Mietola. 2018. "Equality in the Making? Roma and Traveller Minority Policies and Basic Education in Three Nordic Countries." *Scandinavian Journal of Educational Research* 0 (0): 1–18. published online first: doi: 10.1080/00313831.2018.1485735

Helakorpi, J., S. Lappalainen and F. Sahlström. 2019. "Becoming Tolerable: The Subject Constitution of Roma Mediators in Finnish Schools." *Intercultural Education* 30 (1): 51–67.

Heponiemi, T., and S. Silvan. 2017. "Immigrants as Clients and Professionals in Social and Health Care. COPE. Retrieved from: www.stncope.fi/en/whats-new/article-immigrants-as-clients-and-professionals-in-social-and-health-care/

Jensen, L. 2012. "Danishness as Whiteness in Crisis: Emerging Post-Imperial and Development Aid Anxieties." In *Whiteness and Postcolonialism in the Nordic Region: Exceptionalism, Migrant Others and National Identities*, edited by K. Loftsdottír and L. Jensen, 105–118. Surrey: Ashgate.

Keskinen, S., S. Tuori, S. Irni and D. Mulinari. 2016. *Complying with Colonialism: Gender, Race and Ethnicity in the Nordic Region*. London: Routledge.

Kuokkanen, R. 2007. *Reshaping the University: Responsibility, Indigenous Epistemes and the Logic of the Gift*. Vancouver: UBC Press.

Linné, C. von. 1735. *Systema Naturae*. Holmiae: Sweden.

Loftsdottír, K., and L. Jensen. 2012. *Whiteness and Postcolonialism in the Nordic Region: Exceptionalism, Migrant Others and National Identities*. Surrey: Ashgate.

Markkola, P. 2000. "Promoting Faith and Welfare. The Deaconess Movement in Finland and Sweden, 1850–1930." *Scandinavian Journal of History* 25 (1–2): 101–118.

Markkola, P. 2001. "Lutheranism and the Nordic Welfare States in a Gender Perspective." *Women, Gender & Research* 2: 10–19.

Markkola, P., and I. Naumann. 2014. "Lutheranism and the Nordic Welfare States in Comparison." *Journal of State and Church* 56 (1): 1–12.

Mulinari, D., S. Keskinen, S. Irni and S. Tuori. 2016. "Introduction: Postcolonialism and the Nordic Models of Welfare and Gender." In *Complying with Colonialism: Gender, Race and Ethnicity in the Nordic Region*, edited by S. Keskinen, S. Tuori, S. Irni and D. Mulinari.1–16. London: Routledge.

Mulinari, D., and A. Neergaard. 2004. "Systor, du är jo annorlunda: Immigration, institutionell förändring och kön." [Sister, You are Different: Immigration, Institutional Change and Gender] *Framtiden i samtiden: könsrelationer i förändring i Sverige och omvärlden*, edited by C. Florin and C. Bergqvist. Institut for Framtidsstudier: Rapportserien Framtidsstudier, ISSN 1650-8955, vol. 9.

114   *Rebecca W. B. Lund*

Nilsen, A. C. E. (2016): "In-Between Discourses: Early Intervention and Diversity in the Norwegian Kindergarten Sector." *Journal of Comparative Social Work* 11 1: 64–85.

Palmberg, M. 2016. "The Nordic Colonial Mind." In *Complying with Colonialism: Gender, Race and Ethnicity in the Nordic Region*, edited by S. Keskinen, S. Tuori, S. Irni and D. Mulinari, 67–84. London: Routledge.

Petterson, C. 2012. "Colonialism, Racism and Exceptionalism." In *Whiteness and Postcolonialism in the Nordic Region: Exceptionalism, Migrant Others and National Identities*, edited by K. Loftsdottír and L. Jensen, 29–41. Surrey: Ashgate.

Smith, D. 2004. "Ideology, Science and Social Relations: A Reinterpretation of Marx's Epistemology." *European Journal of Social Theory* 7 (4): 445–462.

Smith, D. 2009. "Categories Are Not Enough." *Gender & Society* 23 (1): 76–80.

Statistics Finland. 2017. "Immigrants in the Population." Retrieved on April 14th 2019 from: www.stat.fi/tup/maahanmuutto/maahanmuuttajat-vaestossa_en.html

Thideman-Faber, S., A. Prieur and L. Rosenlund. 2012. *Det Skjulte Klassesamfund [The Hidden Class Society]*. Aarhus: Aarhus Universitetsforlag.

Tuhiwai Smith, L. 1999. *Decolonizing Methodologies: Research and Indigenous Peoples*. London: Zed Books.

United Nations. 2016. Report on the Human Rights Situation of the Sami People in the Sápmi Region. Human Rights Council, Thirty-Third Session. Retrieved on April 14th 2019 from: http://unsr.vtaulicorpuz.org/site/index.php/documents/country-reports/155-report-sapmi-2016

Part 3

Application of institutional ethnography in Nordic countries

9 Institutional ethnography as a feminist approach for social work research

Marjo Kuronen

Introduction

As a feminist social work academic, I have argued over the years that social work practice and research in Finland are rather 'gender blind' (Kuronen et al. 2004) and that social work research has ignored not only gender-specific issues but also feminist theorising and methodology (Kuronen 2009). Even if the interest in gender studies has increased among younger social work researchers, there is still much to do. In this chapter, my aim is to show that institutional ethnography (IE) is a valuable feminist approach for social work research, which should be better known and more widely used in Finland and the other Nordic countries.

For me, IE is primarily 'a feminist sociology' or 'a sociology for women' as Dorothy Smith formulated it in her early work (Smith 1988, 1990a). Since then, it has been used more widely, and Smith herself has more recently defined it as 'a sociology for people' (Smith 2005). Even as a feminist approach, it does not mean studying only women. It is not so much what to study but how. Its main commitment is that instead of abstract scientific concepts and theories, the inquiry should start from a standpoint in the everyday world, where we are bodily and socially acting as knowing subjects. Thus, social sciences should be grounded in the local actualities of people's lives and their material conditions, which is 'a point of entry' to larger social and economic processes and the relations of ruling organising these actualities (Smith 2004, 2005, 54–57).

Ever since my doctoral research project in the 1990s, where I was studying professional advice giving to mothers in maternity and child health services (Kuronen 1999), IE has inspired me. It has provided a feminist approach to study women as service users in different welfare service institutions; first as mothers, and more recently as women in vulnerable and marginalised positions in the Finnish society, as well as their encounters with the welfare service system and how it meets (or fails to meet) their needs.

This chapter focusses on the special value of IE for my own academic field, social work research. To contextualise that, I will first return to the early 1990s to look at how IE found its way to the academic arenas in Finland, and how it has influenced my own research projects.

Institutional ethnography finding its way to Finland

Ever since Smith published her first three books, *The Everyday World as Problematic. A Feminist Sociology* (1988), *The Conceptual Practices of Power* (1990a) and *Texts, Facts, and Femininity* (1990b), IE has been widely adopted, discussed and debated not only in sociology and women's studies (gender studies) but also in education, nursing and social work research (Malachowski et al. 2017). Considering this, it has been surprisingly little recognised and used in Finland, despite Smith's work being introduced through Finnish women's studies in the early 1990s.

Women's studies established itself as an academic discipline in Finland during the 1980s. At that time, the first national research networks were founded (Rantalaiho 1986; Julkunen and Rantalaiho 1989), the first courses were offered at universities and the Finnish journal of women's studies *Naistutkimus-Kvinnoforskning* was established in 1988 (in 2014 its name was changed to Finnish journal of gender studies).

In the 1980s and 1990s, many researchers studied the Finnish welfare state and its history from a gender perspective. Nordic feminist research has been shaped by the notion that the welfare state is woman-friendly, as was argued at the late 1980s by Norwegian researcher Helga Maria Hernes (1987). This means that the state has been perceived as an important ally for the women's movement, and women's concerns, needs and interests have been taken seriously in policymaking. In the Nordic countries, women have historically been important actors in the development of social policy, and the welfare state actively supported professionalisation and labour market participation of women. This woman-friendliness notion stands in opposition to the Anglo-American feminist understanding of the patriarchal state enforcing women's role as unpaid care providers, who are financially dependent on men (e.g. Anttonen 1997; Borchorst and Siim 2008).

These welfare state researchers, many of them doctoral students at that time, were supervised by Professor Liisa Rantalaiho from the University of Tampere and Senior lecturer Raija Julkunen from the University of Jyväskylä (both emerita now). They formed a national network called 'Women of the Welfare State' and made a research proposal 'Gender System of the Welfare State' (Julkunen and Rantalaiho 1989), which received funding from the Academy of Finland and was initiated in the early 1990s. Many doctoral dissertations grew out of that network, and it published two edited volumes based on its findings (Anttonen et al. 1994; Eräsaari et al. 1995). I was then in the early stages of my post-graduate studies, and it was an advantage to join such a network.

Funding from the Academy of Finland allowed the network to organise seminars and invite international established academics. Dorothy Smith was invited to one of these seminars. During that week, she gave lectures, supervised and commented on papers. Meeting her personally and reading her texts influenced and encouraged many of us. However, very few eventually adopted IE as their main research approach. Among the younger generation of social scientists in Finland, there are two noteworthy exceptions: Riikka Homanen (2013) and Rebecca Lund (2015), who both used IE in their doctoral dissertations.

Through the 'Women of the Welfare State' – network IE also found its way into social work research in Finland, but rather marginally. Mirja Satka, currently professor of social work at the University of Helsinki, was the first one to adopt it. In her doctoral dissertation, she used IE in studying the history of social work in Finland (Satka 1995). More recently, together with her colleagues, she has discussed and tested whether and how Foucault's and Smith's methodology and conceptual tools could be used in parallel to study the historical transformation of child welfare social work (Satka and Skehill 2012; Skehill et al. 2012). She has also supervised doctoral students using IE, among them Ulla Jokela (2011) and the forthcoming thesis by Susanna Hoikkala. However, Satka's work is a rare exception in Finland, in that it adopts and discusses IE in the field of social work research. Sometimes any ethnographic case study of a specific institution, such as a hospital, a shelter or a residential institution, is referred to as an IE, even if there is no reference to Smith. This also shows how little IE is known in social work research in Finland.

Institutional ethnography, welfare services and women service users

As mentioned above, it was through the Finnish women's studies network and not social work research that I first learned about IE. In my doctoral dissertation, I studied a topic only indirectly related to social work: namely, how maternity and child health services in Finland and Scotland, and professional advice to mothers, were socially organised, including how motherhood ideologies shaped the work of mothers (Kuronen 1999). I was inspired by the research on mothering and schooling that Smith had done together with Alison Griffith (Griffith and Smith 1990; also Griffith and Smith 2005). Moreover, IE provided an approach to overcome the apparent conflict between the woman-friendliness of the Nordic welfare state, on the one hand, and ideological control of women's mothering, on the other hand. It allowed me to critically analyse the service system and the social organisation of motherhood without placing the blame or responsibility on female professionals as control agents of the state.

My work was particularly influenced by what Smith in her early work called the *ideological circle* and *ideological practices*. The ideological circle is related to her conceptual framework with two 'worlds'. First, there is the 'ruling apparatus', or 'relations of ruling' as she prefers to call it in her more recent work (e.g. Smith 1999, 77), which is a *'complex of management, government, administration, professions, and intelligentsia, as well as the textually mediated discourses that coordinate and interpenetrate it'* (Smith 1988, 108).

Second, there is the 'everyday world', which *we experience directly, and in which we are located physically and socially*' (Smith 1988, 89). Smith also identified different narratives or discourses related to these 'worlds': primary narrative and ideological discourse. Primary narrative uses lived experience as its resource while ideological discourse refers to professional or scientific discourse. This ideological discourse was the main interest in my doctoral dissertation.

Smith described the ideological circle as a process where primary narratives are used as the material of the institutional, ideological discourse (Smith 1990a, 141–173). She has identified it in the process in which the concept of 'single mother' is used as an interpretative schema in defining and explaining children's behaviour and possible problems (Smith 1988, 167–178), or in how SNAF (Standard North-American Family) as an ideological code intervenes in different local sites by influencing how family is understood (Smith 1999, 157–171; Kuronen 2014). I found ideological circle as a useful conceptual tool for analysing how professional definitions and categorisations were used and constructed within the welfare service system in describing their (female) service users, for example as 'lone mothers', 'homeless women' or 'female drug abusers'. Such institutional definitions influence how the women are seen and what kind of services are provided for them.

More recently, Smith has increasingly emphasised the importance of texts, language and discourses as mediators of social relations and their role in creating and maintaining these definitions (Smith 1999, 2005, but already Smith 1990b). My approach in adopting IE has been less focussed on analysing texts or textually mediated relations and has been instead closer to 'traditional' ethnographic research (see also De Montigny 1995; Nichols 2014). In studying mothering and child health services (Kuronen 1999), my point of entry was (participant) observation of the work of health professionals and their encounters with mothers. I combined ethnographic methods in data collection and IE as the general framework of my research. Jonathan Tummons (2017, 150) states that '*An institutional ethnography is not simply an ethnography of or an ethnography that has been constructed within an institution*'. Still, there is often some confusion of what 'ethnography' means in IE as it is not what is more commonly understood as ethnographic research in the methodological literature, which refers either to the method of participant observation or to cultural studies in anthropology and sociology (e.g. Atkinson et al. 2007).

It took many years after my doctoral research project before I got the opportunity to return to IE. Currently, together with my research team, we are studying how the Finnish welfare service system meets the needs of women in vulnerable positions in society.[1] The women whose standpoint we have taken are drug users, lone mothers living on basic social benefits and ex-convicts. We want to find out what they hold in common in terms of their relationship to the welfare service system. The wider context of this project are the recent and ongoing reforms and transformations of the welfare service system in Finland, including new models of service delivery and management, austerity policies and growing requirements for cost-effectiveness, marketisation and prioritising, which might make access to and availability of services even more difficult for these women.

By using the concept of vulnerable life situations, instead of referring to these women as vulnerable individuals or groups, we want to emphasise temporal, situational, relational and structural nature of vulnerability. By using IE, we turn the attention towards the society and its institutions, including social work and the entire welfare service system, which compensate for, but possibly also generate and (re)produce, vulnerability in these women's lives (Fineman 2010; Virokannas et al. 2018).

We have adopted IE also to 'bridge the gap' between two distinct research traditions and to escape their flaws. The first tradition, common in feminist research but also in social work, seeks to give marginalised women or people a voice. However, according to Smith, engaging with women's experiences is not enough. Instead, feminist research should provide them with 'maps' of how their experiences and everyday lives are organised by social relations of ruling (Smith 1988, 151–154, 1999, 96–97). The second tradition can be coined as a more macro-level and social policy-oriented approach. It is important in focussing on structures, processes and alterations of the welfare service system (e.g. Martinelli et al. 2017). However, this approach does not delve into how these systems and policies are experienced in the daily lives of women. We are arguing that as social work researchers, we should critically analyse the welfare service system, but we should do this without losing the standpoint of women and the connection with their experiences as its service users.

The value of institutional ethnography for social work research

I have already discussed the influence of IE for my own research. Besides, I want to consider more generally, what IE has to offer specifically for social work research. Therefore, in this section, I will discuss with and refer to other social work researchers beyond Finland about how they have seen it. These researchers have rarely discussed IE specifically as a feminist approach even if many of them have studied issues such as how mothers are met in child welfare or analysed the work of social workers, a vast majority of whom are women.

Social work research often focusses on the experiences of either service users or social workers or the encounters and interaction between them. What I want to show is that IE can provide an approach for studying and problematising social work instead as a social institution, in its wider social context, where both service users and professionals are positioned in its ruling relations, yet as social actors, they can also resist these positions.

Social work research using IE is often asking how the everyday world and experiences of people who for some reason have become social work service users are transformed into categories, definitions and labels that serve organisational purposes as part of the 'organisational order' (Hicks 2009) or 'ideological practice' (De Montigny 1995) of social work. It demonstrates how ideological discourse shape individual lives and experiences (e.g. Winfield 2003). This has also been the aim of my research projects even if the institutions I have studied have been others than social work. This is comparable in focus to Smith's article 'K is mentally ill' and her other work where she has analysed the processes in how women are diagnosed or defined as having mental illness (Smith 1990a, 1990b). Studying such processes provides possibilities for alternative meanings, which are closer to people's own understanding of their situation (e.g. Brown 2006).

Several researchers have studied how different guidelines and procedures not only organise the lives of the service users, but of the work of social workers as well. Social workers are expected to follow and use, for example, risk reduction strategies in child protection work (Brown 2006) and child custody planning procedures (Kushner 2006), make individual rehabilitation plans (Breimo 2016) or assess who can qualify to be foster carers or adoptive parents (Hicks 2009). These studies show that IE offers a framework to analyse the connections between work with individual service users, the organisational contexts of work and its guiding principles.

In its focus on institutions instead of individuals (Tummons 2017), IE helps to avoid placing service users and professionals against each other, as easily happens in social work research when taking the perspective of one or the other. Instead of blaming individual social workers or other welfare professionals, it is important to show how professionals and service users are embedded within the same institutional relations of ruling (Høgsbro 2017). As Stephen Hicks (2009) has put it in his research on how lesbians and gay men are assessed as possible foster or adoptive parents:

> Institutional ethnography does not ask about 'bad attitudes' towards lesbian, gay, bisexual and transgendered people [or any service users – mk], but rather asks how versions of these categories of knowledge circulate within a given context. That is, rather than seeing the problem as merely 'homophobic individuals', institutional ethnography investigates the complex, frequently disputed, practices in which all of us – to some extent – participate and which are part of the organizational order of social work.
>
> (Hicks 2009, 235)

Using IE, some authors (e.g. Parada et al. 2007; Hicks 2009; Arnd-Caddigan 2012) have also shown how social workers are able to oppose and resist the institutional order and use their professional agency. For example, Margaret Arnd-Caddigan (2012) has studied how clinical social workers respond to evidence-based practice policy they are expected to follow in their work and shows that in their actual practice they adopt to this policy in a selective, reflective and critical manner. I find recognising and analysing possibilities for professional agency important especially as in the Nordic countries social work is one of the female professions of the (woman-friendly) welfare state (e.g. Satka 1995).

Furthermore, IE offers an approach that takes the standpoint of the local and particular actualities of people's lives and begins from their experience. Its approach to experience is still different from most social sciences, including social work research. Studying experiences, narratives or life stories of different service user groups or marginalised people is common in social work research, at least in Finland. I appreciate such research as it might help to see them as 'entire persons', not merely as clients due to their social problems. What is particular about IE, however, is its focus on the social organisation of these actualities, not on the experiences as such (Smith 1988, 151–154, 1999, 96–97). I see this being especially important and valuable when doing research with and for people who are in the most marginalised, vulnerable and powerless positions in society as social work service users often are. This commitment shares the emancipatory and empowering aims and ethical values of social work practice and research, especially those of critical and feminist social work (e.g. Healy 2000).

Related to its emancipatory commitment, Smith's approach is linked to materialism and realism in its aim to tell 'how things work' (Smith 1988, 160–161, 2005, 29–38). I find that this is highly important in social work research in order to make a change in people's lives and to improve social work practice. Smith has criticised not only 'traditional sociology' but also postmodernism (Smith 1999, 96–130) for its relativism, its focus on discourse and performativity and its separation from the actualities of people's lives. Hart and McKinnon (2010) assess that a special value of Smith's work is that she has managed to avoid the opposite dangers of naive empiricism and relativism of social constructionism. According to them, her work *'provides a means of conceiving the discursive nature of social life (and the operations of power) without giving up the notion of "truth"'* (Hart and McKinnon 2010, 1040).

Finally, I find the way in which Smith understands and underlines the role of texts and textually mediated social relations in how the ruling relations work important for social work research. In social work, different texts have a crucial role in categorising and defining the needs of service users, regulating the work of social workers and even organising social work itself and its place in society. Social work depends on legislation, national and local regulations and guidelines, but it also produces documents concerning the lives of its service users. Case files are 'telling the case' and defining and classifying the person behind the 'case' for years or even decades ahead. In Finland, service users have the right to access and read their case files, which can be a traumatic experience, for example, for the clients of child protection, both for parents whose child has been taken into care and for those who have been into care as children. Based on her empirical findings, Tarja Vierula

(2017, 12) concludes, '*the transformation of information not only signifies a linguistic and a conceptual modification of information regarding their personal lives, but it also shifts the control and the ownership of that information*'. That is why documentation in social work should be critically analysed, as should also the role of other texts in organising social work and its professional practice. IE provides an approach to study institutional texts, such as those used and produced in different social work contexts, not just in their written form but also as active texts that coordinate and mediate people's actions translocally (e.g. Smith 2005, 101–122).

Conclusion

In this chapter, I have argued and tried to demonstrate that IE is a valuable approach for social work research. In the other social sciences, it has already made a substantial contribution worldwide, including the Nordic countries, especially Norway. One reason why it has not found its place in social work research in Finland might be that until recently feminist research in general has been rather marginal in this field. Smith originally developed IE as a feminist sociology (Smith 1988, 1990a) but since then it has been adopted more widely and maybe even lost some of its feminist origins. What makes IE a feminist approach is not so much, or not simply, the topics that are studied but rather its commitments and the standpoint in the everyday world.

I have shown, referring to both my own research projects and the views and empirical findings of other researchers, that IE allows studying social work and the whole welfare service system as an institution, which tends to transform the experiences and daily lives of its service users into generalised categorisations and definitions, which can be even stigmatising. This often happens mediated by different texts, written guidelines and procedures and textual practices of recording and documenting. In social work research, it is important to analyse and problematise such institutional categorisations and how they work. In both social work practice and research, we should instead begin from what people tell us about their lives and their needs for support and services.

In its focus on institutions and social relations of ruling, IE also allows to see how social workers and other professionals are positioned in the same institutional relations and practices as the service users. These are difficult but not impossible to resist and change. Social work practitioners often feel that not only the service users but also researchers blame them and criticise their work. Adopting IE could be one solution to avoid this and to do research that benefits both the service users and professionals alike.

In my own research, introducing and using IE has been the way of bridging feminist research and social work research. More than 30 years ago, US social work researcher Barbara G. Collins argued that '*In numerous ways the values, ethical commitments, purposes and philosophical systems of feminism and social work converge and impart added meaning to each other'* (Collins 1986, 214). For me, the strongest argument for using IE is that it shares and fits well with the critical, emancipatory and empowering aims of social work practice and research, especially those of feminist social work.

Note

1 This research was funded by the Academy of Finland research project *Transforming welfare service system from the standpoint of women in vulnerable life situations* (2016–2020, project no. 294407).

References

Anttonen, Anneli. 1997. *Feminismi ja sosiaalipolitiikka* [*Feminism and Social Policy*]. Tampere: Tampere University Press.

Anttonen, Anneli, Lea Henriksson, and Ritva Nätkin.1994. *Naisten hyvinvointivaltio* [*Women's Welfare State*]. Tampere: Vastapaino.

Arnd-Caddigan, Margaret. 2012. "Clinical Social Workers' Response to a State Policy On the Use of Evidence-Based Practice: How Attitudes, Behaviors, and Competing Values Affect Actual Practice." *Smith College Studies in Social Work* 82 (1): 19–38.

Atkinson, Paul, Amanda Coffey, Sara Delamont, John Lofland, and Lyn Lofland, eds. 2007. *Handbook of Ethnography*. London, Thousand Oaks, New Delhi and Singapore: Sage.

Borchorst, Anette, and Birte Siim. 2008. "Theorizing Scandinavian Gender Equality". *Feminist Theory* 9 (2): 207–224. doi: 10.1177/1464700108090411

Breimo, Janne Paulsen. 2016. "Planning Individually? Spotting International Welfare Trends in the Field of Rehabilitation in Norway." *Scandinavian Journal of Disability Research* 18 (1): 65–76. doi: 10.1080/15017419.2014.972447

Brown, Debra J. 2006. "Working the System: Re-Thinking the Institutionally Organized Role of Mothers and the Reduction of "Risk" in Child Protection Work." *Social Problems* 53 (3): 352–370.

Collins, Barbara E. 1986. "Defining Feminist Social Work." *Social Work* 31 (3)· 214–219,

De Montigny, Gerald A. J. 1995. *Social Working: An Ethnography of Front-Line Practice*. Toronto: University of Toronto Press.

Eräsaari, Leena, Raija Julkunen, and Harriet Silius. 1995. *Naiset yksityisen ja julkisen rajalla* [*Women at the Border of Private and Public*]. Tampere: Vastapaino.

Fineman, Martha A. 2010. "The Vulnerable Subject and the Responsive State." *Emory Law Journal* 60 (2): 251–275; *Emory Public Law Research Paper* No. 10–130. Available at SSRN: https://ssrn.com/abstract=1694740

Griffith, Alison I., and Dorothy E. Smith. 1990. "'What Did You do in School Today?' Mothering, Schooling and Social Class." *Perspectives on Social Problems*, vol. 2. Edited by Gale Miller and James A. Holstein, 3–24. Greenwich: Jai Press.

Griffith, Alison I., and Dorothy E. Smith. 2005. *Mothering for Schooling*. New York: RoutledgeFalmer.

Hart, Randle J., and Andrew McKinnon. 2010. "Sociological Epistemology: Durkheim's Paradox and Dorothy E. Smith's Actuality." *Sociology* 44 (6): 1038–1054.

Healy, Karen. 2000. *Social Work Practices: Contemporary Perspectives on Change.* London: Sage.

Hernes, Helga. 1987. *Welfare State and Woman Power: Essays in State Feminism.* London: Norwegian University Press.

Hicks, Stephen. 2009. "Sexuality and the 'Relations of Ruling': Using Institutional Ethnography to Research Lesbian and Gay Foster Care and Adoption." *Social Work & Society* 7 (2): 234–245.

Høgsbro, Kjeld. 2017. "Institutional Ethnography for People in a Vulnerable and Oppressed Situation." *Social Work and Research in Advanced Welfare States.* Edited by Kjeld Høgsbro and Ian Shaw, 117–130. London and New York: Routledge.

Homanen, Riikka. 2013. *Doing Pregnancy, the Unborn, and the Maternity Health-care Institution.* Academic Dissertation. Acta Electronica Universitatis Tamperensis 1273. Tampere: Tampere University Press.

Jokela, Ulla. 2011. *Diakoniatyön paikka ihmisten arjessa* [The Place of Diaconia Work in People's Everyday Life]. Diakonia-ammattikorkeakoulun julkaisuja sarja A, Tutkimuksia 34. Helsinki: Diakonia-ammattikorkeakoulu.

Julkunen, Raija, and Liisa Rantalaiho. 1989. *Hyvinvointivaltion sukupuolijärjestelmä. Tutkimussuunnitelma* [Gender System of the Welfare State. A Research Proposal]. Jyväskylän yliopiston yhteiskuntapolitiikan laitoksen työpapereita no 56. Jyväskylä: Jyväskylän yliopisto.

Kuronen, Marjo. 1999. *The Social Organisation of Motherhood. Advice Giving in Maternity and Child Health Care in Scotland and Finland.* PhD thesis. University of Stirling. http://hdl.handle.net/1893/2302

Kuronen, Marjo. 2009. "Feministinen tutkimus ja sosiaalityön tutkimus – kohtaamisia ja kohtaamattomuutta." [Feminist Research and Social Work Research – Meeting and Not Meeting Each Other] *Sosiaalityö ja teoria [Social Work and Theory].* Edited by Mikko Mäntysaari, Anneli Pohjola, and Tarja Pösö, 111–130. Jyväskylä: PS-kustannus.

Kuronen, Marjo. 2014. "Perheen ideologinen tuottaminen." [Ideological Construction of Family]. *Perhetutkimuksen suuntauksia.* Edited by Riitta Jallinoja, Helena Hurme, and Kimmo Jokinen, 81–98. Helsinki: Gaudeamus.

Kuronen, Marjo, Riitta Granfelt, Leo Nyqvist, and Päivi Petrelius, eds. 2004. *Sukupuoli ja sosiaalityö [Gender and Social Work].* Jyväskylä: PS-kustannus.

Kushner, Margo Anne. 2006. "Is "Best Interests" a Solution to Filling Potholes in Child Custody Planning?" *Journal of Child Custody* 3 (2): 71–90. doi: 10.1300/J190v03n02_04

Lund, Rebecca W. B. 2015. *Doing the Ideal Academic. Gender, Excellence and Changing Academia.* Aalto University publication series. Doctoral Dissertations 98/2015: Helsinki: Aalto University.

Malachowski, Cindy, Christina Skorobohacz, and Elaine Stasiulis. 2017. "Institutional Ethnography as a Method of Inquiry: A Scoping Review." *Qualitative Sociology Review* 13 (4): 84–121.

Martinelli, Flavia, Anneli Anttonen, and Margitta Mätzke, eds. 2017. *Social Services Disrupted. Changes, Challenges and Policy Implications for Europe in Times of Austerity.* Cheltenham: Edward Elgar Publishing.

Nichols, Naomi. 2014. *Youth Work: An Institutional Ethnography of Youth Homelessness.* Toronto: University of Toronto Press.

Parada, Henry, Lisa Barnoff, and Brienne Coleman. 2007. "Negotiating 'Professional Agency': Social Work and Decision-Making within the Ontario Child Welfare System." *Journal of Sociology & Social Welfare* XXXIV (4): 35–56.

Rantalaiho, Liisa, ed. 1986. *Miesten tiede, naisten puuhat. [Male Science, Women's Chores]*. Tampere: Vastapaino.

Satka, Mirja. 1995. *Making Social Citizenship. Conceptual Practices from the Finnish Poor Law to Professional Social Work*. Jyväskylä: SoPhi.

Satka, Mirja, and Caroline Skehill. 2012. "Michel Foucault and Dorothy Smith in Case File Research: Strange Bed-Fellows or Complementary Thinkers?" *Qualitative Social Work* 11 (2): 191–205.

Skehill, Caroline, Mirja Satka, and Susanna Hoikkala. 2012. "Exploring Innovative Methodologies in Time and Place to Analyse Child Protection Documents as Elements of Practice." *Qualitative Social Work* 12 (1): 57–72. doi: 10.1177/1473325011416878

Smith, Dorothy E. 1988. *The Everyday World as Problematic. A Feminist Sociology.* Oxford Open University Press/Milton Keynes.

Smith, Dorothy E. 1990a. *The Conceptual Practices of Power. A Feminist Sociology of Knowledge.* Toronto: University of Toronto Press.

Smith, Dorothy E. 1990b. *Texts, Facts, and Femininity. Exploring the Relations of Ruling.* London and New York: Routledge.

Smith, Dorothy E. 1999. *Writing the Social. Critique, Theory and Investigations.* Toronto, Buffalo and London: University of Toronto Press.

Smith, Dorothy E. 2004. "Ideology, Science and Social Relations: A Reinterpretation of Marx's Epistemology." *European Journal of Social Theory* 7 (4): 445–462.

Smith, Dorothy E. 2005. *Institutional Ethnography. A Sociology for People.* Lanham and Oxford: AltaMira Press.

Tummons, Jonathan. 2017. "Institutional Ethnography, Theory, Methodology, and Research: Some Concerns and Some Comments." *Perspectives on and from Institutional Ethnography.* Edited by James Read and Lisa Russell, 147–162. Bingley: Emerald Publishing. doi: 10.1108/S1042-319220170000015003

Vierula, Tarja. 2017. *Lastensuojelun asiakirjat vanhempien näkökulmasta [Examining Child Welfare Documents from a Parental Perspective]*. Acta Universitatis Tamperensis 2323. Tampere: Tampere University Press.

Virokannas, Elina, Suvi Liuski, and Marjo Kuronen. 2018. "The Contested Concept of Vulnerability – A Literature Review." *European Journal of Social Work*, Published online 12 Aug 2018. doi: 10.1080/13691457.2018.1508001

Winfield, Bonnie M. 2003. "Turning the Kaleidoscope: Telling Stories in Rhetorical Spaces." *Journal of Sociology and Social Welfare* 30 (1): 23–40.

10 Making gendering visible

Institutional ethnography's contribution to Nordic sociology of gender in family relations

May-Linda Magnussen

Introduction

Scholars studying women's lives in Norway in the 1970s were motivated by the fact that women, women's experiences and the social spheres that women were most active in were largely left unexplored (Halsaa 2006a; Koren 2012). Sociologists among them also found motivation in the understanding that to the extent that women's practices *had* been studied, this had been done from the standpoint of men, using concepts for and about the world of men. The sociologists argued that this resulted in women becoming visible and understood mainly through their deficiencies, by what they *did not do* (Wærness 1975; Sørensen 1977). By researching women's everyday lives, sociologists and psychologists made visible work that women *actually did*. They paid particular attention to care work in family relations, and with time they showed the scope and diversity of this work (Wærness 1975; Andenæs 1984; Haavind 1987; Leira 1992). More recent Norwegian sociological studies have continued to explore caregiving, "doing family" and home-making, and the role of gender in this work (Brandth and Kvande 2003; Lilleaas 2003; Aarseth 2008; Stefansen and Farstad 2008; Nadim 2012; Smeby 2017).

The problems raised and the solutions proposed by the first Norwegian feminist sociologists bear resemblance to the problems raised by Dorothy Smith and the solutions she proposes with institutional ethnography (IE). For Smith, however, entering a sociology dominated by the perspectives and concepts of men sparked even more fundamental questions concerning how we, as sociologists, "write the social" (Smith 1987). She argues that adding women to a sociology that objectifies the social world by conceptualising it does not change the fundamental nature of the (men's) game. Instead, sociologists should be critical towards the theoretically driven, conceptualising, objectifying sociology built by men. Using IE to study men's everyday lives in nuclear families in Agder, the southernmost part of Norway, I show that the early Norwegian feminist sociologists adopted a predetermined understanding of paid work instead of exploring it (Magnussen 2015). The consequence was that while *unfolding* family work that women did and still do most of, these scholars simultaneously *concealed* family work that men did and still do most of. Another consequence was that this research, while on the one hand aiming to show that "family life" and "work life" were not separate spheres (Halsaa 2006a), on the other hand portrayed *men's* family life and work life as separate from each other. Even more noteworthy, the same goes for much Nordic research on men and masculinities. What I call *breadwinning work* does not only have low visibility in earlier and contemporary Norwegian sociology. In addition, it is largely left out of public debates about the division of work in the nuclear family in today's Norway. In these debates, men are mainly understood through their deficiencies; through what they *do not do*.

In this chapter, I use the above-mentioned study to demonstrate IE's usefulness in exploring how people's lives are gendered. I argue that Smith's method of inquiry is particularly well-suited for making low-visibility gendering visible. I also argue that making such processes visible is of general importance, but particularly important in gender research in the Nordics today.

Being captured by concepts

Dorothy Smith warns against the "capturing grip" of concepts on the researcher's gaze and consciousness, and IE is designed to help the researcher challenge this grip (Smith 2005). Starting the research process by exploring social phenomena as *work* reduces the risk of the researcher reproducing dominating scientific or lay discourses in her interaction with research participants. Furthermore, it reduces the risk of being caught in discourses dominant in the institutional relations the research participants engage in. In my research on men's family lives, however, I did not start out exploring the everyday and everynight work of my informants. Instead, I used Norwegian sociology on gender in family relations to develop my research questions. Initially, the aim of this research was to show connections between men's "handling of breadwinner responsibility" and their "handling of health", connections substantiated by the work of Norwegian sociologist Ulla-Britt Lilleaas (2003). This meant that my research, even before initiating my data production, was shaped by specific ideas about what constitutes breadwinning. Without fully realising it, I thought that breadwinning was about working long hours and having the highest wage in the family and about worrying about the economic situation of the family.

I interviewed my first ten informants and felt that I had developed good data. Having transcribed most of the interviews and read through them, however, a troubling feeling started to grow. Even when going through transcripts from an interview with a man I thought was very preoccupied with money, I did not see much "handling of breadwinner responsibility". This, of course, also made possible connections between "handling of breadwinner responsibility" and "handling of health" invisible. To link these, I had to use theory, and I did so when I presented my ongoing research to other researchers in the field. My arguments, in which I used theoretical concepts to fill the "empirical gaps" that worried me, were considered credible by my audience. Even so, the troubling feeling prevailed.

Exploring breadwinning as *work*

At this point in my research, I was advised to go through the transcripts of the interviews with the man I found to be preoccupied with money once more, now looking for "breadwinning work" in Smith's understanding of the term. This became a watershed in my research. Going through the transcripts with the same man, I now saw him talk about breadwinning throughout three long interviews. This man did not only work long hours and make more money than his wife. He worked shifts to increase his pay and worked very hard to be considered a good and loyal worker and colleague and eligible for a leadership position in the future, both of which he connected to securing and maximising his income. To be considered a loyal worker, he went to work when he was sick, as long as he "could get out of bed". He had an extra job, so that he could earn extra when the shifts in his main job allowed it. He had much knowledge about maximising earnings and he even made money from buying, fixing and selling cars. He called this a "hobby" but said that if he had not made money from it, he "might as well be fishing". Furthermore, he did not only discipline his body, thoughts and feelings in order to go to work when he was sick. Instead, he altogether tried to avoid what he called "negative thoughts and feelings". Not least, he talked about himself in ways that portrayed him as a good worker and a good breadwinner. He portrayed himself as a man who *had to work*, almost continuously, in order to thrive.

This research participant not only did a lot of physical work that both made and portrayed him as a good income generator but also did most of the income-handling work in his family. The sharing of expenses between him and his wife shaped this work. His wife payed for food and clothes for all family members and for "minor things for the house". My informant paid for everything else. This meant that he did the work of paying bills. He was also the one checking and negotiating prices and conditions in relation to, for example, banks and insurance companies. This way of organising expenses turned my informant into the one with the overview of, and the responsibility for, the largest part of the family economy. He was the one planning future expenses. He *knew* a lot about reducing costs and *did* much to reduce the family's use of money. Trying to steer the family's use of money in a "sensible" direction through discussing – and quarrelling – with his wife and children was one way of doing this. Doing house and vehicle maintenance himself was another. In addition, he spent a lot of time and energy on building, expanding or refurbishing the family's house and cabin. He argued that he did this himself since it was much less expensive than paying someone to do the job. Furthermore, working shifts allowed for this kind of work.

Compared to the rest of my informants, the man I have described here did a particularly broad range of what I call breadwinning work – work that also seemed particularly deeply embodied. I argue, however, that this work and its embodiment also became particularly *visible* in the interviews with this informant. His experience functioned as a kind of analytical key, rendering visible breadwinning work in the experience of my other informants. In the end, this research made me conclude that the men I had interviewed did a considerable amount of physical, mental and emotional breadwinning work that was often deeply embodied and silent. They did not only do this work *for themselves*, but also *for others*. Furthermore, I concluded that breadwinning work was "masculinity work" for most of my informants: It was work that made them feel like and become recognised as "good men" among colleagues, family and friends. Not only making money, but being able to finance a large share of the family's expenses and having a strong say in the family's use of money, contributed to this kind of recognition. This, however, almost exclusively became visible when such practices were threatened, hypothetically or in real life. It became visible, for example, in the experience of a man on disability pension.

Furthermore, this research directed my attention towards the social coordinating of my research participants' breadwinning. I paid particular attention to the men's family relations. Studying these relations, even if only from the standpoint of the men, I could see that their breadwinning work was ways of doing love; of being good fathers and life partners. To pass as a good father and life partner, for example, many of my informants not only financed what they defined as necessities but also less necessary things. I could see that their breadwinning work was not *only facilitated* by their female life partners having part-time paid work and doing much care and house work. In addition, it *made it possible* for their female life partners to mother in ways that were recognised as good mothering in the social relations they engaged in. In other words, doing gender as *cooperative work* became visible. In the end, as I have already indicated, I was also able to connect the men's breadwinning work and "the work of handling one's health", as I had initially aimed to do. Investigating the work these concepts "consist of" enabled me to see such connections in my data.

Exploring research on gender in the nuclear family

After this analytical work, I returned to the Norwegian sociology of gender in family relations that I had started out in. I now, however unknowingly, treated this research as what Smith calls "second-level data". This enabled me to trace my own preconceptions of men's breadwinning. Much of this research, and the Norwegian and Nordic research it refers to, highlights that women are steadily increasing their paid work and income, that men are steadily increasing their house and care work and that the support for the "present" or "involved" "father" and gender equality more generally is gradually on the rise. The research often states that since men still do more paid work and earn more than women, they often continue to be "the family's main breadwinner". Men's greater breadwinning is, however, presented as unimportant, empty of meaning, ungendered and as something that will inevitably wither away with the general social development. It is understood neither as fathering, nor as a way of "doing couple". In this sociology, and in the Nordic sociology it refers to, the difference in men's and women's income generation is often described as a "gap" between a gender equal *ideal* and a gender unequal *practice* (Magnussen 2015).

Norwegian sociologists and Anglo-American researchers often seem to agree that the connections between paid work and masculinity that were established during the modernisation process are alive and well. Paid work is seen as an important way of "doing masculinity", not least because it is seen as central to gaining independence and achieving status as an individual with certain rights. Norwegian sociologists, however, contrary to what many Anglo-American researchers claim, have largely declared the connection between breadwinning and masculinity dead and buried in the post-industrial/modern society (Magnussen 2015). Norwegian sociologists Berit Brandth and Elin Kvande (2003), for instance, write that the fathers they have interviewed do not talk of breadwinning as an important part of being a father. According to them, this is a sign of the disconnection of fathering and breadwinning. Simultaneously, much Norwegian sociology explains the inertia characterising the gendered division of labour in the nuclear family by declaring the connection between *femininity, mothering* and *care work* alive and well. This research claims that men's increasing care for children did not "ungender" such work. Instead, the connections between femininity, mothering and care work are portrayed as increasingly silent, subtle and difficult to see.

I argue that the silence surrounding men's breadwinning in contemporary Norway is not only a sign of more gender equal breadwinning, of breadwinning being less important for being a father and a life partner and of weaker connections between breadwinning and masculinity. It is also a sign of the *silencing* of this work. This silencing has and is being done, in sociology, in public debate and in policy documents about gender equality in the nuclear family, by reducing breadwinning in two rounds. First, breadwinning is reduced by being equalled to paid work. Second, paid work is reduced by being equalled to self-interest. It is defined as a right, a privilege, an asset and a way of gaining influence (Slottemo 2009). The early women's studies and the women's movement, being closely connected in Norway in the 1970s (Halsaa 2006b), defined paid work as "self-realisation", "the right to money of one's own" and "economic liberation" (Koren 2012). This understanding also underpins Norwegian gender equality policies, from the 1970s and up until today (The Norwegian Ministry of Children and Equality 2012).[1]

This definition is understandable from the standpoint of women, and in particular from the standpoint of the middle-class women who, to a large degree, shaped Norwegian gender equality policies as feminist scholars and/or activists (Magnussen 2015). Seeing paid work as *only* self-interest, however, conceals the duties, burdens, care and responsibility for others that this work can entail (Slottemo 2009). We have good reason to believe that this experience of paid work is men's more than women's, both historically and today. Still, the understanding of paid work as pure self-interest also seems to have been adopted by the Nordic research on men and masculinities. This probably has to do with this research growing out of women's studies and its tight connections to gender equality policies (Lorentzen 2006; Hearn et al. 2012). In 1998, Norwegian sociologist Øystein Gullvåg Holter wrote that "men, as women saw them, became part of the basis for the Nordic research on men and masculinities" (my translation) (Holter 1998, 228). The research on men and masculinities that concerns family and work life, however, shows few signs of having taken this insight into account (Magnussen 2015).

Understanding this reduction of breadwinning and paid work, the focus on what men *do not do* in contemporary Norwegian public debate about gender equality in the nuclear family becomes understandable. Not understanding the diversity – and the relational and gendered aspects of – men's breadwinning, much Norwegian sociology and Nordic research on men and masculinities has missed out on important aspects of many men's everyday lives in the Nordics. The same seems to be the case for much of the Nordic sociology to which the aforementioned Norwegian sociology refers.[2] This has, no doubt, impeded the understanding of family practices more generally, including their gendered aspects – but also their classed and raced aspects. It has concealed the fact that even if men as a group can be said to be more privileged than women, men are not only and always privileged in the social relations they engage in. It has obscured the costs that may follow so-called privilege. Not least, it has concealed women's contributions to reproducing gender inequality in the nuclear family. In addition, I believe it has exaggerated the difference between the everyday lives of men in the Nordics and men living elsewhere. Several Anglo-American studies understand breadwinning as family work and, for instance, understand it as fathering being done alongside, and coordinated with, "newer" ways of fathering, like I do (Palkovitz 1997, 2002; Townsend 2002; Henwood & Procter 2003; Doucet 2006; Miller 2010). It is probably easier to discover such "traditional fathering", and the connectedness of people's actions more generally, outside of the discourses of individualism and gender equality so dominant in the Nordics (Gullestad 2002). The capturing power of such discourses suggests that using IE to study gender may be particularly useful in the Nordics. It might also be particularly useful for studying class and race relations here, taking dominant discourses about equality more generally into account (ibid.).

Exploring trans-local gendering of family practices

Hopefully, the previous sections have demonstrated how easily social scientists can end up "writing the social" in ways that reproduce dominating scientific, institutional or lay understandings. These understandings can concern both *work*, like breadwinning, and *social categories* that we often sort people into, such as gender. Wanting to "do good", for instance by aiming to contribute to gender equality, in no way removes the risk of reproducing dominating understandings. I argue that researchers that have such ambitions, and who in addition start out in well-established concepts and social categories, probably run a particularly high risk of systematically not seeing experiences that do not fit into these. Norwegian sociologist Karin Widerberg (2015) claims that Smith's concern about concepts is probably more relevant than ever, seeing that so much human action is conceptualised – and apparently exhaustively understood. I argue that the widespread use of intersectionality theory also contributes to this relevance (Lund & Magnussen 2018), an argument similar to that of Norwegian sociologist Helene Aarseth (2017).[3] Starting out research with intersectionality theory, social categories like gender, class and race might end up not only looking like they are *acting*, but even *interacting*. Furthermore, the more – and the more finely tuned – categories we are able to find "effects" and "interacting effects" of, the more seductive, and concealing, the analysis might be.

Being a feminist scholar investigating the everyday lives of white, Norwegian, heterosexual men, many of them middle class, I was at high risk of concealing experiences that did not fit with established ideas of privilege – or a lack of such. As I have tried to show, starting research in people's everyday experiences proved efficient in developing knowledge that could challenge dominant understandings of gender in the nuclear family of today's Norway. Doing gender research using IE, exploring people's work/ work knowledge is usually the starting point. Looking for possible traces of gendering of this work is secondary, helping the researcher to avoid exaggerating possible effects of gender. Using IE to study gender, gendering is an *empirical* question rather than a *theoretical* one. The ultimate aim is to discover whether gender categories *do* something and if so, *what*; how they organise actions and knowledge and how they are activated and lived in ways that have a generalising effect on people's lives – and contribute to producing certain privileges for certain groups (Lund & Magnussen 2018).

My research on men's breadwinning showed that my informants' everyday lives were shaped by gender ideals that became dominant in the Nordics and in the Western world during the modernisation process (Magnussen 2015). To put it in Smith's words, my work substantiated that the ideal of the male breadwinner *rules* many men's everyday lives, even in contemporary Norway – the "land of gender equality". However, much of men's breadwinning work and this work as "masculinity work" is concealed by another ruling understanding; the understanding of paid work as pure self-interest. This gendered, and presumptively middle-classed, understanding seems to have been promoted by the women's movement, the Norwegian welfare state and its gender equality project as well as by Norwegian sociology on gendered family practices. It also seems to have been adopted by much Nordic research on men and masculinities. Much Nordic research on gendered family practices aims to show connectedness between the Nordic welfare states and family practices. IE offers understandings and tools that enable us to make such connectedness and its gendering visible.

Notes

1 Björnberg and Kollind (2005) claim that the gender equality ideal in itself sees the individual as separate and independent.
2 See Magnussen (2015) for some exceptions.
3 In 2017, Aarseth initiated a debate about intersectionality. She claimed that intersectionality theory increasingly takes the form of a paradigm that all qualitative researchers in some way must conform to.

References

Aarseth, H. 2008. *Hjemskapingens moderne magi. [The modern magic of home-making]*. Oslo: The University of Oslo, Department for Sociology and Human Geography.
Aarseth, H. 2017. "Den rette lære i academia." [Dogma in academia]. Retrieved on April 23rd 2019 from: www.stk.uio.no/om/aktuelt/i-media/2017/den-rette-lere-i-akademia.html
Andenæs, A. 1984. "Hverdagsliv i småbarnsfamilien." [Everyday life in families with small children]. 75–94, *Barns oppvekstmiljø [Children's childhood environment]*, edited by E.M. Skaalvik. Oslo: Aschehoug/Tanum-Norli.
Björnberg, U. and A.K. Kollind 2005. *Individualism and families. Equality, autonomy and togetherness*. London: Routledge.
Brandth, B. and E. Kvande 2003. *Fleksible fedre. Maskulinitet, arbeid, velferdsstat [Flexible fathers. Masculinity, work, welfare state]*. Oslo: Universitetsforlaget.
Doucet, A. 2006. *Do men mother? Fathering, care, and domestic responsibility*. Toronto: University of Toronto Press.
Gullestad, M. 2002. *Det norske sett med nye øyne [The Norwegian seen with new eyes]*. Oslo: Universitetsforlaget.
Haavind, H. 1987. *Liten og stor. Mødres omsorg og barns utviklingsmuligheter [Small and big. Mothers' care and children's developmental possibilities]*. Oslo: Universitetsforlaget.
Halsaa, B. 2006a. "Kvinneforskning". [Women's studies]. 95–105, *Kjønnsforskning. En grunnbok [Gender research. A primer]*, edited by J. Lorentzen and W. Mühleisen. Oslo: Universitetsforlaget.
Halsaa, B. 2006b. "Fra kvinneforskning til kvinne- og kjønnsforskning." [From women's studies to women's and gender studies]. 108–119, *Kjønnsforskning. En grunnbok [Gender research. A primer]*, edited by J. Lorentzen and W. Mühleisen. Oslo: Universitetsforlaget.

Hearn, J., M. Nordberg, K. Leifson, D. Balkmar, L. Gottzén, R. Klinth, K. Pringle, and L. Sandberg 2012. "Hegemonic masculinity and beyond. 40 years of research in Sweden." *Men and Masculinities* 15(1):31–55.

Henwood, K. and J. Procter 2003. "The "good father". Reading men's accounts of paternal involvement during the transition to first-time fatherhood." *The British Journal of Social Psychology* 42(3):337–355.

Holter, Ø.G. 1998. "Mansforskningen 1970–1997." [Research on men 1970–1997]. *213–253, Han, hon, den, det. Om genus och kön* [*He, she, it. About gender and sex*], edited by B. Westerberg. Stockholm: Ekerlids Förlag.

Koren, C. 2012. *Kvinnenes rolle i norsk økonomi.* [*The women's role in Norwegian economy*]. Oslo: Universitetsforlaget.

Leira, A. 1992. *Welfare states and working mothers. The Scandinavian experience.* Cambridge: Cambridge University Press.

Lilleaas, U.B. 2003. *Fra en kropp i ustand til kroppen i det moderne.* [*From a body that is not working to the body in the modern*]. Oslo: The University of Oslo, Department for Sociology and Human Geography.

Lorentzen, J. 2006. "Forskning på menn og maskuliniteter." [Research on men and masculinities]. *121–133, Kjønnsforskning. En grunnbok* [*Gender research. A primer*], edited by J. Lorentzen and W. Mühleisen. Oslo: Universitetsforlaget.

Lund, R.W.B. and M.L. Magnussen 2018. "Intersektionalitet, virksomhedskundskab og styringsrelationer. Institutionel Etnografi og hverdagens sociale organisering." [Intersectionality, work knowledge and ruling relations. Institutional ethnography and the social organising of everyday life]. *Tidsskrift for kjønnsforskning* [*Journal for Gender Research*] 4(42):268–283.

Magnussen, M.L. 2015. *Familieforsørgelse i menns hverdag.* [*Family breadwinning in men's everyday lives*]. Oslo: The University of Oslo, Department for Sociology and Human Geography.

Miller, T. 2010. *Making sense of fatherhood.* Cambridge: Cambridge University Press.

Nadim, M. 2012. "Mellom familie og arbeid. Moralske forhandlinger blant kvinnelige etterkommere." [Between family and work. Moral negotiations among female descendants of immigrants]. *289–306, Velferdsstatens familier. Nye sosiologiske perspektiver* [*Families of the welfare state. New sociological perspectives*], edited by A.L. Ellingsæter and K. Widerberg. Oslo: Gyldendal Akademisk.

Palkovitz, R. 1997. "Reconstructing "involvement". Expanding conceptualizations of men's caring in contemporary families." *200–216, Current issues in the family series, Vol. 3, Generative fathering. Beyond deficit perspectives*, edited by A.J. Hawkins and D.C. Dollahite. Thousand Oaks, CA: Sage Publications.

Palkovitz, R.J. 2002. *Involved fathering and men's adult development. Provisional balances.* Mahwah, NJ: Lawrence Erlbaum Associates.

Slottemo, H.G. 2009. "Ansvarlighetens menn – Normer for maskulinitet i etterkrigstidas industrisamfunn." [Men of responsibility – Masculinity norms in industrial societies after the second world war]. *Tidsskrift for kjønnsforskning* [*Journal for Gender Research*] 1–2(33):64–81.

Smeby, K.W. 2017. *Likestilling i det tredje skiftet? Heltidsarbeidende småbarnsforeldres praktisering av familieansvar etter 10 uker med fedrekvote* [*Gender equality in the third shift? Full-time working parents' practising of family responsibility after 10 weeks of paternal leave*]. Trondheim: Norwegian University of Science and Technology, Department of Sociology and Political Science.

Smith, D.E. 1987. *The everyday world as problematic. A feminist sociology.* Boston, MA: Northeastern University Press.

Smith, D.E. 2005. *Institutional ethnography. A sociology for people.* Lanham, MD: AltaMira.

Stefansen, K. and G.R. Farstad 2008. "Småbarnsforeldres omsorgsprosjekter. Betydningen av klasse." [The care projects of parents of small children. The impact of class]. *Tidsskrift for samfunnsforskning [Journal of Social Research]* 3(49):343–372.

Sørensen, B.A. 1977. "Arbeidskvinner og verdighet." [Working women and dignity]. 33–53, *I kvinners bilde. Bidrag til en kvinnesosiologi [In women's image. Contributions to a women's sociology]*, edited by A.M. Berg, Å. Berge, A. Kalleberg and A. Leira. Oslo: Pax.

The Norwegian Ministry of Children and Equality 2012. *NOU 2012:15, Politikk for likestilling.* [Official Norwegian Report 2012:15, Policies for gender equality]. Retrieved on April 23rd 2019 from: www.regjeringen.no/no/dokumenter/nou-2012-15/id699800/sec1

Townsend, N.W. 2002. *The package deal. Marriage, work, and fatherhood in men's lives.* Philadelphia, PA: Temple University press.

Widerberg, K. 2015. "En invitasjon til institusjonell etnografi." [An invitation to institutional ethnography]. 13–25, *I hjertet av velferdsstaten. En invitasjon til institusjonell etnografi [In the heart of the welfare state. An invitation to institutional ethnography]*, edited by K. Widerberg. Oslo: Cappelen Damm akademisk.

Wærness, K. 1975. *Kvinners omsorgsarbeid i den ulønnete produksjon [Women's care work in the unpaid production].* Bergen: Levekårsundersøkelsen.

11 Collaboration and trust
Expanding the concept of ruling relations

Siri Yde Aksnes and Nina Olsvold

Introduction

Over the last decades, institutional ethnography (IE) has inspired and informed an increasing volume of social research, turning IE into a widely recognized methodology. Its commitment to exploring people's actual doings and rejecting objectifying theorizing has appealed to researchers who want to bring about research *for* people. When the first author was introduced to IE, she was soon convinced that her field of research, vocational rehabilitation for people with disadvantages, could benefit from its rich analytical and conceptual "toolkit" (Deveau 2008). Understanding the complexities of street-level practices within vocational rehabilitation requires an account of what kind of knowledge underpins and organizes these practices. By tracing processes from micro to macro, institutional ethnographies can show how ideological contexts shape vocational rehabilitation practices (Townsend 1996).

This chapter draws on data from a project about new forms of collaboration in vocational rehabilitation. The project had two groups of key informants: counsellors who support jobseekers in vocational rehabilitation programmes and job agents who initiate and coordinate collaboration processes between vocational rehabilitation enterprises and employers in a recruitment programme called Ripples in the Water (RiW). The analysis focused on the counsellors' experiences of a disjuncture between their caring and empowering commitments towards the jobseekers and a ruling discourse of accountability (Aksnes 2017). Further, the job agents' approach to employer engagement was interpreted as brokering between a welfare discourse and a market discourse (Aksnes 2018). What primarily organized the job agents' practices, we argued, was their position in-between employers and vocational rehabilitation providers.

During the process of data analysis, we were puzzled by a major difference in the counsellors' and the job agents' experience of their work. The counsellors had to balance between conflicting requirements on a daily basis, and institutional regulations were rather easy to discern. The job agents, on the other hand, did not refer to specific requirements or scripts that regulated their everyday actions. They saw themselves as actively engaged in developing and co-creating the RiW programme. This made it harder for us to discern how the job agents' work knowledge was coordinated within relations of ruling. What exactly could explain this difference in the counsellors' and the job agents' experience of their scope of action? Moreover, what kind of ruling underlies the job agents' experience of self-governance, given that they work within the same overarching framework as the counsellors? In this chapter, we take this problematic as a starting point for a discussion about how we can understand ruling relations in organizational contexts where partnerships and co-production are prominent, and new, autonomous forms of coordination and integration are required. Discussing this, we argue, can have relevance beyond the specific case under scrutiny here, as the challenges of today's welfare societies require the formation of new networks and partnerships that collaborate in but also shape and influence relations of ruling (Taylor 2007). The continuous but shifting character of ruling relations demands us to pay close attention to the emergence of new ways of coordinating activities in contemporary society as well as to how they are articulated and performed in local sites of action.

As "ruling relations" is a key subject of discussion here, we will start with a brief unpacking of the concept. Dorothy Smith (1999, 73) defines ruling relations as "the complex of objectified social relations that organize and regulate our lives in contemporary societies". IEs explicate the processes through which power is routinely organized (Smith 1987) by focussing analytic attention on *how* people (more or less consciously) coordinate their activities in compliance with particular ruling relations. As the concept itself indicates, ruling relations are *relational* and not necessarily experienced as dominating or oppressive in a traditional sense. People may disagree with them or resist them, but they still activate institutional processes as part of their everyday work (Smith 2005). For Smith, ruling relations are mostly restricting or regulatory, instead of productive or enabling (Satka and Skehill 2012, 200) and IEs tend to be oriented towards problematics that occur between the particularity of people's doings and sayings in local contexts and a constraining institutional order. Importantly, relations of ruling are envisaged as text-mediated and text-based systems of coordination and control that are built into objectified forms of discourse (Smith 1987, 2005, 2006). By privileging texts and discourse in her understanding of "ruling relations" Smith appears to put more emphasis on how peoples actions are *coordinated* (externally) than on how they are *performed* as local practices. That is, the local is taken as a point of departure for mapping "just how people's doings in the everyday are articulated to and coordinated by extended social relations that are not visible from within any particular local setting and just how people are participating in those relations" (Smith 2005, 36). The direction of the mapping is from the local outwards and upwards in what, we argue, often becomes a one-way process that obscures the agentic and innovative aspects of peoples' local practices. In this chapter, we depart from the local practices of job agents in RiW and argue for the need to explore the complexities of the relational in ruling relations and for a need to re-emphasize the openness of the concept.

In the following section, some contextual background is provided to situate RiW as a case of new ideas and approaches in vocational rehabilitation. To write out our problematic, we describe and compare the work of the counsellors and the job agents in relation to the concept of ruling relations. We then move on to consider how IE can draw on perspectives from governance literature to capture ways of working and relating in new and evolving systems of ruling.

Norwegian activation services: towards a joined-up approach to social organization

For decades, the employment policies known as the *Work line* has been a cornerstone in the Norwegian welfare state. The work line is founded on the idea that paid work is beneficial to good health and promotes social inclusion for the individual, and that an active, employed population is best for society (Fossestøl 2007; White Paper No. 9 [2006–2007]). Norway also has a strong tradition of public responsibility for improving job prospects for disadvantaged groups, and the work line constitutes a guiding principle for activation services in Norway. *Activation* refers to all social policy interventions aimed at improving employment. The goal is that also people with health problems or other support needs shall be part of the work force. Thus, activation programmes are hooked into a particular ideology of what constitutes a good life.

The Norwegian Labour and Welfare Administration (NAV) is the key agent in implementing the work line. NAV is the result of a large and ambitious reform process, merging the three main welfare administrations – national insurance, employment services and municipal social services. Because NAV covers such a wide range of services, it has increased its procurement of services from private vocational rehabilitation enterprises. These enterprises function as NAV's "extended arm" (Kasin and Sannes 2012, 22) as NAV regulates and places demands on the services (NOU 2012, 6, 88–99). The counsellors in my study are employed in these enterprises.

Norwegian activation policies and services are inevitably influenced by international activation trends. The past two decades have brought about welfare reforms across the globe involving substantive changes at the intersection of formal and operational policy (Brodkin and Marston 2013; van Berkel and Borghi 2007). Despite national and political variations, the reforms target the management of the activation trajectory, emphasizing effectivity, output and outcome, and performance measurement strategies associated with the ideology of New Public Management (NPM) (van Berkel and Valkenburg 2007, 10–11). In Norway, disappointing outcomes of the activation programmes over time has led to increased demands from the authorities to enhance the activation services (e.g. Andreassen and Fossestøl 2014). One central response to this, of particular importance in this chapter, concerns the gradual "opening up" of activation services to a wider range of actors, including public agencies, private enterprises, employer organizations, labour unions and the third sector in an effort to improve the design and delivery of activation policies (McQuaid 2010, 1–2). The result is a more joined-up approach to the social organization of activation services, with new spheres of responsibilities and inter-organizational cooperation. The most comprehensive and well-known collaboration in this respect is the Cooperation Agreement on a More Inclusive Working Life (the IA Agreement), signed in 2001 by the government (the Minister of Labour), the employer organizations and the labour unions. A core idea in the IA Agreement is that measures to prevent labour market exclusion must be anchored in the labour market and implemented in collaboration between the *social partners* – the government, the employers' organizations and the labour unions (e.g. Ose et al. 2013). A more collaborative approach to labour market inclusion, forwarded by both Norwegian and global reform processes, has paved the way towards an increased emphasis on employers' roles in activation. This is the context of the RiW, launched in 2012 by the main employers' federation in Norway, NHO.

In RiW, private enterprises and vocational rehabilitation enterprises, which are both members of NHO, collaborate on recruiting jobseekers enrolled in vocational rehabilitation programmes. The organizational framework of RiW is designed to improve dialogue between vocational rehabilitation enterprises and employers, and between the different vocational rehabilitation enterprises participating in RiW (referred to as the RiW network).The initiative is considered to be an innovative approach, as it takes employers' actual recruitment and competence needs as starting points for inclusion processes. By doing this, they turn "traditional vocational rehabilitation", that has the needs and wishes of the individual jobseekers in focus, on its head. A main strategy is job agents providing employers up-front and long-lasting assistance in order to reduce their perceived sense of risk associated with recruiting people with disadvantages (Tøssebro et al. 2017). RiW is a time-limited strategy targeting the transition from job training to paid employment. Its foundation in NHO is supposed to make the recruitment strategy appealing and accessible for private enterprises. In this way, we can say that RiW has one foot in the business sector (NHO) and one foot in the welfare administration (NAV).

Method

The data collection for this research project took place in Oslo and the surrounding area between December 2015 and May 2017. The project was designed as a fieldwork where the first author sought insight in the social organization of RiW through participant observation. Fieldwork in modern organizations is often centred on meetings (Garsten and Nyqvist 2013), and in RiW various meetings, events and seminars proved to be a natural place to start. The first author also had lengthy conversations and semi-structured interviews with job agents, counsellors, employers, jobseekers and people working elsewhere in the field of vocational rehabilitation. After starting out with a broad, holistic approach, the focus gradually narrowed down to explore the job agents' role and work.

The counsellors and the job agents

The counsellors and the job agents were employed in vocational rehabilita-tion enterprises. As the core task of these enterprises is to support people with difficult life situations, the counsellors, who work directly with job-seekers, are often educated within health, social work, pedagogics and psy-chology (Møller & Sannes, 2009; Qvortrup, 2014). All the job agents had previously worked as counsellors (some of them still worked part-time as counsellors), and some also had a background within sales and marketing work. The job agents were responsible for outreach activities and contacting employers. Despite different primary work tasks, however, the counsellors' and job agents' work also overlapped, counsellors also contacted and col-laborated with employers, and job agents also assisted jobseekers. Yet, de-spite closeness and overlap between the two groups, there were considerable differences in how their work was organized.

In the analysis of the counsellors' work knowledge, three institutional discourses were identified about how to *do* vocational rehabilitation. These were evident in the counsellors' talk and in what they took for granted in their everyday practices. First, a discourse of empowerment appeared as a guiding principle. The counsellors understood vocational rehabilitation as a process of comprehensive change and were concerned with the clients' health, their social and economic needs and their life quality, resources and wishes. Second, to secure a holistic, individualized and empowering coun-selling, the counsellors embraced a discourse of inter-professional collabo-ration. In each individual process, the counsellor had to engage with other professionals, like the client's caseworker at NAV, a general practitioner (GP), a psychologist and potential employers. They represented different fields of expertise and interest and had their own viewpoints of what was in the best interest of the client. The discourse of empowerment and the dis-course of inter-professional collaboration could be challenging to conform to, but both were deeply integrated and presupposed in the counsellors' practices and understandings of vocational rehabilitation. Third, due to new regulatory requirements, the counsellors had to organize their work in compliance with a discourse of accountability. Standardized timelines and targets obliged them to report, count and evaluate their work. The coun-sellors conceived the discourse of accountability as a demand that was im-posed on them from "the outside", and as something that brought tensions and paradoxes into their daily work. When a counsellor had less time to talk to and get to know a jobseeker, and hurriedly placed the jobseeker in a more or less random work placement, the accountability practices appeared to have overruled the other two discourses. This "disjunctive space" (Rankin and Campbell 2006, 180) between discourses on a collision course made up the ruling context of the counsellors' everyday world. As such, their roles can be interpreted within the framework of a traditional street-level bureaucracy (Lipsky 1980). Although the counsellors experienced a certain degree of discretion in their work, their potential to act was regulated by policy.

The job agents held a key role in RiW as responsible for developing a strategy to involve employers in the project. Besides their outreach activities of promoting RiW and visiting employers, their everyday work consisted of sharing information about vacancies with counsellors in their own enterprises and job agents in the RiW network (in web-based recruitment programmes), interviewing potential candidates and keeping regularly in touch with employers during job training and recruitment processes. We came to understand the job agents as having three main approaches to employer engagement: building relations, coaching and negotiating. These concerned the job agents' way of talking and acting towards employers, emphasizing the value of being professional, predictable, accessible and service-minded. The job agents saw the turn towards employers' needs and viewpoints as a necessary and longed-for response to what they called the "ineffectiveness of traditional vocational rehabilitation". In their own enterprises, they taught the counsellors how to approach and communicate with employers. Despite a more "business-inspired" approach to vocational rehabilitation, the job agents were concerned not to compromise with the social work anchored approach that informs vocational rehabilitation. They tried to create alignment in values between the two fields. For example, RiW's guiding principle "job match" could be approved both from a business perspective and from a social work perspective, as promoting job match was in the interest of both jobseekers and employers. The job agents spoke warmly about their work and apparently believed in the RiW strategy. They appeared as self-governing in the conduct of their work. As one of them explained: "I very much create my own workday. I initiate different projects and look for opportunities where labour market inclusion is still unknown territory. I try to think 'outside the box'. It is great fun". Perhaps due to this, there were hardly any discontentment or frictions to track in their accounts. The job agents had plenty of opportunities to influence their own work. One of them even stated that "us job agents continually create and recreate RiW".

Looking for ruling in the job agents' practices

Despite different topics and institutional settings, IE research often takes place in "environments that are politically highly charged" (Campbell and Gregor 2008, 16) and aim to uncover what consequences institutional power

has on people. A recurring issue is the way in which ruling relations operate to displace other forms of knowledge, especially knowledge from experience (Smith 2005, 120). For instance, Widerberg and colleagues' (2015)
empirical studies from different Nordic welfare state institutions, all track
down how increased emphasis on effectivity and accountability in the institutions' work practices represent a breach with knowledge grounded in
people's embodied activities. Because the concept of ruling relations in institutional ethnographies has been used in a tradition of explicating social
problems, constraining forms of ruling are often given attention. However,
the concepts of IE are empirically empty and constructed to open up rather
than prematurely categorize the empirical world (Lund 2015, 180). In order
for the concept of ruling relations to be useful in our analysis of the job
agents' practices, we had to free ourselves from interpretations of ruling as
constraining and consider it as open, empty and enabling.

Subsequently, this insight enabled us to see that the joined-up approach
of current activation policies functioned as a ruling relation. "Collective action" was conceived as the solution to the failure of the publicly driven policies and an important underlying idea organizing the job agents' practices.
Several times during first author's fieldwork, she had to ask the job agents
to specify who they referred to when saying "we". "We" did not only refer
to the group of job agents or the vocational rehabilitation enterprises but
included a wide range of public and private stakeholders. Their work was
given direction horizontally, in a network of relations with employers and
their own colleagues and with the collaboration between vocational rehabilitation enterprises, NAV and NHO as organizational framework. The broad
sense of "we" illustrated that the job agents had incorporated the new forms
of partnership and ownership of activation. They saw RiW's positioning in
both the public welfare services and the business sector as privileged and
enabling. NAV provided a range of useful policy instruments, and it was
clearly beneficial to be associated with NHO when recruiting employers. "In
this field, there is no doubt that we are getting stronger together", a job agent
stated in the focus group interview, followed by the consent of the others.

The ruling relations of collective action allowed the job agents to act as
co-creative and innovative problem-solvers. As one of them put it: "I function as a door opener between NHO-enterprises (employers), counsellors,
jobseekers and NAV. *How* I proceed to open these doors however, vary from
time to time". To work in a context of multiple actors at the intersection of
the welfare discourse and the market discourse demanded comprehensiveness, flexibility and adaptability. From their key position as trusted inter-
mediaries, they very much developed their own particular working style in
the course of learning and doing the job. In this regard, the regular meetings between the job agents[1] were an important arena for discussion and
exchange of ideas. In one of the meetings the first author attended, the job
agents reflected upon how RiW was gradually taking shape: While they in
the start-up of the programme had been "too eager to please the employers",

they were now getting better at "negotiating and demanding something back from the employers". This serves as an illustrative example of how the job agents spoke of RiW as a dynamic and changeable programme that they actively contributed to shape and reshape.

As the research project developed, we realized that the job agents' responsibility in RiW went far beyond their everyday practices of contacting employers and facilitating inclusion processes. We were fascinated by the level of ambition, enthusiasm and positivity they brought into their work. The job agents were on a constant lookout for new collaboration partners and projects in what one of them referred to as a field of "endless possibilities". Simultaneously, they wanted to change vocational rehabilitation enterprises from within, not necessarily the counselling of the jobseekers but their outward activities and communication practices. Their overall aim was to reposition vocational rehabilitation enterprises to become professional and equal cooperation partners for employers, and thereby bridging the gap between vocational rehabilitation and employers. In this way, they acted as change agents attempting to transform the design and delivery of vocational rehabilitation.

In the following, we try to expand the notion of ruling relations by introducing and "writing in" ideas and concepts that capture the enabling and innovative side of ruling relations. These relations are seldom highlighted in IE studies. In working with the first author's empirical material and digging into the job agents' work knowledge, what struck us as interesting was the job agents' eagerness to communicate that they were creating something new within vocational rehabilitation, which they believed took both the jobseekers' and the employers' interests into account. From their standpoint, the ruling context of collective action was open, enabling and constantly evolving in an ongoing dialogue with their practical experience. The dynamics of this type of horizontal, co-constructive practices are often left out of view in institutional ethnographies. We therefore turned to literature on governance where we found concepts that spoke more directly to the empirical material.

RiW as a case of co-production

> The idea of a sovereign state that governs society top-down through laws, rules and detailed regulations has lost its grip and is being replaced by new ideas about a decentred governance based on interdependence, negotiation and trust.

This quote by Sørensen and Torfing (2005, 195–196) illustrates that public authorities' dependency upon other stakeholders to achieve their goals does not only apply to activation policies but is also increasingly becoming the "essence of the Nordic society model" (Sørensen and Torfing 2005, 13). Røiseland and Vabo (2008, 86) propose that governance, in the Nordic context, is best understood as "the non-hierarchical process through which public and private actions and resources are coordinated and given a common direction and meaning". Thus, governance involves a movement towards more complex forms of democracy (Peters, 2011) with "networks", "partnerships" and "corporations" as important elements.[2] To describe the nature of governance *practices*, the governance literature frequently use so-called co-concepts, like co-initiation, co-design, co-creation, co-production, cooperation and co-implementation (e.g. Voorberg et al. 2015). These practices are linked to different phases in the course of policymaking and implementation, but they share some basic ideas of significance here. As the prefix "co" indicates, they point to joint efforts, mutuality and "horizontal relationships" (Hill and Hupe 2014, 155). They involve knowledge- and resource-sharing as well as negotiation across boundaries. Ultimately, co-practices make social innovation possible (Voorberg et al. 2015).

The job agents' abilities to influence the design and delivery of RiW made us reflect upon the dynamics between work knowledge and ruling relations in the context of the job agents as opposed to the counsellors. Insights drawn from Osborne's (2006) contrasting of key characteristics of NPM and New Public Governance (NPG) can shed light on the organization of the counsellors' and the job agents' work. Osborne (2006, 380) criticizes NPM for being a "partial theory" about implementing private-sector techniques to public services and for a narrow focus on intra-organizational management in an increasingly plural world. The counsellors experienced the new accountability requirements as a threat to their holistic and inter-professional work with the clients. They had less time to talk to their clients and collaborators, they increasingly "rushed" clients into work placements, and they felt they had to defend their use of time, towards their leaders. In line with Osborne's critique, the counsellors experienced NPM strategies as partial and reductive and not adapted to the complexities of vocational rehabilitation. "New truths in the field", as one of them described it, dominated and sought to displace the counsellors' professional and embodied knowledge about vocational rehabilitation (Aksnes 2017).

In a contrasting way, Osborne describes NPG as acknowledging the fragmented and pluralistic nature of todays' public services. NPG focusses on inter-organizational relationships, where trust and relational contracts act as governance mechanisms (2006, 383–384). The RiW programme is a *case* of NPG in vocational rehabilitation. The job agents shaped their role in the middle of a myriad of actors, interests and compromises. The "open-ness" of the ruling relations enabled them to develop new knowledge and practices over time, together with other central actors. In this way, the dynamics between work knowledge and ruling relations in the context of RiW were explicitly co-constructive.[3]

The governance literature functioned as a tool we used to understand what guided the job agents in their work. Concepts like "collaborative working", "mutual dependency" and "responsibility" that frequently occur in this literature can contribute in understanding the nature of the ruling at play in RiW and other contemporary institutional arrangements. Social practices are always both coordinated and performed (Halkier and Jensen 2008). In mapping social relations, we can choose to foreground the coordinative or the performative elements of a practice. If we foreground the coordinative or scripted aspects, we risk placing the social outside of social actors in larger chains of texts and discourses that rule. Foregrounding the performative, elements of peoples' doings and sayings, not just as organized and shaped by a ruling discourse, might allow us to play more analytic attention to agency as the meeting point of complex configurations of coordinative and performative elements of social action.

Conclusion

We started this chapter by introducing our puzzle regarding what seemed to be an essential difference in the ways in which the counsellors' and the job agents' work was organized. Whereas ruling in the context of the counsellors corresponded to how ruling is often presented in institutional ethnographies, ruling in the context of the job agents had a character we did not understand. To make sense of it, we had to redefine the concept of ruling relations as open and empirically empty. However, we still felt that something was missing in order to understand the organizing ideas behind the job agents' work. Literature on governance offered concepts that captured the processes of collaboration, mutual dependencies and trust that characterized the ruling context of the job agents.

The aim of this chapter has been to explore the observed differences in the counsellors' and the job agents' scope of action, and find ways to articulate RiW as a ruling context. By critically reflecting on the concept of ruling relations in light of the job agents' work practices, we have argued that more responsive forms of ruling require us to be sensitive to how relations of partnerships, networks and co-production shift and change the way in which people's everyday-everynight activities are coordinated. To maintain its openness and avoid social determinism in the way we use the concept of ruling relations analytically, we must remain open to the complex ways in which ruling interconnects with people in a two-directional manner. By this, we mean that as we map the social in IE, we must simultaneously move outwards from local sites of action and upwards to the impersonal arena of discourse, and inwards to people's know-how, motivations, states of emotion and senses of responsibility. This chapter has aimed to be a reminder to step in both directions.

Notes

1 It was only one job agent employed in each vocational rehabilitation enterprise. Around 20 job agents across these enterprises met 34 times a year.
2 "The shifts in governance" is subject of a variety of disciplines (Kersbergen and van Waarden 2004; Newman, 2001; Pierre and Peters, 2000), and the concept of governance has been given a great number of definitions (see Hill and Hupe

2014; Rhodes 1997). We will not go into these definitions here but focus on how new forms of governance influence the work of the job agents.

3 It might seem strange to place the counsellors and the job agents, who work in the same enterprises, in different organizational ruling contexts. However, as we have shown, the differences in ruling have to do with the counsellors' and the job agents' positioning in their organizations. Whereas the counsellors have a classic street-level bureaucrat position, the job agents function as autonomous brokers between vocational rehabilitation and employers. Moreover, Osborne explains that elements of NPM and NPG can coexist and overlap, and we find both in the vocational rehabilitation enterprises (e.g. Kasin and Sannes, 2012).

References

Aksnes, S. Y. 2017. "Rethinking Vocational Rehabilitation through Institutional Ethnography." *Journal of Comparative Social Work* 12(2): 1–23.

Aksnes, S. Y. 2018. "Engaging Employers in Vocational Rehabilitation: Understanding the New Significance of Knowledge Brokers." *Journal of Vocational Rehabilitation* 12(12): 1–12.

Andreassen, T. A., and Fossestøl, K. 2014. "Utfordrende inkluderingspolitikk: Samstyring for omforming av institusjonell logikk i arbeidslivet, helsetjenesten og NAV." [Challenging Inclusive Politics Using Governance to Reshape Institutional Logic in the Labour Market, Health Service and Labour and Welfare Administration.] *Tidsskrift for samfunnsforskning* 55(2): 173–202.

Brodkin, E. Z., and Marston, G. (Eds.). 2013. *Work and the Welfare State: Street-Level Organizations and Workfare Politics.* Washington, DC: Georgetown University Press.

Campbell, M. and Gregor, F. 2008. *Mapping Social Relations: A Primer in Doing Institutional Ethnography.* Walnut Creek, CA: Altamira Press.

Deveau, J. L. 2008. "Examining the Institutional Ethnographer's Toolkit." *The Journal of the Society for the Socialist Studies* 4(2): 1–20.

Fossestøl, K. 2007. *Den revitaliserte arbeidslinja- én linje eller to? [The Revitalized Work Line- One Line or Two?]* AFI-note 5/2007. Oslo: Arbeidsforskningsinstituttet.

Garsten, C. and Nyqvist, A. (Eds.). 2013. *Organisational Anthropology: Doing Ethnography in and Among Complex Organisations.* London: Pluto Press.

Halkier, B., and Jensen, I. 2008. "Det sociale som performativitet – et praksisteoretisk perspektiv på analyse og metode." [The Social as Performativity. A Practice-Theoretical Perspective on Analysis and Method.] *Dansk Sociologi* 3(19): 49–68.

Hill, M., and Hupe, P. 2014. *Implementing Public Policies: An Introduction to the Study of Operational Governance.* London: SAGE Publications.

Kasin, M., and Sannes, B. 2012. *Fra vernet bedrift i et vernet marked, til tiltaksbedrift i et konkurranseutsatt marked: framtidige tjenesteleveranser i et uforutsigbart marked. [From Vocational Rehabilitation Enterprise in a Protected Market, to Vocational Rehabilitation Enterprise in a Competitive Marked: Future Service Delivery in an Unpredictable Market.]* Master thesis. Oslo: Høgskolen i Oslo og Akershus.

Kersbergen, K. V., and van Waarden, F. 2004. "Governance as a Bridge between Disciplines: Cross-Disciplinary Inspiration Regarding Shifts in Governance and Problems of Governability, Accountability and Legitimacy." *European Journal of Political Research* 43: 143–171.

Lipsky, M. 1980. *Street-Level Bureaucracy: Dilemmas of the Individual in Public Services.* New York: Russell Sage.

Lund, R. W. B. 2015. *Doing the Ideal Academic: Gender, Excellence and Changing
Academia.* Doctoral thesis. Aalto University.

McQuaid, R. W. 2010. "Theory of Organizational Partnerships: Partnership Ad-
vantages, Disadvantages and Success Factors." *The New Public Governance: Critical Perspectives and Future Directions,* edited by Osborne, S. P., 125–146. London:
Routledge.

Møller, G., and Sannes, J. 2009. *Evaluering av arbeidsmarkedstiltak i skjermede virk-
somheter. [Evaluation of Employment Programmes in Sheltered Enterprises.]* Report 253/2009. Bø: Telemarkforskning.

Newman, J. E. 2001. *Modernizing Governance: New Labour, Policy and Society.*
London: SAGE Publications.

NOU 2012:6. 2012. *Arbeidsrettede tiltak. [Employment Programmes.]* Retrieved
on August 15th 2018 from: www.regjeringen.no/no/dokumenter/nou-2012-6/
id672029/

Osborne, S. P. 2006. "The New Public Governance?" *Public Management Review*
8(3): 377–387.

Ose, S. O., Dyrstad, K., Slettebak, R., Lippestad, J., Mandal, R., Brattlid, I., and
Jensberg, H. 2013. *Evaluering av IA-avtalen (2010–2013).* [Evaluation of the
IA-agreement (2010–2013).] SINTEF Report 2013.

Peters, G. B. 2011. "Governance as Political Theory." *Critical Policy Studies* 5(1):
63–72.

Pierre, J., and Peters, G. B. 2000. *Governance, Politics and the State.* London:
MacMillan.

Qvortrup, J. 2014. *Kompetanse i attførings- og vekstbedrifter.* [Expertise in
Vocational Rehabilitation Enterprises] Attføringsbedriftenes skriftserie
report 3/2014. Retrieved on October 10th 2018 from: https://asvl.no/filestore/
Kompetansekartlegging-11-3-2014.pdf

Rankin, J. M., and Campbell, M. L. 2006. *Managing to Nurse: Inside Canada's
Health Care Reform.* Toronto: University of Toronto Press.

Rhodes, R. A. W. 1997. *Understanding Governance. Policy Networks, Governance,
Reflexivity and Accountability.* Maidenhead: Open University Press.

Røiseland, A., and Vabo, S. I. 2008. Governance på norsk. Samstyring som empirisk
og analytisk fenomen. [Governance on Norwegian. Governance as Empirical and
Analytical Phenomenon.] *Norsk Statsvitenskapelig Tidsskrift* 24(1–2): 86–107.

Satka, M. E., and Skehill, C. 2012. "Michel Foucault and Dorothy Smith in Case
File Research: Strange Bed-Fellows or Complementary Thinkers?" *Qualitative
Social Work* 11(2): 191–205.

Smith, D. E. 1987. *The Everyday World as Problematic: A Feminist Sociology.* Boston, MA: Northeastern University Press.

Smith, D. E. 1999. *Writing the Social: Critique, Theory, and Investigations.* Toronto:
University of Toronto Press.

Smith, D. E. 2005. *Institutional Ethnography: A Sociology for People.* Oxford:
AltaMira Press.

Sørensen, E., and Torfing, J. 2005. "The Democratic Anchorage of Governance
Networks." *Scandinavian Political Studies* 28(3): 195–218.

Taylor, M. 2007. "Community Participation in the Real World: Opportunities and
Pitfalls in New Governance Spaces." *Urban Studies* 44(2): 297–317.

Tøssebro, J., Wik, S. E., and Molden, T. H. 2017. *Arbeidsgivere og arbeidsinkludering: Ringer i Vannet- et bidrag til økt rekruttering av personer med nedsatt funksjonsevne.* [*Employers and Labour Market Inclusion: Ripples in the Water – A Contribution to Increased Recruitment of People with Reduced Work Capacities.*] NTNU Samfunnsforskning.

Townsend, E. 1996. "Institutional Ethnography: A Method for Showing How the Context Shapes Practice." *Occupational Therapy Journal of Research* 16(3): 179–199.

Van Berkel, R., and Borghi, V. 2007. "Contextualising New Modes of Governance in Activation Policies." *International Journal of Sociology and Social Policy* 27(9/10): 353–363.

Van Berkel, R., and Valkenburg, B. 2007. "The Individualisation of Activation Services in Context." *Making it Personal: Individualising Activation Services in the EU*, edited by Van Berkel, R. and B. Valkenburg, 3–21. Bristol: The Policy Press.

Voorberg, W. H., Bekkers, V. J. J. M., and Tummers, L. G. 2015. "A Systematic Review of Co-Creation and Co-Production: Embarking on the Social Innovation Journey." *Public Management Review* 17(9): 1333–1357.

White Paper No. 9 (2006–2007). *Arbeid, velferd og inkludering.* [Work, Welfare and Inclusion.] Arbeids- og sosialdepartementet. Retrieved on June 12th 2018 from: www.regjeringen.no/no/dokumenter/stmeld-nr-9-2006-2007-/id432894/sec1

Widerberg, K. (Ed.). 2015. *I hjertet av velferdsstaten: En invitasjon til institusjonell etnografi.* Oslo: Cappelen Damm akademisk.

12 Institutional paradoxes in Norwegian labour activation

Helle Cathrine Hansen

Introduction

In Nordic countries, labour market participation is considered important, not only as a means of income security or revenue for the state but also as a means of social inclusion and individual self-realisation for the citizens (Halvorsen 2012). Therefore, social policies in the Nordic countries are closely connected to active labour market policies (ALMP), which, in the Norwegian context, are referred to as "the workline policy" (as outlined in the introduction chapter). Following its development from the beginning of the 1990s, workline policy has gone from favouring strict and coercive measures to employing more enabling strategies (Lødemel and Moreira 2014) to include various groups of service users in the labour market. The policy is now referred to as *activation policy*.

The aim of this chapter is to explore how activation policies are realised in practice. More specifically, I explore, from the standpoint of service users and their collaboration with social workers how service users' activation processes and social workers' activation work are coordinated through the institutional framing of a human resource development (HRD) programme, and how institutional framing may shape activation work in complex ways. The study context is the Norwegian Qualification Programme (QP), a state-initiated municipal programme that aims to bring service users who face particular difficulties in obtaining paid employment into work. The QP is a good example of activation policy from the Nordic context because it represents a particular feature of the Nordic welfare states, namely activation policy carried out with an HRD approach and the inherent enabling strategies that are compatible with social work.

This chapter contributes to the body of knowledge on activation practice research by showing how the institutional framing of an activation programme may inhibit social workers from providing adequate measures and support to service users according to *individual users*' defined needs. I have applied institutional ethnography (IE) as an analytical and methodological approach, in combination with a street-level bureaucracy perspective. IE enabled me to see the extent to which social workers' practice was coordinated by the institutional and structural settings of the QP and how they navigated within these settings.

Helle Cathrine Hansen

The institutional context of the Norwegian Qualification Programme

The QP targets long-term unemployed people who have significantly reduced work capacity due to complex challenges such as mental or physical health problems; substance abuse; lack of formal education, work experience, and/ or relevant skills; insecure housing situations; and family issues and therefore face difficulties in acquiring employment. Hence, the target group is diverse, needing various degrees of support to obtain paid employment.

A fundamental principle of the QP is that activation measures and activities should be tailored to each participant's individual needs, abilities, and limitations. Therefore, individual programmes should be planned in close collaboration with social workers, and participants should be offered personalised measures to improve their employment prospects (Norwegian Ministry of Labour and Inclusion 2006–2007a and 2007b; Norwegian Ministry of Labour and Social Affairs 2011). Even though paid employment is the ultimate goal of the QP, enhanced quality of life and self-efficacy are also important outcomes, regardless of whether participants obtain paid employment or not. Thus, an individual programme might include a variety of activities, such as work placement, courses (e.g. CV writing, work-life knowledge, clergy work, computer skills, care work skills, truck driving), motivational training, social and physical training, medical treatment, and recreational activities (Norwegian Ministry of Labour and Social Affairs 2012, §30).

Social workers are granted considerable discretion when it comes to determining regarding participants' needs, and according to policy intentions, they have the power to offer a wide range of measures – as long as those measures are relevant to the service users' needs. Nevertheless, social workers are limited in what they actually *can* offer participants based on legal regulations, local policy practice, or financial situations. Normally, the availability of measures depends on municipal finances. Work placement is easily obtainable and cost-effective, both for the labour and welfare services (Norwegian Labour and Welfare Administration (NAV)) and for employers, and therefore commonly offered to QP participants. Work training in sheltered workshops may be an alternative for participants who have limited work capacity due to health problems. But again, this opportunity depends on availability in the local area. Courses that are contracted and purchased by the regional or central labour and welfare administration are also commonly used. However, the local selection of courses may also depend on municipal finances. In the study, one NAV office offered a variety of employment preparation courses, including CV writing, basic computer skills, job search, work-life knowledge, and communication skills, while others offered only a couple of courses, namely Norwegian language courses and basic computer skills. The problem with these contracted and prepaid courses is that few of them provide formal qualifications, and they therefore have limited value in the ordinary labour market. Simultaneously, participation in higher education that would be formally qualifying is not permitted as a programme activity (Norwegian Ministry of Labour and Social Affairs 2012, §1–4.30.2.9).

Previous research contends that broad framework laws and extensive use of discretion on the part of local authorities in implementing the QP seem to limit the intended scope of a programme that should be tailored to users' individual needs (Gubrium et al. 2014, 39). The extent to which service users are granted individualised measures strongly depends on local NAV office personnel and municipal resources (Gubrium et al. 2014, 34). Correspondingly, the Norwegian health board's audit indicates a lack of individual tailoring and user involvement in the implementation of the QP in the municipalities (Norwegian Board of Health Supervision 2015). Moreover, since the QP's implementation in 2007, restrictions on individualised activities have grown, requiring at least the second half of the estimated programme time to be dedicated to employment-oriented activities (Norwegian Ministry of Labour and Social Affairs 2011, 2012). Notwithstanding, many QP social workers experience that they have insufficient knowledge of and connections to local labour markets (Malmberg-Heimonen et al. 2016; Schafft and Spjelkavik 2011), which, in turn, may impede service users in obtaining paid employment. This previous research points to challenges in activation policy implementation and practice besides the individual deficiencies that often are ascribed to service users with complex and multiple challenges (e.g. adversity related to health, social network, family, housing, language, skills, and education) vis-à-vis the labour market.

A bottom-up perspective on activation policy implementation

Lipsky's (2010) street-level bureaucracy perspective represents a bottom-up perspective on public policy implementation, in which frontline workers' discretionary practices play an important part. Elaborating on Lipsky's (2010) street-level perspective, Hupe and Hill (2007) argued that not only is policy implementation a result of frontline workers' autonomy and discretionary practices, but it is also shaped in a *multidimensional web* of horizontal and vertical *relations*, through which frontline workers are held accountable for the outcomes of their actions with colleagues, managers, and other stakeholders inside and outside the organisation. However, as pointed out by Hupe and Buffat (2014), the traditional street-level perspective does not consider the influence of the wider context in which street-level practice takes place: "In most street-level bureaucracy studies, the nature of the macro-institutional setting involved and the impact of specific institutional factors are ignored (…) the impact of other sets of potentially explanatory factors, particularly those regarding institutional settings, remain understudied" (Hupe and Buffat 2014, 554–555). Within the field of activation policy studies, Van Berkel et al. (2017) answer this call by acknowledging that various contexts (i.e. policy, governance, organisational, and occupational) may influence how activation service delivery takes place.

Building on these scholars' work, I sought to understand the complex dynamics embedded in QP practice and implementation. IE, in combination with Lipsky's street-level approach, proved to be a fruitful analytical and methodological approach for understanding the complexity of QP practice because it allows for the inclusion of service users as well as institutional and structural settings. The point of investigating QP from the standpoint of service users and their collaboration with social workers is to connect service users' everyday experiences and activities in the QP activation programme back to the programme's processes of administration and governance (Devault and McCoy 2012, 381). IE enabled a wider understanding of the social relations in which QP service users' and social workers' practices are embedded and thereby facilitated a better understanding of the complexity involved in the local implementation of activation policy, going beyond Lipsky's street-level approach. With IE, it was possible to show how the multidimensional web of relations in which QP is embedded shapes activation practice, as well as how the ordering of these relations may have unintended consequences for service users' activation processes and social workers' activation work.

Data and methods

The study was carried out as a field study in four NAV offices in 2013. Data is based on observations of 33 meetings between QP participants and social workers, 15 individual interviews with QP participants, and informal conversations with staff in four NAV offices.

The institutional ethnographic approach implies a bottom-up perspective which aims at mapping the social relations of the phenomenon under investigation in order to trace how people's everyday practices and activities are trans-locally governed (Smith 2005). Hence, the point of departure for my analysis was the experience of the QP participants, especially their collaboration with social workers. In the first step of the analysis, through interviews and observations of meetings between QP participants and their social workers, I explored how the participants experienced the qualification programme in terms of their expectations of obtaining paid employment and/ or getting assistance in meeting other needs. Second, I looked more closely at the participants' experiences to reveal how the social relations embedded in the QP might obstruct or promote QP participants' activation processes. To accomplish this second step, I used a dialogical strategy of asking analytical questions of the data (McCoy 2006, 111; Smith 2005, 135–139), for instance, where did the practice of work placement referral come from? Based on issues that emerged from the interviews and the observational data, I found that certain chief texts concerning the QP – policy documents and legal texts, parliamentary reports, regulations, and directives (Norwegian

Ministry of Labour and Inclusion 2006–2007a and 2007b; Norwegian Ministry of Labour and Social Affairs 2011, 2012) – shaped both the work social workers were doing and the service users' qualification processes.

Mapping the social relations in the QP led me to extend the contextual frame of my analysis beyond QP documents to include other trans-local conditions, such as the municipal economy and the labour market situation. By asking analytical questions of the data, I found that these extra-local conditions governed participants' activation processes in ways that both promoted labour market inclusion of participants yet seemed to inhibit the process of becoming employed.

The third step comprised an analysis of how social workers navigated the structural and institutional framings of the QP while following up on participants and their processes of labour market inclusion. This stage of analysis looked at how social workers interpreted and carried out the programme and how their work was shaped by directive texts, local NAV office policy, municipal finances, and local labour market situations. The ways in which social workers navigated these institutional and structural settings in their follow-up work with QP participants highlighted the relations governing QP practice.

Institutional paradoxes

The policy goal of the QP is to improve participants' labour market prospects; therefore, participants should be offered measures that suit their needs and preconditions. However, the findings of the study suggest that QP participants' need for certain types of assistance and adjustments regarding their work-life potential, *as well as* the programme's work-oriented requirements, inhibited activation work in various ways. The analysis underscores the paradox that this finding appears to contradict the policy goal of the programme: to move QP participants into paid employment.

The qualification paradox

Several of the participants in the study expressed a need for specific and qualifying measures in order to become employed. However, it could be a challenge for social workers to provide service users with relevant and qualifying measures, as demonstrated in the following extract from a conversation between a social worker and a QP participant:

PARTICIPANT: They [employers] told me if I had the driver's license [I would get a job], but I cannot, because I do not have enough money. I passed the theoretical part, but I cannot afford the rest.

SOCIAL WORKER: Yes, I see that it is much easier to get a job with a driver's license, but I cannot help you with that ... unless you get an employment guarantee from an employer, then I could try.

PARTICIPANT: So if I get a confirmation from an employer that he would hire me, 99 per cent sure, then ...

SOCIAL WORKER: Then it *may* be easier, but I cannot promise you anything. But, yes, I do agree that your possibilities of getting a job would have been much better with a driver's license.

The participant is enrolled in the QP because he was not able to get a job on his own and therefore needed assistance from NAV, but he could not get what he needed from NAV without already having a job offer. This paradoxical situation emanated from a retrenchment in municipal finances that led the local NAV office to refrain from granting individual measures entailing financial commitments unless the participant had a job guarantee. However, in this case, local economic retrenchment also made it difficult for the participant to find a job guarantee.

An alternative activation measure might have been work placement. However, as this participant had already attended several work placements without being hired, the social worker supported him in continuing his job search through personal networking instead. This strategy required travelling and overnight stays out of town and the service user had already spent his monthly QP benefit on travelling expenses. The social worker provided him with what assistance she could within the institutional limits: covering his travelling expenses for another month and giving advice on accommodation while away from home. Acknowledging that this strategy would hardly improve his labour market prospects because the people in his network were also unemployed and therefore lacked labour market contacts, covering the travel expenses was a way – seemingly the only way – for the social worker to provide the service user with some kind of activation-related assistance without having expectations in terms of employment-related outcomes.

This case demonstrates how the social worker navigated within a multi-dimensional web of relations comprising the service user's needs, organisational policy, municipal finances, the local labour market, and QP rules and regulations, and how these relations shaped the social worker's incapacity to assist the service user towards labour market inclusion. The example points to the extent to which social workers are caught between the needs of service users and the constraints of institutional settings, and how their discretionary power may be limited by higher-order internal and external relations.

The work placement paradox

Work placement refers to a temporary position as a trainee in the ordinary public or private sector labour market, and the social workers in this study valued work placement as an important means to improve participants' labour market prospects.

"Work placement is the entrance ticket, you know", said one social worker to a participant. "You need to have work placement. This is how you can show them that you are good, that you are reliable". It was also the case that some participants in the study experienced benefits from work placement because they learned new skills, were able to use their competencies, and did valuable work (see also Hansen 2018). Nevertheless, although work placement occasionally led to paid employment,[1] most study participants did not experience it as beneficial. One participant said,

> I had been on three different work placements, not only for a month or two, but I was there for six months, and I didn't get the job. I was in X for four months and in Y for two months. I worked 12 months for free [the participant received benefits and the employers didn't pay] ... I did a good job, everybody was satisfied, and he [employer] promised to hire me, but he said I just needed to do one more month on work training ... and then [after the four months], he said they could not afford to hire me, but later they hired a Norwegian guy. Now I just want a job, no more work placement.

The quote from this participant indicates that he experienced work placement as exploitation rather than as a job opportunity. Another participant expressed similar feelings:

> I was happy because I got to use my competency and I got to do valuable work which [the employer] needed ... setting up systems that saved them a lot of money, a job that somebody should have done a long time ago. It is obvious that they lack either competency or employees to do this [work] ... however, after a year, it was clear that there was no possibility of getting employed on ordinary terms, and under those circumstances, I quit.

Both participants felt that they had contributed favourably to their work placement employers, and despite this they were not permanently hired. The employers seemed to blame their failure to hire on lack of financial resources. Hence, these participants' employment prospects were related to how the employers perceived their own financial situations. But they were also connected to regional economic retrenchment, which affected the general labour market by creating a decrease in jobs, both for people with higher education and for low-skilled workers.

The social workers' continued promotion of work placement may have been related to a lack of alternative employment-oriented measures due to the retrenchment in municipal finances. Or it may simply have been the result of a narrow interpretation of "employment-oriented measures" as work placement. Regulations state that the QP should be employment oriented, with a particular emphasis on compulsory employment-oriented measures during the last six months of a year-long individual programme (Norwegian Ministry of Labour and Social Affairs 2011). However, employment-oriented measures are not specified in any particular form. Hence, social workers can use their discretion to determine what measures might be considered work oriented for each individual participant. Nevertheless, as demonstrated in the previous case, their discretionary power is negotiated in relation to the policy of the local NAV office, in other words through vertical social relations. At the same time, their discretionary power is also negotiated in relation to their colleagues or through horizontal social relations (see Hupe and Hill 2007). Hence, referral to work placement may represent a routine way to handle QP participants' needs for qualification that fellow social workers have adopted without questioning its relevance for the individual service user (see also Fossestøl et al. 2016, 26, 28).

Nevertheless, the institutional paradox of work placement seems to have led to a de-individualised activation practice that conflicts with the intention of tailoring measures to achieve labour market inclusion, as expressed in policy papers. Coupled with employers' need for labour and their failure to hire, the practice of work placement referral may have resulted in further demotivation and lost opportunities for participants to qualify for the labour market (Hansen 2018).

The work test paradox

The work test paradox is an example of a paradox that appears when participants claim reduced work capacity and therefore are not able to fulfil the programme's requirements regarding taking part in work-oriented activities on a full-time basis or at all. Several of the participants in the study attended work training in sheltered workshops, either to prove their lack of work capacity or to fulfil the QPs work-oriented activity requirement despite being unable to work. The following example demonstrates the paradox of having to prove one's incapacity to work through a work test because the official diagnosis system does not acknowledge certain health problems (in this case tinnitus) as conditions that qualify for health-related benefits.

SW: You know, if you are going to be with us [in the QP], you have to try it,
PARTICIPANT: I don't know, I don't know ... it is difficult, but I do not have a choice ... let's try, I have told you I will try.
SW: You will get help for your hearing problems and the pain, they are specialized in hearing problems, ... and you will get your work capacity tested, and then you will see what you are able to do ... or it might strengthen the application for disability pension.

In this case, the social worker tried to find the best possible solution to the user's problem, given the institutional limitations. Sheltered work training in a company specialised in the user's health problem was chosen based on the user's individual situation. Thus, when faced with the competing demands of the participant's expressed needs and the work-oriented QP requirements, the social worker accommodated the measures and offered the participant the best available alternative. While she acknowledges the user's situational self-understanding – namely not being able to work – she nevertheless addresses the QP's work-oriented requirements directly by also referring to the opportunity of having his work capacity tested in a specialised environment. Still, it is paradoxical that the social worker has to insist on these conditions and that the only solution she can offer a man who perceives himself unable to work is a work test to prove his incapacity.

The paradox in this case is created by the intersection of the QP rules and regulations, which require full-time participation and work-oriented measures, and the diagnosis system, which does not acknowledge tinnitus as a condition that entitles a person to health-related benefits. The social worker navigated within this institutional framework in an attempt to offer something that would partly remedy the participant's problem – getting help to deal with his pain. Moreover, in the long run, the work testing might also help to strengthen the participant's application for disability pension. Nevertheless, the case demonstrates how social workers may be caught between the competing demands of participants' problems and needs on the one hand, and the institutional settings that limit their capacity to offer the most appropriate forms of assistance on the other hand.

From paradoxes to objectifying policy practice

Embedded in the QP's institutional framing, I found that a multidimensional web of relations created paradoxes that set limits for social workers' discretionary practice in activation work, which, in turn, obstructed participants' qualification processes. The paradoxes point to inflexibility of programme practice and limited possibilities for social workers to provide measures that correspond with participants' individual needs. QP policy documents emphasise individually tailored programmes with relevant measures as key to obtaining employment (Norwegian Ministry of Labour and Inclusion 2006–2007a and 2007b). However, my findings point to how trans-local settings – such as budgetary restrictions or contradictory rules and regulations – limit social workers' discretionary power and their ability to offer service users individualised, relevant and qualifying measures.

The results from this study align with previous research from Nordic countries indicating that social work practice tends to respond to administrative and organisational requirements rather than to service users' needs (Caswell and Larsen 2017; Thoren 2008), and that labour activation has become increasingly standardised and fails to deliver individualised and tailored services (Fossestøl et al. 2016; Fuertes and Lindsay 2016, 539–540; Wright 2013). The findings from this study, however, add to previous research by demonstrating *how* this happens and *how* it concretely affects service users' qualification processes. Following Lipsky's (2010) perspective, QP social workers may have the autonomy to find solutions to *their* professional everyday challenges, for instance through work placement referrals.

However, as explicitly shown in this study, they have limited means and authority to respond adequately to service users' needs. Hence, the study indicates that policy implementation in the activation field may be more of a top-down, objectifying process than a street-level creation.

The study underscores the complex relationship between local and trans-local levels in activation policy implementation and how institutional and structural settings may have the unintended consequence of creating a standardised and objectifying policy practice. An important implication of these findings for policy and practice is that the institutional framing of activation programmes may obstruct policy outcomes and prolong activation processes for participants. The findings further suggest that activation policy fails to reach its goal because there is a gap between policy ambitions and the opportunity service users and social workers have to realise these ambitions in practice. To conclude, in order to improve activation policy and service delivery, we must acknowledge the institutional complexity in which activation policy is embedded.

The methodological implication of the study is that research in policy implementation should be conducted contextually from a bottom-up perspective to include service users' and frontline workers' interactions and experiences. However, the study also suggests that street-level research should move beyond the frontline setting to consider the multidimensional web of social relations through which policy implementation occurs. IE was useful as a means of investigating how trans-local social relations shaped QP practice and how the ordering of these relations had consequences that contradicted the QP's policy goal of moving service users into work. Hence, this wider methodological scope calls for policy and practice to address unemployment and activation not only at the individual level with an HRD approach but also at the institutional level.

Note

1 Only two participants in this study obtained paid employment through work placement: One got a fixed job with a limited amount of working hours – four hours per week – while the other found temporary work with unstable hours and was employed only for a short period.

References

Caswell, Dorte, and Flemming Larsen. 2017. "Frontline Work in the Delivery of Danish Activation Policies." In *Frontline Delivery of Welfare-to-Work Policies in Europe. Activating the Unemployed*, edited by Rik Van Berkel, Dorte Caswell, Peter Kupka, and Flemming Larsen, 163–180. New York: Routledge.

Devault, Majorie L., and Liza McCoy. 2012. "Investigating Ruling Relations: Dynamics of Interviewing in Institutional Ethnography." In *The Sage Handbook of Interview Research*, edited by Jaber F. Gubrium, James A. Holstein, Amir B. Marvasti, and Karyn D. McKinney, 381–395. Thousand Oaks, CA: Sage Publications.

Fossestøl, Knut, Helene Berg, Elin Borg, Audun Gleinsvik, Tatiana Maximova-Mentzoni, and Eirin Pedersen. 2016. *Idealer og Realiteter i Forvaltningen av Arbeidsrettede Tiltak i NAV* [*Ideals and Realities in Administration of Employment-oriented Measures in NAV*]. Oslo: Work Research Institute.

Fuertes, Vanesa, and Colin Lindsay. 2016. "Personalization and Street-level Practice in Activation: The Case of the UK's Work Programme." *Public Adminstration* 94 (2): 526–541.

Gubrium, Erika, Ivan Harsløf, and Ivar Lødemel. 2014. "Norwegian Activation Reform on a Wave of Wider Welfare State Changes." In *Activation or Workfare? Governance and the Neo-liberal Convergence,* edited by Ivar Lødemel and Amilcar Moreira, 19–46. New York: Oxford University Press.

Halvorsen, Knut. 2012. "Lønnsarbeid – vår tids sekulære religion." [Wage Work – The Secular Religion of our Time] In *Arbeidslinja: arbeidsmotivasjonen og velferdsstaten* [*The Workline: Work Motivation and the Welfare State*], edited by Steinar Stjernø and Einar Øverbye, 188–198. Oslo: Universitetsforlaget.

Hansen, Helle Cathrine. 2018. "Recognition and Gendered Identity Constructions in Labour Activation." *International Journal of Social Welfare* 27: 186–196.

Hupe, Peter, and Aurelien Buffat. 2014. "A Public Service Gap: Capturing Contexts in a Comparative Approach of Street-level Bureaucracy." *Public Management Review* 16 (4): 548–569.

Hupe, Peter, and Michael Hill. 2007. "Street-Level Bureaucracy and Public Accountability." *Public Administration* 85 (2): 279–299.

Lipsky, Michael. 2010. *Street-Level Bureaucracy. Dilemmas of the Individual in Public Services.* New York: Russel Sage Foundation.

Lødemel, Ivar, and Amilcar Moreira, eds. 2014. *Activation or Workfare: Governance and the Neo-liberal Convergence.* New York: Oxford University Press.

Malmberg-Heimonen, Ira, Sidsel Natland, Anne Grete Tøge, and Helle Cathrine Hansen. 2016. "The Effects of Skill-Training on Social Workers' Professional Competences in Norway: Results of a Cluster-Randomised Study." *British Journal of Social Work* 46 (5): 1354–1371.

McCoy, Liza. 2006. "Keeping the Institution in View: Working with Interview Accounts of Everyday Experience." In *Institutional Ethnography as Practice,* edited by Dorothy Smith, 109–125. Oxford: Rownman and Littlefield.

Norwegian Board of Health Supervision. 2015. *Qualified to Qualify? Summary of Countrywide Supervision in 2013 and 2014 of Job Training Programmes.* Oslo: Norwegian Board of Health Supervision. Available from www.helsetilsynet.no.

Norwegian Ministry of Labour and Inclusion. 2006–2007a. *Work, Welfare and Inclusion. Parliamentary Report 9.* Oslo: Ministry of Labour and Inclusion.

Norwegian Ministry of Labour and Inclusion. 2006–2007b. *Concerning the Act Changes to the Social Welfare Services Law and Individual Other Acts.* Parliamentary Proposition 70. Oslo: Ministry of Labour and Inclusion.

Norwegian Ministry of Labour and Social Affairs. 2011. *Regulations Concerning Qualification Program and Qualification Benefit.* Oslo: Ministry of Labour and Social Welfare.

Norwegian Ministry of Labour and Social Affairs. 2012. *Directive 35 Concerning the Social Services Act.* Oslo: Ministry of Labour and Social Welfare.

Schafft, Angelica, and Øystein Spjelkavik. 2011. *Evaluering av Kvalifiseringsprogrammet. Sluttrapport* [*Evaluation of the Qualification Program. Final Report*]. Oslo: Arbeidsforskningsinstituttet (AFI) and Work Research Institute (WRI).

Smith, Dorothy. 2005. *Institutional Ethnography, a Sociology for People*. New York: Altamira Press.

Thorén, Katarina H. 2008. *Activation Policy in Action. A Street-Level Study of Social Assistance in the Swedish Welfare State*. Doctoral diss. Groningen: Växjö University Press.

Van Berkel, Rik, Dorte Caswell, Peter Kupka, and Flemming Larsen. 2017. *Frontline Delivery of Welfare-to-Work Policies in Europe. Activating the Unemployed*. New York: Routledge.

Wright, Sharon. 2013. "On Activation Workers' Perceptions: A Reply to Dunn." *Journal of Social Policy* 42 (4): 829–837.

13 The transition of care work

From a comprehensive to a co-created welfare state

Guro Wisth Øydgard

Introduction

Norway and the other Nordic countries are well-known for their comprehensive welfare states. Since both women and men participate in the workforce, the state has taken responsibility for the care of old, ill or disabled people (HOD 2011). In recent policy documents, this policy and practice has been challenged (HOD 2011, 2013). Due to an increasing number of elderly and people living with illness or disability, the state has initiated a plan to share the responsibility for caregiving between publicly funded formal services and informal carers, or, as the white paper says, *"the totality of society's care resources"* (HOD 2013). This initiative is referred to as *co-creation*. The concept of co-creation is based on the idea that informal carers voluntarily take part in the care work for the elderly, ill and disabled, driven by the presumed feeling of a common responsibility (Bason 2010; HOD 2013). Drawing on Dorothy Smith's concept of work (Smith 2005), I explore in this chapter how informal care work related to people with dementia is carried out and how it is coordinated with the access to formal care. Given an ageing population, the informal carers are becoming increasingly essential in solving the future challenges with regard to care resources (HOD 2011, 2013; OECD 2011; WHO 2012), and there is a need for knowledge that can contribute to a broader understanding of how shared care actually works.

Using a generous concept of *work* (Smith 2005), institutional ethnography (IE) is an approach that makes it possible to explore the activities and actions of people who partake in care work and allows me to explore how informal and formal care work are interconnected. Therefore, the aim of this chapter is to illustrate how IE can be used to investigate how shared care is done by investigating the work of informal carers and administrators at allocation offices. The exploration shows how administrators' work of translating the informal carers' experienced needs in everyday life into written texts and grants is done within the framework of institutional regulations and boss texts that the administrators are held accountable to.

Current research on informal care work

Informal carers' effort is quite stable in Norway. Despite the fact that informal carers do not have any legal obligation to care for next of kin above the age of 18 (Kaasa 2011; Kildal and Kuhnle 2005), informal carers contribute a considerable part of the overall care for persons with dementia (HOD 2013; Kaasa 2011). Related to the development of a comprehensive welfare state over the past decades, a form of shared care has developed; informal carers carry out practical tasks, while the publicly funded formal care service's contribution is mainly concentrated on nursing tasks (Daatland and Herlofson 2004; HOD 2013; Jakobsson et al. 2012). Furthermore, previous studies show that informal carers' contribution is closely connected to the possibility of getting help from formal services when needed (Aksøy 2012; Daatland and Herlofson 2004; HOD 2011, 2013). Receiving formal care and support in Norway requires that the patient or the informal carers ask for it explicitly. Since the cognitive reduction that follows with dementia makes this difficult, this task is often left to the informal carers (Health Directorate 2007; Health Directorate 2016; HOD 2011; Jakobsen and Homelien 2011). Asking for help on behalf of the person with dementia is therefore a care task facilitated by the welfare state, and a necessary step in accessing the formal care work (Gautun 2003).

Nevertheless, studies show that informal carers are dissatisfied with the formal care system, and that the formal help does not fulfil informal carers' needs (Aasgaard et al. 2014; Jakobsen and Homelien 2013; Larsen et al. 2017; Nordhagen and Sørlie 2016). Previous studies show that informal carers are driven by mixed feelings and a combination of choice and duty (Al-Janabi et al. 2017; Carlsen and Lundberg 2017; Lethin et al. 2015). Previous studies have focussed mainly on how individual factors such as system knowledge, coping resources and cultural and language barriers affect persons with dementia and their informal carers' access to formal services (Clemmensen et al. 2016; Giebel et al. 2015; Mukadam et al. 2011; Mukadam et al. 2013; Pratt et al. 2006; Robinson 2009; Stensletten et al. 2016). However, given the particular relationship between formal and informal care, there is a need for more knowledge about how the shared care is actually carried out. Therefore, this chapter investigates shared care, not as a question of individual resources and informal support of a person with dementia, but explores the interconnection between individuals and the welfare state.

Unpacking informal care work and administrators' judgements – the concept of work

Using IE, my research investigates how informal carers' contribution to care and access to formal services are negotiated with administrators at allocation offices and the ruling relations that, in turn, shape their work. The everyday practical knowledge of informal carers and administrators at the allocation offices knowledge is what Dorothy Smith calls *work knowledge* (Smith 2005, 151). Work in IE refers not only to paid work but is used in a "generous sense" as "anything done by people that takes time and effort, and they mean to do, that is done under definite conditions and with whatever means and tools, and that they may have to think about" (Smith 2005, 151–152). In turn, I use this knowledge to bring into view the institutional field which the informal carers and the administrators are located in, and how it shapes their work (McCoy 2006).

The empirical data comes from qualitative interviews with 26 informal carers and 7 administrators working at municipal allocation offices. Among the informal carers, 3 of them were male and 23 female. Thirteen were children of the person with dementia, nine were their spouses and four had another relationship to the person with dementia: one sister, two cousins and one friend. The persons with dementia whom the informal carers cared for lived in 12 different municipalities in Norway. Of these, I selected five municipalities with variation in size and number of inhabitants. Seven administrators were interviewed: five female and two male.

I asked the informal carers about their everyday lives as informal carers and about their efforts to involve formal carers, for example home care nurse, security alarm or placements in care facilities. I asked them what they did, who they talked to, how they proceeded and why. Similar questions were directed to the administrators; how did they get to know about inhabitants needs for help, who told them, what did they do, who did they talk to, how was grants written and why? This way, I did not only get to know what they should do, or what their routines were, but I got access to their reflections about what they actually do. This way the generous concept of work helped me as researcher to include the invisible work, or as Devault et al. (2014, 181) puts it: "the things people do as *is rarely acknowledged as work*".

The experiences of Jane, a woman whose mother had dementia, illustrate how such invisible work can proceed over a long period of time. She explained to me during an interview how she talked to the administrators at the allocation division several times about applying for a long-term placement in a nursing home for her mother:

> My mother got sicker, and I saw that she couldn't cope at home by herself anymore. I talked to the administrator at the allocation office, but they told me that there was no point in applying for a long-term placement. The municipality had no available placement, so the best option was to grant some more time from the home care nurses. So, they did. But my mother's health got worse. I visited her several times a day. Changed her bed linen, helped her get dressed and made sure she ate. Again, I turned to the administrator at the allocation office and asked for a long-term placement, but the answer was the same; there was no

point in applying. Instead she was granted several short-term stays at a nursing facility. Three years after the first talk about a long-term facility placement, my mother was granted a long-term placement. (...) I never understood how the allocation works. Who is deciding and based on what? I tried to give them medical commentary from doctors, but they said they did not need it. They said that the home care nurses reported that everything was fine when they visited my mother (...) but they were there for 20 minutes, four times a day (...).

I asked administrators working at allocation divisions how they acted when they were notified about inhabitants' needs for help. I asked them what they did when they were notified, who they talked to, what they said, wrote and so on. The stories of the administrators bore witness of approaches to the proposed needs that in different ways made certain needs *accountable* (Smith 2005, 179). Figure 13.1 illustrates the translation of needs as it is done by the administrators. Presented as an *accountability circuit* (Griffith and Smith 2014b, 14), this figure illustrates the process from the informal carers' presentation of a need for help, to granting an application. The accountability circuit illustrates how administrators, as Griffith and Smith (2014a, 340) explain it, "*make performance or outcomes produced at the front line accountable in terms of managerial categories and objectives*".

As this figure illustrates, when administrators map out needs, they *translate* needs for help in daily life into performable services. The administrators can therefore be said to do their work where *individual needs meet the institutional framework* of public health and care services. However, as state employees, the administrators are also held responsible to the institution they work within. The concept of *ruling relations* (Smith 1987, 3) brings us closer to an understanding of how the work of the administrators is carried out.

Figure 13.1 Accountability circuit for the translations from needs to services (Øydgard, 2018, 36).

Ruling relations are forms of consciousness constituted externally to particular places and people and shape people's action to take a distinctive character that is not fully within their scope of knowledge (Smith 1987). In other words, ruling relations can be said to be internalized in people's doings and consciousnesses. *Boss texts* (Griffith and Smith 2014b, 12) is an analytic concept used to describe how ruling relations *rule;* how people's doings are coordinated with higher level texts, such as guidelines, policy documents, principles or procedures. Such texts are not necessarily present in a material form but are textually mediated because they are formed and maintained within textual forms (Griffith and Smith 2014b). Exploring the accountability circuit for translating needs into decisions, two ruling boss texts appeared to be connected to the translation process as they coordinate the transition of requirements: *necessary, justifiable needs* and *lowest effective level of care*. Both boss texts are connected to Norwegian municipalities' duty to offer health and care services to the inhabitants but are also closely connected to new public management-inspired principles that during the last three decades have had a large influence on the public sector in Norway. Due to increased efficacy, fair distribution of scarce goods and a commitment to reduce costs, a stronger control of service allocation has developed (Vabø 2011, 2012). The *ruling* of these boss texts was made visible through the administrators' work of translating needs in a certain way, so that the needs the administrators write down and grant, *accounted to* the boss texts. The first boss text as the answer to why certain needs released services and others did not. The second boss text as the reason how the administrators argued that certain needs should get covered.

The work of translating needs

The work of allocating services often starts with a home visit where the administrators also help users and informal carers filling in an application for help. Administrators reported how they guided informal carers or patients towards less comprehensive services.

> If I'm at a first-time home visit, I may suggest a security alarm. Then they can get in contact with a home care nurse when needed. It's often, usually the informal carers who want us to check in on their older parent because they worry when they are alone (...) but if I think that a security alarm is enough in that particular case, I may suggest that we try that first.
>
> (Administrator)

In contrast, information about certain other services, such as individual plans and coordinators, is seldom a topic in these conversations. Individual plans and coordinators are individual follow-up tools for patients with need for long-term services that include more than one provider. According to an administrator:

> (...) [there are] very few, I think, that have an individual plan or a co-ordinator. These services are more common among our younger users. The elderly don't apply for this. I think that they do not know their rights, and it is not a topic I usually bring up (...) Because, you know, you have to apply to get it.

In another municipality, there were vacancies in long-term nursing home places. However, the administrator told me they did not want to say this out loud, fearing someone would claim the place without "really" needing it. This could, in turn, lead to a lowering of the threshold for long-term placement. Administrators withholding information. Another informal carer also told me how she experienced that administrators withheld information about possibilities. She had taken her father to the general practitioner's office every other week for a whole year to get his regular blood samples, believing that there was no other option. By coincidence, this informal carer got information from a friend working in health care, telling her that home care nurses could take blood samples at home. When she asked the allocation division about this, they immediately granted regular blood samples at home provided by home care nurses.

As these quotes illustrate, the translation of needs begins already in the work filling in the application and continues through the process and dialogue between the administrator and the informal carer. The principle of lowest effective level of care has been central within welfare services in Norway for a long time and is often illustrated by the picture of a staircase (HOD 2009). The least demanding services form the lowest step and starting point, followed by more comprehensive services, with long-term nursing home as the highest step. In the administrators work of translating needs to accountable categories, this boss text is activated when they emphasize services at the lowest step, such as a security alarm, for instance. The fact that there are vacant long-term places in nursing homes is not mentioned. Services such as individual plans and coordinators are seldom allocated because no one asks for them, and the administrators do not suggest it. This way, only the information given in home visits and in dialogues with informal carers is made visible in the written notes by the administrator, and, in turn, they form the basis upon which judgements can be made accountable.

The calculated risk of informal carers submitting a complaint was also a factor the administrators took into account. *"If we believe that the risk for a complaint is high, we are usually extra thorough"*, one of the administrators said, and continued: *"Then we get statements from the doctor, the home care nurses and from the nursing home before we discharge them"*.

At the same time, previous outcomes of complaints guided the administrators work.

It's uncommon that we reject an application for long term stay in nursing homes when it comes to a person with dementia. Usually, the complaint board doesn't agree with us in those cases, so I have had to rewrite several grants for long term nursing home placements for persons with dementia. So, you can say I have learned from past mistakes, and now I almost never reject the applications when dementia is involved.

(Administrator)

The demand for offering *necessary, justifiable needs* is regulated by the legislation of health and care services in municipalities (2012). Supplementary to this, the legislation of patient and user rights (1999) regulates the user's right to receive necessary services developed to justify the individual user's needs. The administrator's allocation of services relating to the calculated risk of complaints and experiences with previous complaints can be seen as a negotiation of how little they can allocate within the framework of necessary, justifiable needs. By testing their written decisions for the complaint board, they negotiate what is to be defined as an acceptable judgement.

Returning to everyday life

The question mark in Figure 13.1 is questioning if the grant covers the proposed need. Returning to Jane, the woman who had asked for the placement of her mother at a nursing home for three years, the illustration in Figure 13.1 also maps the process Jane went through as an informal carer.

Jane asked for a long-term placement in a nursing home due to the fact that her mother needed help to manage her everyday life. Nevertheless, no formal application was written. Jane was told that the possibility for a long-term placement is small, so the administrator instead writes down and grants a need for more home care services. At the same time, Jane increases her effort helping her mom with the household and the number of times she visits her mother. The condition of Jane's mother worsens. Jane talks to the home care nurses, and they tell her that the time has come to apply for a long-term placement. They recommend her to contact the allocation division to form an application. Jane asks for a meeting with the allocation office but receives the same answer: There is no available places in long-term facilities, so there is no point in applying. A new grant allocating more time with home care nurses is made.

Jane's mother is now getting even worse. She can no longer dress herself and walks naked around in the apartment. The home care nurses help her get dressed, but they are not there when her mother gets out of bed. At night she wets her bed, because getting up and going to the bathroom is too challenging. One time she falls on her way to the bathroom. Jane found her there in the morning and no one knows how long she had been lying on the floor. Jane visits several times a day, washing bed sheets when her mother has wet the bed at night, helping her in the house, organizing meals. She is in despair over the situation. In a new meeting with the administrator at the allocation division, she asks for a long-term placement again, but no application is written this time, either. A series of short-term stays at a nursing home is granted, and from then on, the mother lives partly at home and partly at the nursing home. It becomes Jane's job to bring her there. *"She did not want to go, and I had to trick her into going out to the car"*, Jane told me. *"When she came to the nursing facility, she cried and got mad. After two weeks, she was used to being there, but then it was time to go home"*. Jane was frustrated. *"I felt like my mother was transformed into a package that was sent back and forth because I could not manage"*. After three years, Jane was so tired that she couldn't manage anymore. She called the administrator and told them that she was going away for a while. Two hours later, the administrators called back and told her that her mother had been granted a long-term placement in a nursing home.

According to the formal decision letter Jane received from the allocation division on behalf of her mother, it looks like the mother gradually got more help as the illness progressed. In the end, she also got a long-term placement, granted within three hours. According to guiding principles the administrators told me about, the grants looked perfect representing a timeline where Jane's mom is gradually granted more comprehensive help. From Jane's standpoint, the process consisted of an endless line of meetings, frustration and guilty conscience. *"I asked for meetings all the time"*, Jane told me. (...) *"hoping to get something"*.

Previous research on informal carers' access to formal services highlights the need for better and adapted information about the services, improving the informal carers' ability to navigate within the system (Courtin et al. 2014). The insight into Jane's everyday life reveals that there is also a need to pay attention to the application and granting process itself; as Jane's account has shown, a meeting with administrators does not necessarily lead to an application, and without an application, they will not get a grant, and without a grant, they cannot submit a complaint.

We do not know what would have happened if Jane actually had applied for a long-term place in a nursing home, but it could be the case that she actually would have received the place sooner, and if not, maybe the complaints board would have agreed with her. Either way, if Jane had known that the administrators would not treat meetings as an application, she might have experienced less frustration during the process. Jane turned up outside the administrator's office, waiting in her coat until the administrator had to let her in. If she had submitted an application, at least she would have got an answer, an answer where she also could submit a formal complaint. She would have got an answer, instead of being *given gibberish*, as Jane herself described it. Instead of chasing useless discussions with the administrators, Jane could have spent more meaningful time with her mother. As it was, she already spent a lot of time with her mother. She walked her to the general practitioner and to the dentist. She took messages from the home care nurses about her mother's need for appointments, new clothes and other practical tasks. The home care nurses did not have time to take the mother to the doctor, they told her. It would only cause the other patients to suffer. Jane shopped groceries, because the home care services could not help her with things that involved money. She visited, she talked, she comforted. At night, she always kept her phone on the night table, in case her mother or the home care services called her if something had happened. She also reduced her job hours so that she could spend more time with her mother.

Jane's everyday life consisted of a long line of care work. When the needs of her mother and herself were handled by the administrators, however, they were reduced to needs fitting with the guiding and predefined standards and principles that administrators were held accountable to in their everyday work. As a result, individual needs were made invisible. Seen from the standpoint of Jane, it is not difficult to understand the chaos and exhaustion she is describing. Looking at the process in light of the accountability circuit of administrators' translation of needs, helps us understand *why* Jane's experiences became the way they did. The interaction with the administrators, the tasks Jane took on to take care of her mother, can all be seen as *doings coordinated with other doings*, in other words as *work*.

Concluding discussion

A maintaining legitimacy of the welfare state is, as stated by Lund and Nilsen in the introduction chapter, based on people's experience of a balance between benefit and dependence, which, in turn, promotes people's obligation to pay tax (Esping-Andersen 1990). Several researchers have studied the relationship between formal and informal care. They have questioned whether formal care suppresses informal care and the other way around, or if informal and formal care complement each other. In the case of Norway, the literature reports on a complementarity where a certain division of tasks has developed. The public services generally take care of the most burdensome care responsibilities, and the family provides practical help and supervision (Daatland and Herlofson 2004; Jakobsson et al. 2012; HOD 2013).

The discourse of co-creation rests on an ongoing trend of individualization of the responsibility to pay, not only taxes but also to share the care burden. People are no longer to be seen as passive consumers of welfare services, but rather as active participants in providing common solutions to growing demands for care and welfare tasks (Bason 2010). Informal carers coping is, within this individualization trend, related to psychological coping theories such as Antonovsky's sense of coherence. Within these theories, it is assumed that individuals can improve their management of their care burden by increasing their ability to cope or their sense of coherence (Stensletten et al. 2016). Clear traces of this individualization trend are also to be found in Norwegian policy documents stating the expectations towards informal carers. A central part of the political direction towards a co-creative welfare state is therefore to provide support to informal carers, in turn, to increase their ability to cope as informal carers (HOD 2013). Guidance for public sectors' interaction with informal carers was launched in 2017 (Health Directorate 2017). *Plan for dementia* (Health Directorate 2015) highlights support groups and educational programmes for informal carers as important measures. In 2017, the commitment for municipalities to offer support to informal carers with great care burdens was imposed by law (Prop.49L 2016–2017).

This chapter has shown how I used IE in an investigation of the dynamics between formal and informal care. This examination of the work of translation of needs in the allocation process shows that the care work made accountable is not consistent with the actual experiences of informal carers' everyday life. Because of the starting point in informal carers' everyday life, and the investigation of their work in a generous sense, my research makes visible a broader sense of care work than previous research has given attention to. All the things that informal carers are told that formal services cannot do is one part of it. The work of looking into, asking and talking to others about possibilities for help is another. Enduring emotional outbursts and rage from their loved ones that have become ill with dementia and sometimes act like a stranger, is a third. To smooth over and adjust the situation so the person with dementia does not lose face is a fourth. And so, the list can proceed – when the starting point is in everyday life. None of these tasks is highlighted in the distinction between formal and informal care made in political documents. The invisibility of care work and need for help as it is actually done and experienced in everyday life is, in this chapter, made visible through the examination of the translation process as it is carried out by the administrators. In this translation process, the experiences of everyday life are not accountable.

There is no doubt that the welfare state needs informal carers to maintain its current level of welfare provision. However, previous research shows that the quite comprehensive effort of informal carers in Norway is dependent on the reliance that the welfare state will help them *when they need it*. As the legitimacy of the welfare state rests on a balance between benefit and dependence, it therefore also relies on people's ability to trust a balance between formal and informal care. Experiences like Jane's, of chaos and an endless fight for recognition of actual experienced needs, do not contribute to this trust. In order to maintain the trust and legitimacy of the welfare state, the formal service system and the development of formal services need to be based on the *actual everyday lives*. Therefore, this investigation of informal carers' work argues for a broadening of the concept of informal care work. As Smith (2005) uses a generous concept of work, *informal care work* should also be acknowledged as anything done by informal carers that takes time and effort.

References

Aasgaard, Heid Svenkerud, Per Gunnar Disch, Lisbeth Fagerström, and Bjørg Th Landmark. 2014. "Pårørende til aleneboende personer med demens – Erfaringer fra samarbeid med hjemmetjenesten etter ny organisering." *Nordisk sygeplejeforskning* 4 (2):114–128.

Aksøy, Helene. 2012. "Inn i sykehjemmet. Trinn for trinn eller i store sprang? Pårørendes fortellinger om en eldre slektnings omsorgsforløp fram til tildeling av sykehjemsplass." In *Bærekraftig omsorg? Familien, velferdsstaten og aldringen av befolkningen*, edited by Svein Olav Daatland and Veenstra Marijke, 147–156. Oslo: NOVA.

Al-Janabi, Hareth, Fiona Carmichael, and Jan Oyebode. 2017. "Informal care: Choice or constraint?" *Scandinavian Journal of Caring Sciences*. doi: 10.1111/scs.12441.

Bason, Christian. 2010. *Leading public sector innovation: Co-creating for a better society*. Bristol: Policy Press.

Carlsen, Benedicte, and Kjetil Lundberg. 2017. "'If it weren't for me...': Perspectives of family carers of older people receiving professional care." *Scandinavian Journal of Caring Sciences* 32 (1):213–221. doi: 10.1111/scs.12450.

Clemmensen, Trine H, Laila M Busted, Jane Søborg, and Poul Bruun. 2016. "The family's experience and perception of phases and roles in the progression of dementia: An explorative, interview-based study." *Dementia* 18 (2):490–513. doi: doi:10.1177/1471301216682602.

Courtin, Emilie, Nadia Jemiai, and Elias Mossialos. 2014. "Mapping support policies for informal carers across the European Union." *Health Policy* 118 (1):84–94. doi: 10.1016/j.healthpol.2014.07.013.

Daatland, Svein Olav, and Katharina Herlofson. 2004. *Familie, velferdsstat og aldring*, edited by NOVA. Oslo: Norsk institutt for forskning og oppvekst, velferd og aldring (NOVA).

Devault, Marjorie, Murali Venkatesh, and Frank Ridzi. 2014. ""Let's be friends": Working within an Accountability Circuit." In *Under new public management. Institutional ethnographies of changing frontline work*, edited by Alison I. Griffith and Dorothy E. Smith, 177–198. Toronto, Buffalo and London: University of Toronto Press.

Esping-Andersen, G. 1990. *Three Worlds of Welfare Capitalism*. New Jersey: Princeton University Press.

Gautun, Heidi. 2003. "Økt individualisering og omsorgsrelasjoner i familien. Omsorgsmønstre mellom middelaldrende kvinner og menn og deres gamle foreldre." In *Fafo-rapport 420*. Oslo: FAFO.

Giebel, Clarissa M., Maria Zubair, David Jolley, Kamaldeep Singh Bhui, Nitin Purandare, Angela Worden, and David Challis. 2015. "South Asian older adults with memory impairment: Improving assessment and access to dementia care." *International Journal of Geriatric Psychiatry* 30 (4):345–356. doi: 10.1002/gps.4242.

Griffith, Alison I., and Dorothy E. Smith. 2014a. "Conclusion." In *Under new public management. Institutional ethnographies of changing frontline work*, edited by Alison I. Griffith and Dorothy E. Smith, 339–349. Toronto, Buffalo and London: University of Toronto Press.

Griffith, Alison I., and Dorothy E. Smith. 2014b. "Introduction." In *Under new public management. Institutional ethnographies of changing frontline work*, edited by

Alison I. Griffith and Dorothy E. Smith, 3–22. Toronto, Buffalo and London: University of Toronto Press.

Health Directorate. 2007. *Forgetful, but not forgotten.* Norwegian Directorate of Health.

Health Directorate. 2015. *Plan for dementia care 2020.* Norwegian Directorate of Health.

Health Directorate. 2016. Veileder for saksbehandling. Tjenester etter helse- og omsorgstjenesteloven §§ 3-2 første ledd nr. 6, 3–6 og 3–8, edited by Helsedirektoratet.

Health Directorate. 2017. *Veileder om pårørende i helse- og omsorgstjenesten*, edited by Helsedirektoratet. Oslo.

HOD. 2009. The Coordination Reform. Proper treatment—at the right place and right time, edited by Ministry of Health and Care Services (HOD): The Norwegian Ministry of Health & Care Services.

HOD. 2011. Innovation in the Care Services, edited by Ministry of Health and Care Services (HOD): The Norwegian Ministry of Health & Care Services.

HOD. 2013. Future Care edited by Ministry of Health and Care Services (HOD): The Norwegian Ministry of Health & Care Services.

Jakobsen, Rita, and Siri Homelien. 2011. *Pårørende til personer med demens – om å forstå, involvere og støtte.* Oslo: Gyldendal Akademisk.

Jakobsen, Rita, and Siri Homelien. 2013. "Å forstå pårørende til personer med demens." [Understanding the relatives of people with dementia] *Geriatrisk sykepleie* [Geriatric Nursing] 1-2013:22–28.

Jakobsson, Niklas, Thomas Hansen, and Andreas Kotsadam. 2012. "Er det en sammenheng mellom formell og uformell omsorg i Norge?" [Is there a connection between formal and informal care in Norway?] *Tidsskrift for velferdsforskning* [Journal for Welfare Research] 15 (3):168–175.

Kaasa, Karen. 2011. *To tell the truth about informal caregiving*, edited by Ministry of Health and Care Services: Health and Care Department (HCD).

Kildal, Nanna, and Stein Kuhnle. 2005. "The nordic welfare model and the idea of universalism." In *Normative foundations of the welfare state. The Nordic experience*, edited by Nanna Kildal and Stein Kuhne, 13–33. New York: Routledge.

Larsen, Lill Sverresdatter, Hans Ketil Normann, and Torunn Hamran. 2017. "Processes of user participation among formal and family caregivers in home-based care for persons with dementia." *Dementia* 16 (2):158–177. doi: 10.1177/1471301215584702.

Legislation of health- and care services in municipalities. 2012. Available from https://lovdata.no/dokument/NL/lov/2011-06-24-30.

Legislation of patient- and users rights. 1999. Available from https://lovdata.no/dokument/NL/lov/1999-07-02-63.

Lethin, Connie, Ingalill Rahm Hallberg, Staffan Karlsson, and Ann-Christin Janlöv. 2015. "Family caregivers experiences of formal care when caring for persons with dementia through the process of the disease." *Scandinavian Journal of Caring Sciences* 30 (3):526–534. doi: 10.1111/scs.12275.

McCoy, Liza. 2006. "Keeping the institution in view." In *Institutional ethnography as practice*, edited by Dorothy E. Smith, 109–125. Lanham, MD: Rowman & Littlefield.

Mukadam, N., Claudia Cooper, Behzad Basit, and Gill Livingston. 2011. "Why do ethnic elders present later to UK dementia services? A qualitative study." *International Psychogeriatrics* 23 (7):1070–1077. doi: 10.1017/S1041610211000214.

Mukadam, N., Claudia Cooper, and Gill Livingston. 2013. "Improving access to dementia services for people from minority ethnic groups." *Current Opinion in Psychiatry* 26 (4):409–414. doi: 10.1097/YCO.0b013e32835ee668.

Nordhagen, Vera Kristin Lumkjær, and Venke Sørlie. 2016. "Pårørendes erfaringer med kommunal hjemmetjeneste til personer med demens." *Geriatrisk sykepleie* 8 (2):8–14.

OECD. 2011. *Together for better public services*, edited by OECD public governance reviews: Paris: OECD Publishing.

Øydgard, Guro W. 2018. Judgements for the individual service user or standardized service? An institutional ethnography on local government administrators' transition from requirements to decisions. *Tidsskrift for omsorgsforskning* [Journal for Care Research] 4 (2):27–39. doi: 10.18261/ISSN.2387-5984-2018-01-04

Pratt, R., Linda Clare, and Vincent Kirchner. 2006. "'It's like a revolving door syndrome': Professional perspectives on models of access to services for people with early-stage dementia." *Aging and Mental Health* 10 (1):55–62. doi: 10.1080/13607860500307530

Prop.49L. 2016–2017. Endringer i helse- og omsorgstjenesteloven m.m. (styrket pårørendestøtte). Helse- og omsorgsdepartementet.

Robinson, A. 2009. "Information pathways into dementia care services: Family carers have their say." *Dementia* 8 (1):17–37. doi: 10.1177/1471301208099051.

Smith, Dorothy E. 1987. *The everyday world as problematic. A feminist sociology.* Boston, MA: Northeastern University Press.

Smith, Dorothy E. 2005. *Institutional ethnography: A sociology for people.* Lanham, MD: AltaMira.

Stensletten, Kari, Frøydis Bruvik, Birgitte Espehaug, and Jorunn Drageset. 2016. "Burden of care, social support, and sense of coherence in elderly caregivers living with individuals with symptoms of dementia." *Dementia* 15 (6):1422–1435. doi: 10.1177/1471301214563319.

Vabø, Mia. 2011. "Changing governance, changing needs interpretations: Implications for universalism." *International Journal of Sociology and Social Policy* 31 (3/4):197–208.

Vabø, Mia. 2012. "Norwegian home care in transition – Heading for accountability, off-loading responsibilities." *Health & Social Care in the Community* 20 (3): 283–291. doi: 10.1111/j.1365-2524.2012.01058.x.

WHO. 2012. *Dementia. A public health priority,* edited by World Health Organization: World Health Organization.

14 The potential of Institutional Ethnography in Norwegian development research and practice

Exploring child marriage in Nepal

Naomi Curwen, Hanne Haaland and Hege Wallevik

Introduction

> My friend had fallen in love with a guy, and I used to accompany her as a friend when they met. Another guy also used to come with her boyfriend, and that is the guy I fell in love with. Friends of friends you know?
>
> (Curwen 2016, 54)

This quote is taken from Curwen's (2016) fieldwork in Nepal, where she explored the practice of child marriage. Although trying to keep an open mind before conducting fieldwork, Curwen's presumption was that child marriage was a form of forced marriage and that the young girls in question had little or no say in the matter. Meeting a girl who attempted to explain how she got married at age 17 because she fell in love was an experience very far from what Curwen expected to encounter. Several girls explained how they wanted to marry a man of their own choice and decided to marry young, before their parents had time to arrange a marriage for them. Curwen also talked to parents who were concerned and frustrated with this trend because they wanted their girls to finish their education before marrying. Although a narrative of force was part of her findings as well, the situation described above challenged what Curwen thought she knew about the practice of child marriage. She realised that exploring child marriage through girls' own experiences complicates a generalised picture gained from the development literature on the topic.

This chapter is a call for new perspectives in the gender and development research and discourse. We want to explore what we can learn about development issues by starting with the experience and knowledge of local subjects. Gender equality is at the heart of Norwegian development efforts. In the Action Plan for Women's Rights and Gender Equality in Foreign and Development Policy, for the period 2016–2020, it is stated that "the fundamental aim of Norway's gender equality efforts is to increase the opportunities available to women and girls, promote their right to self-determination, and further their empowerment" (UD 2016, 5). Through teaching gender and development, Haaland and Wallevik have for years worked to overcome practices of reproducing simplified narratives of marginalised women in the Global South. Part of their aim as lecturers has been to make sure students engage in overarching issues within gender and development debates from the standpoint of people's own experiences and lifeworlds, acknowledging cultural diversity and situated knowledge (Haaland and Wallevik 2016). Such an approach, they argue, is needed if we want to critically engage with mainstream understandings of gender in development research as well as in practice.

When Norwegian development actors aim at empowerment and enhancing women's rights, we think it is crucial to include the voices and experiences of the girls and women who are to be empowered. There is a need to look into the production of development knowledge, on which we base our development policies and interventions for social change, that, in turn, impact local people's lives. In this chapter, we argue that institutional ethnography (IE) has the capacity to challenge dominant understandings and bring new perspectives into development research and practice. Our discussion draws on empirical findings from Curwen's (2016) IE of child marriage in two districts of Nepal. Curwen's study was conducted through a girls' empowerment project run by a Norwegian non-governmental organisation (NGO). We use some of her findings to discuss how an IE approach enables us to reveal ruling relations and institutional captures that leave certain parts of people's experiences in the blind. Exploring these blind spots through a focus on everyday practices and activities can alter the way we think about child marriage and how to address it. It may also, we hold, result in new insights that can enable new entry points for how we *think about* and *do* gender and development in the Global South in general.

A call for complexity and context

Development research is an interdisciplinary field. In the Norwegian context, much development policy is underpinned by research carried out from "system-based" approaches, which tend to start with theoretical frameworks determining how the social world will be attended to (Stokke 2010; Sørbø 2017). For the last 30 years, hegemonic approaches have dominated development discourse about how to intervene in the Global South, influencing practitioners and actors in the field. The hegemonic discourses tend to rest upon neo-liberal reasoning often reflecting Western ideas and ideals. Jackson (1996, 2) argues that many anthropologists have criticised the way

> Western intellectual traditions tend to be privileged over all others, as though no edifying account of human social life could be rendered by using African, Islamic, Indian, Chinese or Polynesian traditions of thought.
>
> (Jackson, 1996, 2)

As such, anthropologists and feminist researchers have argued the case for complexity when engaging in development research and practice for years (e.g., Mohanty 1991). A general challenge in mainstream development debates is that there is not sufficient recognition of the importance of context. Thus, there is a lack of focus on intersectionality where other aspects such as class, race, caste and age have been taken out of the more generalised equation (Win 2007; Chant 2008; Cornwall et al. 2008). Acknowledging context and including the complexity of people's experiences seems to complicate the picture to an extent that makes it difficult to act. Consequently, development practitioners often turn to more generalised knowledge as a foundation for policies and strategies for intervention that are believed to work irrespective of specific local contexts. According to de Bruijn et al. (2007, 15), this is not only a way to manage complexity but also an approach that rests upon the conviction that there are "deep structures that would render the predictability of social behaviour possible". Within development research and practice, we thus struggle with universalised ideas that through narration gain hegemony and end up being taken-for-granted truths. These "truths" or institutional captures, in turn, become important for formulating policies for intervention (Haaland 2008; Wallevik 2012; Curwen 2016).

The business scholar Michaelson (2010, 242) has a similar concern about a Western ethical and economic bias in global business ethics, where in particular the economic bias is not sufficiently challenged in scholarship. He points out how "as much as the global ethics question appears to be culturally neutral, many of those who ask it do so with a culturally specific lens shaped by prevailing conditions of Western economic strength" (Michaelson 2010, 239). Similarly, Mosse (2014) critiques the power of development knowledge, based on his experiences from studying agricultural practices in India and development efforts trying to change those practices. He argues that it is unlikely that the needs of local farmers match what development experts think the local farmers need (Mosse 2014, 519). Important scholarship is now emerging, analysing the social relations of development and challenging the gap between local people's lives and externally designed and managed development programmes (e.g., Li 2007; Bexell 2012; Campbell and Kim 2018; Nilsen and Steen-Johnsen 2019). What knowledge is and what type of knowledge is considered valid in research becomes important in this regard. According to Rankin (2017, 5), reading topical literature is important in an IE study, but instead of being taken at face value, this research should be read with the social organisation of knowledge in mind:

> Right from the outset, the researcher should develop a critical position and pay attention to how the literature rests on a scaffold of concepts and theories that have been "abstracted" from any concrete descriptions of people doing things. The IE analyst pays attention to how the

issue is known about within the ruling relations and discursive practices of knowledge production. Positioning this way to the literature is one of the biggest challenges for scholars trained in other approaches.

(Rankin, 2017, 5)

We argue that there is a need to try to understand local people's agency and the performance and outcome of such agency in specific places. Starting the inquiry in people's own experiences will help us to put theoretical arguments, causal explanations, concepts, policies and interventions into context and further enable our understanding of various ways of life. A foundation in local realities provides a point of entry for identifying and analysing

the taken-for-granted order of things, hierarchies and structures that offer default privilege to certain people and perspectives, while simultaneously excluding and downplaying others.

(Lund 2015, 32)

Norway: a pioneer for gender equality and empowerment

Norway is one of the world's most gender-equal countries, and in our development policies on gender we often emphasise what can be learned from Norwegian experiences. For instance, it is stated that Norway is a pioneer for gender equality in the Action Plan for Women's Rights and Gender Equality, and that the priority areas of the Action Plan are areas where Norway has strengths and can make a difference (UD 2016, 5). The first Norwegian policy on gender and aid was launched in 1985, followed by a long-term strategy in 1997, focussing on women alone, and finally by a gender Action Plan in 2007 (Selbervik and Østebø 2013). In 2008, Norway was the first donor country to present a White Paper to its parliament on gender and aid. Today five main thematic priorities are listed in the Action Plan for 2016–2020, including girls' right to education, political rights and empowerment, economic rights and empowerment, sexual and reproductive health rights and finally violence against women. The emphasis on empowerment is not only a result of Norwegian gender and equality politics. Selbervik and Østebø (2013) argue that Norwegian gender and equality politics, when exported to the Global South, are influenced by an international development agenda. Within the international development discourse, a focus on the independent, individual change agent is prevalent, leading to interventions aiming at empowerment at the individual level. Haaland and Wallevik (2016) argue that there within gender and development practice still is a bias since the individual in focus is almost always a woman. Thus, even though the stated primary focus is on gender equality, the main point is still about strengthening women's individual positions and women's rights, highlighting for example economic independence as an important way to empower women and also a need to empower women and girls to overcome oppression from patriarchal structures (Kabeer 2005). Thus, it has been difficult to bring men back into the arena (Cornwall and White 2000; Chant and Gutman 2002; Jones 2006).

The concept of empowerment has become an institutional capture determining how we understand and evaluate local, political, social and economic development. The meaning of empowerment seems to be taken for granted and is not truly problematised in development policy documents. According to Cornwall (2009), empowerment was once seen as a radical concept. Today however, it has been mainstreamed and is commonly understood in terms of an individualistic, neo-liberal way of doing development. Cornwall (2009) argues that an independent change agent, empowered through development efforts, should not be confused with a process of empowerment that comes from within. Bexell (2012, 399) finds that the voices of women and girls who are to be empowered by UN-business partnerships are not adequately taken into account. Rankin (2001, 2002) further states that neo-liberal ideas of empowerment can turn women into instruments for development and put a heavy burden on their shoulders, instead of bettering their lives. Abu-Lughod (2006) adds to this when she argues that we need to acknowledge that people may make different choices than what we anticipate. A general critique against interventions for empowerment is that such interventions assume that a particular way of organising society and living in the world can be a model for understanding and intervening in the lives of others (Wallevik 2012). When accepting that others may choose differently, we should explore and learn from them why they do so (Smith, 2005; Barth 2000). We agree with Campbell and Kim's (2018, 4) reflections that those who do or study transnational development, such as Norwegian actors, should learn more about themselves and the standpoints they carry into the development relationships with others and seek to learn what needs changing from the local subject. Only then can experiences inform the use of concepts, such as empowerment, and give insights beyond predefined connections (Wallevik 2012).

The case of child marriage in Nepal

Child marriage is a practice that occurs across cultures, regions and religions, and affects approximately 12 million girls each year. United Nations Children's Fund (UNICEF) (2019) defines it as "any formal marriage or informal union between a child under the age of 18 and an adult or another child". Within the international development discourse, it is considered a human rights violation and a form of social violence that denies girls choice and participation. The practice of child marriage can have severe implications for the girls themselves and their communities, and it impacts development in areas such as education, health, gender equality and poverty alleviation. Consequently, it is identified as an important development issue to address if sustainable development goal 5, related to gender equality and the empowerment of all women and girls, is to be achieved. Sub goal 5.3 is to "eliminate all harmful practices, such as child, early and forced marriage and female genital mutilation" (UN 2019). In connection to this the Norwegian Action Plan on gender equality states that "the aim of Norway's efforts is to help eliminate child and forced marriage within a generation. Our efforts span across several thematic areas and are channelled through various organisations" (UD 2016, 23). The main drivers of child marriage have been identified as a combination of tradition, poverty, gender roles, lack of education, security concerns and weak law enforcement (World Vision 2013; Lemmon 2014, Girls not Brides 2019).

Understanding child marriage as being forced and caused by tradition, poverty or gender norms is the same as assigning agency to abstracted concepts. Smith (2005, 69) argues that such concepts cannot be differentiated from people's activities, and research must empirically show how they exist as local practices. Instead of starting with a theoretical framework based on the international development discourse, Curwen (2016) wanted to explore what can be learned about child marriage beginning with the experiences of local Nepali girls and their families. She sought to learn from their situated knowledge, by interviewing them about what they do and about the circumstances of their activities. When much development work stresses the importance of empowering women and girls, it becomes an important contribution of IE to make sure the research process itself does not objectify people but rather values their knowledge. Furthermore, using people's work knowledge as data gives room for descriptions of activities that might otherwise not have been considered relevant in the research. For Curwen (2016), an IE approach resulted in a detailed account of what child marriage entails for some of the people involved, and how young girls reasoned with local practices and negotiated these practices through their activities. The findings from Curwen reflect a reality much more complex than what an understanding of child marriage as the result of poverty, tradition or gender norms offers.

Curwen (2016) did her fieldwork in villages in two different districts of Nepal: One district in the western hill area and one on the boarder to India. Child marriage is prevalent in both places, but people's work knowledge gave interesting insights as to why. Part of Curwen's (2016) findings is that even within the same country the social organisation of child marriage looks different. The quote cited at the beginning of this chapter is from the first interview with a girl who we call Nirmala from the hill area. She got married at the age of 17 but was 24 at the time of the interview. She described her experience of child marriage as her own choice against her parents will, much to Curwen's surprise. Nirmala said she fell in love with a friend of a friend, and that they used to meet without her parents knowing. One day the boy wanted to bring Nirmala home with him for marriage. After considering whether she should stay with her own family or go, Nirmala ended up going with the boy without informing her parents. She explained that she did not ask her parents because she knew they would disagree with her:

> If I told my parents, they would advise me to wait with marriage until I was older. Child marriage is prevalent in the village, but my parents would want me to wait and finish my studies. But, I loved him so much and wanted to go with him.
>
> (Curwen 2016, 54)

Nirmala's story turned out to be common in this area. Other girls described similar experiences of discovering they liked a boy and eventually deciding to marry him. Running away to the boy's home to be together was referred to as "eloping". They did this when they were between 14 and 17 years old, against their parents will. Arranged marriage, where parents choose a suitable companion on behalf of their children, was the accepted marriage practice in this area. However, in this particular village, the parents also valued education and wanted to delay marriage until the girls had finished school. Thus, forcing a child marriage on their daughters was not their wish. One mother explained:

> I don't agree with the ways girls in this village elope. It's not good. They just get into more trouble by doing it. They get tortured and cannot even tolerate it because they are immature. Both physically and mentally, they cannot handle the pressure. They are not ready for what they have to face in the boy's home after marriage. They don't listen and then they regret. It is much wiser to wait and get married in your twenties, 22 is a good age. You are more mature and more able to stand up against violence and other social problems in the in-laws home.
>
> (Curwen 2016, 55)

Many parents in the hill area expressed concern for their daughters and were aware of the negative impacts a child marriage can have. The data from this area does not conform to the common understanding of child marriage as forced by ignorant parents or what some project reports call "backward traditions". Even in a context of arranged marriage, these girls did not have to get married as adolescents. However, they expressed a wish to fall in love and choose their own partner, which in turn resulted in child marriage organised by themselves. It is an interesting paradox that exercising choice and independence, as opposition to the tradition of arranged marriage, can result in child marriage. Nirmala and other girls from the hill area are performing agency, they are choosing someone to marry. So, on the one hand, they can be understood as empowered because they choose their own life partner. On the other hand, the outcome of their independence is defined as child marriage, a practice which development practitioners are trying to address by empowering girls and women. The example illustrates how dominant discourses on child marriage as a forced practice or "backward tradition" can stop us from seeing what other rationalities may potentially guide local practices and decision-making processes. These young girls and boys were also shaped by a love discourse that was external to their local village setting, a discussion we return to below.

Child marriage occurs in the border area of Nepal as well, but the experiences of people who live there were quite different compared to the hill area. According to Curwen (2016, 61–72), many of the girls and their mothers explained how girls are taught to keep silent and not voice their opinions, and how they are mostly kept inside the house. This is to control their behaviour and ensure that they do not initiate love affairs or relationships with boys on their own. Such behaviour is referred to as "the wrong track" because it will damage their social reputation and make it difficult for the parents to get them married and secure their future. The girls often receive less education, because preparing them for life in the in-laws' house by teaching them household work is considered more necessary. Child marriages were arranged by parents so that they did not have to worry about their girls, and for economic reasons connected to dowry practice. The dowry demand was set based on the boys' qualifications as a provider. The older the boy, the more education and work experience he has, and thus he is considered more qualified. Therefore, the dowry price often becomes higher with age, and in a context of poverty many parents married away their daughters early to be able to manage the dowry price. This was different in the hill area where what they call "offerings" were more common. There the parents usually gave something to their daughter, for her to bring into her marriage (Curwen 2016, 57).

Accounts of work knowledge and descriptions of local realities are only the starting point of an IE. Some of this so-called entry-level data could also have been found using more traditional ethnographic approaches. However, it is the focus of the analysis that sets IE apart (e.g., Rankin 2017). In more traditional ethnographic approaches, a researcher often starts grouping informants into types or identifies recurring words or events from the data that, in turn, are coded to reference certain meanings. The researcher then runs the risk of detaching social concepts from specific places and people in the analysis. Jackson (2005) reminds us that concepts do not transcend lifeworlds. Hence, we cannot assume that the way we give meaning to concepts will be the same in other lifeworlds. Child marriage occurs across contexts that are as different as those of West Africa and South Asia. It is likely that the experiences related to the practice are vastly different, and research findings should reflect this complexity and give insight into what rationales are at play in specific places. Additionally, the focus of the analysis can easily shift to individuals and their characteristics as causal explanations, following the approach mentioned above. In Curwen's case from Nepal, child marriage could be interpreted as a characteristic of being Dalit or low caste, of being poor, uneducated or from a rural village. This is because the places where the prevalence of child marriage is high are the rural places where Dalits reside and where education levels are low (Curwen 2016, 72). Blaming the practice on people and their characteristics maintains typologies and stereotypes that inhibit our ability to understand others and their circumstances. Consequently, it allows for understandings common within the development field; traditions and cultures as barriers to development. Crewe and Harrison (1998) argue that practitioners often talk and write much about "traditional ways of life" as a hindrance to development. They explain that:

> Traditionalism is partly attributed to economic or ecological conditions but is often conceived of as being linked to a psychological or cultural disposition that is in some sense backward and prevents people from embracing modernity.
>
> (Crewe and Harrisson 1998, as quoted in Edelman and Haugerud 2005, 232)

Twenty years later, the idea of "traditions holding people back" is still persistent across the development industry. This understanding informs empowerment interventions aimed at the individual or community level. Culture or tradition is reduced to fixed entities imposing ideas on people. Through empowerment efforts, it is thought that people can break out of tradition. We wish to emphasise that we are not arguing against efforts to assist people experiencing social violence. Rather, our argument is that the way to meet people in difficult situations is to explore the causes of difficulties and that this exploration must reflect the experiences of people, acknowledging culture as ever-changing and negotiable. This may enable a perspective where culture is seen as inherent to development rather than as a hindrance (Wallevik 2012).

Within IE, it is not people as such who are at the centre of the analysis, but social organisation, meaning how people's actions are coordinated both locally and trans-locally. For the IE researcher, it is imperative to move from ethnographic description and empirically show how local activities and experiences are connected and shaped by trans-local, ruling relations. According to Smith (2005, 228), people's activation of different texts and discourses is often part of such coordination across time and space. When people engage with a discourse and align their actions according to it, they act discursively. Sometimes this ruling occurs through legally binding discourses, other times it is less explicit as people act on their own understanding of dominant discourses (Campbell and Gregor 2002, 40). The data in Curwen's (2016, 74–75) work reveals that many informants talked about their experiences by using terms such as "falling in love", "a limited concept of love", "arranged marriage", "love marriage", "eloping" and "love affair". To have a so-called love marriage, where the union is based on mutual feelings and personal choice, is discursive activity connected to a different discourse than that of arranged marriage. The informants' mobile phones, it turned out, were the devices through which both girls and boys hooked into different perspectives on love and marriage. They accessed Facebook, watched Korean dramas, Hindi soap operas and music videos. They listened to various love songs with stories of young couples in love, choosing to be with each other. This love marriage discourse was at play in both areas, but interestingly it coordinated action differently depending on how people interacted with the discourse. In the hill area, it organised child marriage because of the girls' activation of the love marriage discourse. In the border area, although eloping occurred there as well, it was mostly the parents who arranged child marriages to avoid love affairs and protect their girls from what they called "the wrong track". Using an IE approach allows the researcher to explore how various informants navigate between the dominant discourse of arranged marriage and new influences on love and marriage from media. Concepts such as gender roles, culture or tradition are often presented as static and non-negotiable within international development discourse. Curwen's (2016) findings show that customs and culture are dynamic and continuously changing.

IE is an approach for both scholarship and activism (Rankin 2017, 2). As development research feeds into development policy and practice, the tight link IE offers between scholarship and activism becomes particularly interesting. We argue that studying development issues by beginning with the experience and knowledge of local people who are being affected can provide new discoveries that allow us to engage in meaningful discussions concerning the practice of child marriage itself and contribute to debates of overall development policies, and why they potentially fail (e.g., Campbell and Kim 2018, 4). Having said that, development management is a complex of standardised tools and approaches, driven by results-based management, accountability to tax payers, donors and stakeholders (Curwen 2016, 84–87; OECD 2019; Norad 2019a, 2019b). As IE does not aim to produce results responding to such universality, the question is whether IE and its complexity will be well received within development management and how we best can advocate for the need to introduce IE.

Concluding remarks

Communicating lived realities into a development debate is a recurring challenge. Much development policy is underpinned by hegemonic discourse that tends to rest upon neo-liberal reasoning and Western ideas and ideals. The overall focus on gender equality and empowerment within Norwegian development support leans on experiences from a Norwegian context and is also influenced by the international development discourse where the independent, individual change agent is emphasised as an important driver for development. Having the power to set the development agenda and design programmes for social change that impact local people's lives comes with responsibility. Development research and practice is a field packed with institutional concepts, understandings and theories that might not match the needs, wishes and experiences of local subjects in different contexts. To avoid that these understandings become institutional captures, there is a specific need for reflexivity and a focus on the language and concepts used within this field. Institutional captures blur our understanding of what informs people's decisions and actions. Thus, we argue it is vital to explore underlying assumptions and allow for new questions and new answers within the gender and development discourse. If we agree with Smith's argument that the social is happening in and through coordinated activities, we need to include the researcher and development practitioner in this socially coordinated work and critically examine the production of development knowledge on which we base our development interventions. In this chapter we have argued that there is much to be learned about current development issues by beginning with the experience and knowledge of local people. Curwen's journey into Nepali village life is a beautiful example of IE's potential in development research and practice. Her shift from a theoretical approach to child marriage to an IE-inspired study demonstrates the strength of IE. It has the capacity to make visible what is left invisible by institutional discourse. Consequently, more research is needed in the field of gender and development to explore how institutional discourse, concepts and understandings mediate ruling relations in ways that replace actual experiences and rationales with predefined notions and ideas of what is at stake.

References

Abu-Lughod, Lila. 2006. "The Muslim Woman. The Power of Images and the Danger of Pity." *EUROZINE*, 2006–09-01.

Barth, Fredrik. 2000. *Andres liv – og vårt eget*. Oslo: Universitetsforlaget.

Bexell, Magdalena. 2012. "Global Governance and Gender." *International Feminist Journal of Politics* 14(3), 389–407.

Campbell, Marie and Frances Gregor. 2002. *Mapping Social Relations. A Primer in Doing Institutional Ethnography*. Ontario: Garamond Press.

Campbell, Marie. L. and Elena Kim. 2018. "The (Missing) Subjects of Research on Gender and Global Governance: Toward Inquiry of the Ruling Relations of Development." *Business Ethics: A European Review* 27(4), 1–11. doi: 10.1111/beer.12189/

Chant, Sylvia. 2008. "The 'Feminisation of Poverty' and the 'Feminisation' of Anti-Poverty Programmes: Room for Revision?" *The Journal of Development Studies* 44(2), 165–197.

Chant, Sylvia and Matthew Gutmann. 2002. "'Men-Streaming' Gender? Questions for Gender and Development Policy in the Twenty-First Century." *Progress in Development Studies* 2(4), 269–282.

Cornwall, Andrea. 2009. "New Narratives of Women's Empowerment" Retrieved 15th June, 2011, Audio from Andrea's Sussex Development Lecture at the University of Sussex from www.ids.ac.uk/go/news/new-narratives-of-women-s-empowerment/

Cornwall, Andrea, Ann Whitehead and Elisabeth Harrison. 2008. *Gender Myths and Feminist Fablesthe Struggle for Interpretive Power in Gender and Development.* Malden, MA: Blackwell Publishing.

Cornwall, Andrea and Sarah C. White. 2000. "Men, Masculinities and Development Politics, Policies and Practice." *IDS Bulletin* 31(2), 1–6.

Crewe, Emma and Elisabeth Harrisson. 1998. "Is Culture a Barrier to Change?" in Mark Edelman and Angelique Haugerud. 2005 (eds.) *The Anthropology of Development and Globalization: From Classical Political Economy to Contemporary Neoliberalism*, 406. Malden, MA: Blackwell.

Curwen, Naomi. 2016. Doing and Undoing Child Marriage in Nepal. An Exploratory Study Using Institutional Ethnography. Master thesis., University of Agder. Accessed at https://brage.bibsys.no/xmlui/handle/11250/2414509

de Bruijn, Mirjam, Rijk van Dijk and Jan-Bart Gewald. 2007. "Social and Historical Trajectories of Agency in Africa" in Patrick Chabal, Ulf Engel & Leo. d. Haan (eds.) *African Alternatives*, 185. Leiden: Brill.

Girls not Brides. 2019. "Why Does Child Marriage Happen?" Accessed 01.04.2019 at www.girlsnotbrides.org/why-does-it-happen/

Haaland, Hanne. 2008. Narrating History, Negotiating Rights: A Discussion of Knowledge, Land Rights and Matters of Identity in Madjadjane, Mozambique. Noragric, PhD thesis.

Haaland, Hanne and Hege Wallevik. 2016. "Reflections on Gender and Diversity in Cross-Cultural On-line Teaching." *Kvinder, Køn & Forskning* 25(1). doi: 10.7146/kkf.v25i1.97068

Jackson, Michael. 1996. *Things as they are. New Directions in Phenomenological Anthropology.* Bloomington: Indiana University Press.

Jackson, Michael. 2005. *Existential Anthropology. Events, Exigencies and Effects.* New York: Berghahn Books.

Jones, Adam. 2006. *Men of the Global South. A Reader.* London: ZED Books.

Kabeer, Naila. 2005. "Gender Equality and Women's Empowerment: A Critical Analysis of the Third Millennium Development Goal 1." *Gender & Development* 13(1), 13–24.

Lemmon, Gayle Tzemach. 2014. "Fragile States, Fragile Lives: Child Marriage amid Disaster and Conflict" Council on Foreign Relations. Accessed 03.09.15 at www.cfr.org/global/fragile-states-fragile-lives/p33093/

Li, Tania Murray. 2007. *The Will to Improve: Governmentality, Development and the Practice of Politics.* Durham, NC: Duke University Press.

Lund, Rebecca W. B. 2015. Doing the Ideal Academic. Gender, Excellence and Changing Academics. PhD Diss., Aalto University.

Michaleson, Cristopher. 2010. "Revisiting the Global Business Ethics Question." *Business Ethics Quarterly* 20(2), 237–251.

Mohanty, Chandra Talpade. 1991. "Under Western Eyes: Feminist Scholarship and Colonial Discourses." in Ann Russo & Luordes Torres (eds.) *Third World Women and the Politics of Feminism*, 51–80. Bloomington: Indiana University Press.

Mosse, David. 2014. "Knowledge as Relational: Reflections on Knowledge in International Development." *Forum for Development Studies* 41(3), 513–523.

Nilsen, Ann-Christin and Tale Steen-Johnsen. 2019. "The ECCD Mission and the Institutional Circuit of Evidence." *Journal of Early Childhood Research*

Norad. 2019a. "Norges resultatfokus i bistanden." Accessed 03.04.2019 at https://norad.no/resultater/norges-resultatfokus/

Norad. 2019b. "Om evaluering av bistand." Accessed 03.04.2019 at https://norad.no/evaluering/om-evaluering/

OECD. 2019. "DAC Criteria for Evaluating Development Assistance." Accessed 03.04.2019 at www.oecd.org/dac/evaluation/daccriteriaforevaluatingdevelopmentassistance.htm

Rankin, Janet. 2017. "Conducting Analysis in Institutional Ethnography: Analytical Work Prior to Commencing Data Collection." *International Journal of Qualitative Methods* 16(1), 1–9. doi: 10.1177/1609406917734472/

Rankin, Kathrin. 2001. "Governing Development: Neoliberalism, Microcredit, and Rational Economic Woman." *Economy and Society* 30(1), 18–37.

Rankin, Kathrin. 2002. "Social Capital, Microfinance, and the Politics of Development." *Journal of Feminist Economics* 8(1), 1–24.

Selbervik, Hilde and Marit Tolo Østebø. 2013. "Gender Equality in International Aid: What has Norwegian Gender Politics Got to Do With It?" *Gender, Technology and Development* 17(2), 205–228.

Smith, Dorothy. 2005. *Institutional Ethnography. A Sociology for People.* Lanham, MD: Alta Mira Press.

Sørbø, Gunnar. 2017. "Kriser og kriger – er det bruk for oss nå?" *Norsk antropologisk tidsskrift* 28(1), 7–19.

Stokke, Olav. 2010. "Utviklingsforskningen i Norge gjennom 50 år: Rammevilkår, diskurs og praksis." *Internasjonal Politikk* 68(4), 495–568.

UD (Utenriksdepartementet/Norwegian Ministry of Foreign Affairs) 2016. "Freedom, Empowerment and Opportunities. Action Plan for Women's Rights and Gender Equality in Foreign and Development Policy 2016–2020." Accessed at www.regjeringen.no/globalassets/departementene/ud/vedlegg/fn/womens_rights.pdf/

UN (United Nations) 2019. "Goal 5: Achieve Gender Equality and Empower all Women and Girls." Accessed 03.04.2019 at www.un.org/sustainabledevelopment/gender-equality/

UNICEF 2019. "Child Marriage." Accessed 03.04.2019 at www.unicef.org/protection/child-marriage/

Wallevik, Hege. 2012. The Complexity of Generalisation: A Phenomenological Approach to Women and their Economic Affairs in Zanzibar Town. Noragric, PhD thesis.

Win, Evelyn. 2007. "Not Very Poor, Powerless or Pregnant The African Woman Forgotten by Development" in Andrea Cornwall & Ann Whitehead (eds.) *Feminisms in Development: Contradictions, Contestations and Challenges*, 253. London: ZED Books.

World Vision 2013. "Untying the Knot: Exploring Early Marriage in Fragile States". Accessed 04.09.15 at www.worldvision.org/resources.nsf/main/press-reports/$file/Untying-the-Knot_report.pdf/

Part 4

The transformative potential of IE in the Nordics

15 Challenging behaviour and mental workload at residential homes for people with cognitive disorders

Kjeld Høgsbro

Introduction

In 2009, a resource centre dealing with social services for people with autism asked me to find out if it was possible to investigate the relation between pedagogical strategies and mental workload at residential homes for people with autism and some kind of challenging behaviour. At first, I was a little sceptical about this. Several investigations had already investigated pedagogical strategies for handling challenging behaviour at residential homes for people with cognitive disorders. There were also investigations which had focussed on the mental workload of staff members who were confronted with different forms of challenging behaviour. However, after a while it became clear to me that no investigations had hitherto explored on the relation between the two (Høgsbro et al. 2012).

I became increasingly dedicated to the idea and found that it could be interesting to see if an investigation inspired by institutional ethnography (IE) could contribute to a better understanding of the relation between discourses, guidelines and mental stress in these rather extreme cases. Accordingly, in 2010 Leena Eskelinen (Anvendt Kommunalforskning (AKF), Denmark) and I together with a team of research assistants contacted six residential homes and asked them to help us finding out if it was possible to define such a relation. The institutions were all well known, experienced and had a reputation for having a high level of expertise in the field. They were deliberately selected to ensure that the problems we were dealing with were not based on 'ignorance' but anchored in the best knowledge of recent pedagogical methods and approaches. The field studies were carried out in collaboration between AKF and Aalborg University in Denmark (Høgsbro et al. 2012). Later this was followed by an IE of two residential homes for people with different kinds of dementia and challenging disorders (Høgsbro and Burholt 2015). This chapter summarises the issues and findings from these different investigations. IE was used as a research design because the everyday life and interaction between staff members and residents was the focal point of the study and we further wanted to find out how trans-local relations such as hegemonic discourses, forms of conduct and organisation as well as regulating texts sustained challenging behaviour and mental workloads.

After having analysed in detail the different forms of challenging behaviour, the discourses and the workload, an unexpected problematic appeared to challenge the most widespread and accepted pedagogical discourses. This chapter is a story about the process of investigation and the impact of it. The aim is to show how IE can be used in cases when professionals have come to a dead end, knowing that there are something wrong in the interaction between staff members and residents, but being unable to identify where the problem stems from.

The guidelines for our research

According to Dorothy Smith, the aim of IE is to identify the essential problematic in the relation between citizens and the public institutions. As she expresses it in her book from 2005 (Smith 2005, 41):

> A problematic is a territory to be discovered, not a question that is concluded in its answer. Exploration opens up an institutional complex, as it is relevant to the problematic. In opening up an institutional complex it participates in institutional ethnography's more general discoveries of the workings of institutions and the ruling relations in contemporary western societies.

This thus became our first research guideline. The 'problematic' was distinguished from 'issues', the latter being defined by the researchers before initiating data production, and the first being something we had to identify during the course of field work. Accordingly our issue was the relationship between pedagogical discourses, paradigms and concepts on the one hand and the psychological strain on the other hand. The problematic was yet to be discovered.

The second guideline for our research process, we drew from the concept of 'institutional complex'. We had to be aware of the ways in which the residential homes were hooked in to a wider institutional complex. We had to explore the workings of that complex through identification of discourses, regulating texts, relations in a wider institutional field and the conditions of management in different residential homes. Thus, we expected that the problematic would say something significant about the everyday world of residents and staff members, while simultaneously connecting their experiences with trans-local dynamics 'at once present and absent in the everyday' (Smith 2005).

The investigation also had a third guideline, which was to root the research process in the 'lifeworld' of the residents. In this context, the lifeworld includes life history, future perspective and the whole experience within the horizon of a human being from which the everyday world is being understood (Habermas 1981; Schutz and Luckmannn 1989). This commit-ment turned out to be complicated, first because some of them were not able to express their experience in a systematic way and second, their experiences and life situation were so radically different from our own that we could not rely on an intuitive understanding (Høgsbro 2017).

We were not left without equipment to help us engage the field. In our tool-box, we had a wide range of sociological theories and ethnographic meth-ods. We were going to carefully observe the relation between actors, actions and sites in a systematic way (Spradley 1980). We were going to be engaged in small-talk as well as focussed individual interviews as an entrance to the experience of residents and staff members (Spradley 1979). We were at a later stage of the investigation going to make focus-group interviews to iden-tify an existing hierarchy of discourses in the field (Fairclough 2003). And in the end, we would produce a questionnaire to identify the distribution of experiences expressed in the talk and interviews with staff members. This was meant to ensure that we had sufficient knowledge of the general experi-ences of staff members in the field. As a side benefit, it also made us able to determine the relation between certain incidents and discourses on the one hand and certain levels of mental strain on the other hand.

Challenging behaviour and cognitive disorders

When a person is not able to regulate his/her behaviour in a way that local authorities can manage. When the home-care worker refuses to visit the care receiver. When the local shops refuse to accept his or her presence. When the police are called upon twice a week and the psychiatric hospital has received the person twice within a month. Then the person is transferred to the kinds of residential homes we chose for our inquiry. This might be the only thing the residents have in common.

In order to understand the challenging behaviour, staff members referred to recent models of how the brain works and the possible cognitive defi-cits the disturbance of this system can create. This involved considerations about their ability to remember the consequences of action, the ability to control impulses and the ability to imagine what other people might think or feel (Goldberg 2001).

The situation of the residents is basically understood as characterised by constant stress and anxiety when trying to find out what is happening around them, why other people are acting the way they are and what other people expect from them. This way of understanding the basic problem characterised all the residential homes. One of my colleagues came up with the expression 'when the map does not fit the terrain' (Ringø 2012), and this serves as a perfect metaphor for the situations in which the residents are situated. In short, the major problem for the residents is that their cognitive map does not fit the social reality or the way cognitively normally function-ing people perceive and experience social reality.

The structure of time and space might also differ. A man with Alzheimer told that he had lost his driver licence after colliding with a truck. He was driving on the highway in his car and was passing a truck when the truck suddenly moved into the fast lane and he drove right into the side of the truck. There was just one problem with this perception of the incident: The truck had kept its direction and never moved into the fast lane. His own sense of space had been disturbed and altered by the Alzheimer.

The mother of a boy with autism asked for professional advice because her young boy displayed panicky behaviour when attending birthday parties (Høgsbro 2007). He would lay down in the hallway, scream and refuse to spend time with the other children. The professional advisor told the mother to contact the host of the birthday celebration, ask for details about what would be happening at the party and then pass it on to her son. This proved to be a successful strategy and her boy was now able to enjoy the party together with his peers. When the mother told me about this, she regretted that she had to spoil the surprise. In Denmark, and most of the Western world, surprises are an important part of birthday and Christmas celebrations. But for people with autism surprises cause panic and discomfort (Happé and Frith 1996). Interacting with other people is complicated enough as it is without the additional complications caused by surprises.

Having observed this and identified the understanding of challenging behaviour as an expression of stress and anxiety as a particular professional discourse, we turned towards the workload of the professionals.

The professional situation

The situation of the professionals was not easy. They were exposed every day to many different kinds of physical and mental harassment. Between 20% and 30% were on a weekly basis exposed to aggressive behaviour and varying degrees of physical assault as well as verbal threats and devaluation. A small percentage of the professionals had been exposed to serious assaults, but these could have lasting effects in the form of post-traumatic stress disorder (PTSD).

The reaction to these sometimes unpredictable incidents was a relatively high level of stress and a constant awareness of sounds and movements. It was worth noticing that self-harming behaviour by residents caused as much stress for the professionals as when they were themselves exposed to aggression. On a certain level, our qualitative as well as quantitative data showed that mental strain was not so much related to the concrete physical assault as it was related to situations the staff members had not been able to predict. Thus, we were able to define the connection between professional discourses and mental workload: The discourses made staff members able to foresee what was going to happen, and this ability was both their personal security and their professional pride or identity. So, when something happened that they did not foresee, both the personal security and professional identity were threatened.

Realising that discourses played an important role in the conduct of risk and security led us to distinguish between two forms of conduct: 'conduct of' and 'conduct within'. Conduct *of*, on the one hand, is the top-down regulated work conditions, explicitly based on manuals and prescriptions. This includes, for instance, evidence-based models for preventing dangerous behaviour. Conduct *within*, on the other hand, is primarily based on local discourses of what constitutes good social work. This refers, on a trans-local level, to some national and international professional discourses for pedagogical intervention.

There were basically two concepts which characterised the professional discourses as a part of the 'conduct within': Autonomy and shielding. 'Autonomy' meant that the residents ought to decide what they wanted to do during the day. They could go wherever they wanted to go and they could choose freely between different activities. 'Shielding' meant to protect them from ending up in situations, they could not manage, get into conflicts with other residents or get disturbed by too many impressions.

Shielding residents from impressions often meant reducing access to activities or reducing the amount of options as well as hinder access to specific activities. In general, the staff members tried to make the daily schedules simple and recognisable and ensure that interaction between residents and staff members followed strict guidelines. These guidelines referred specifically to autism theories but nonetheless seemed to be commonly accepted and used among staff members at residential homes for people with dementia and challenging behaviour (Happé and Frith 1996).

Accordingly, actions labelled 'shielding' were potentially in conflict with actions focussing on 'autonomy'. This seemed to be the core of a number of disagreements and regular conflicts among the staff members. Some of our staff informants thought that the amount of specific guidelines was exaggerated, and this made us aware of a certain level of heterodoxy among the staff members within the residential homes. More specifically, it indicated the existence of a professional discourse emphasising resident autonomy and access to activities, which challenged dominant shielding strategy.

It became clear from our observations that shielding played a dominating role in the regulation of everyday life to prevent the residents from hurting each other, protect them from overwhelming stimuli and stress induced by memories and complicated choices. The professionals where often confronted with difficult decisions between demands on autonomy and shielding strategies: between what they *wanted* to do to tackle a situation and what they felt they *had* to do in accordance with residential home guidelines and dominating discourses.

> I remember BB – she also attended activities and she was out on excursions and she really enjoyed it so much to participate in all that, but afterwards she screamed all night. So, there was a bill to be paid and

it can be rather frustrating to listen to. Sometimes you have to realise that she needs this amusement at this moment and then tolerate that it has a price.

(Høgsbro and Burholt 2015)

This resulted in difficult discussions about shielding, motivation, autonomy and self-determination. There seemed to be unsolved disagreements about the need for more activities and autonomy on the one hand, and the need for shielding, on the other. The staff members intensively tried to decode the expressions of the residents and used their own personal and professional experience to build up confident interactions with each resident. This was sometimes in conflict with general guidelines. Sometimes the interaction between residents and staff members took an unforeseen course and resulted in serious forms of stress among staff members as well as residents.

To further identify these elements in what now was regarded as a general problematic we had to include some of the quantitative data from the questionnaires to understanding how the staff experienced situations that resulted in heightened stress levels among staff members. We found out that the most significant stress factor was, as mentioned above, not the specific physical threats from residents, but rather it was the situations when the staff members did not understand what was going on and could not predict the course of action. Interestingly, a multiple regression analysis of the data showed that trained pedagogues were more seriously stressed in such situations than the unskilled staff members. This made us aware of a rather close connection between pedagogical premises and mental stress. When comparing the results from questionnaires and interviews, we came to the conclusion that a skilled ability to understand the residents and predict their reactions to specific situations was essential for the feeling safeguarded from serious incidents. When this understanding was not established, professional identity as well as safety was challenged, causing heightened stress levels.

The next puzzle to solve was then if it was possible to change a feeling of uncertainty into a feeling of personal professional competences. When looking at the data from the questionnaires, we noted that 15% felt 'helpless' when exposed to challenging behaviours while 53% felt 'professionally challenged'. The question became thus whether the experience of helplessness could be turned into an experience of being professionally challenged and how such a transformation of reception and identity could take place? A possible way of transforming helplessness into a feeling of being professionally challenged could be identified in the following segment from a qualitative interview with a staff member from one of the residential homes for people with dementia:

INTERVIEWER: Do you all agree about how to approach her? How to help her?

STAFF MEMBER: Yes, generally we do. Also when she beats us, if we don't do the things that prevents her from beating us or hitting us at least, stand beside her and wait or stand really close or keep her hand while you feed her. If you don't do that, the result is that she is hitting us and we are getting angry with her, and she does not deserve that because we actually know what to do to prevent her from hitting us. So no one is to be blamed, and we always think this way. Not so much because I cannot stand a few chats, but I do not want to have her regarded as a violent person, because she does not deserve that. She just cannot do anything about it.

(Høgsbro and Burholt 2015)

This explanation seems overwhelmingly tolerant, however, the quote illustrates a professional shift from a focus on violent behaviour to a focus on the lifeworld behind the behaviour. Curiosity towards the lifeworld of the resident replaces fear and anxiety. Thus, it transforms helplessness to a feeling of being professionally challenged.

Coping strategies like this are not developed by the individual staff member but developed as a kind of collective cultural invention dependent on the existence of certain professional discourses among the staff members. These discourses are, in turn, shaped by national and international literature and local courses, local management, personal experiences, supervision and the surrounding context of the institutional setting. So we had to investigate this 'territory' before we could identify the influence of all these actors. Before doing so, however, we took a closer look at the heterodoxy mentioned above, between shielding strategies and autonomy discourses.

When looking at the results from this questionnaire, we could see a striking disagreement about the need for activities and shielding. When asked if it was important that the schedule for the day was the same every day, 54% of the staff members agreed and 20% disagreed at the residential homes for people with dementia. At the residential homes for people with autism, the figures were 70% against 7%. This pattern was repeated in similar questions, and we were able to identify between 10% and 20% as 'dissidents' of the organisation. In the interviews, the disagreements were sometimes openly expressed. But at some of the residential homes, it seemed to be a part of a deeper conflict among the staff members and the dissidents seemed to be suppressed.

One of the dissidents had a certain authority in the organisation of a specific residential home because of his position as chief manager. He told us about an incident that took place shortly after he had taken office. A young man with autism was considered aggressive and dangerous, and the staff members tried to convince their new chief manager that only three staff members were able to handle him. These three staff members followed some strict rules for their contact, following specific guidelines for every step they took and every position they held when approaching him and supporting him in everyday activities. One day when the three staff members were not present, the chief manager took over and decided to break all the rules and guidelines they had been following, and he did not get into any conflict with the young man.

We received similar reports from several of our informants who could be regarded as 'dissidents' of the organisation. It was stories about breaking rules and building trust and personal relations from understanding the individual residents' lifeworld, history and cognitive uniqueness.

We hypothetically drew the following Figure 15.1 to encapsulate what had possibly become the consequence of a structural pedagogy emphasising extreme forms of shielding (Høgsbro et al. 2012).

The point in presenting this model is that structural pedagogy may result in a *vicious circle* where staff members, on the one hand, try to strengthen the shielding and reduce stimuli (impressions and activities) in order to prevent challenging behaviour in accordance with the discourse on the connection between stimuli and challenging behaviour. On the other hand, residents may react to the efforts of regulating their everyday life because they feel bored and restricted, and they react in a way that the staff members perceive as an escalated challenging behaviour. The staff members' response is to further strengthen the 'shielding' guidelines of the structural pedagogy, which, in turn, escalates the conflict level. Simultaneously the many rules they have to observe stress the staff members even more. As a result, they face an escalation of challenging behaviour, structural restrictions and stress.

This was not a critique of the staff but rather a critique of the international tradition for structural pedagogy. When we presented the results at the final meeting at the first residential home, there was silence for some minutes and we beginning to get quite nervous until one of the staff members said: 'I think you are right' and the rest of the staff members agreed.

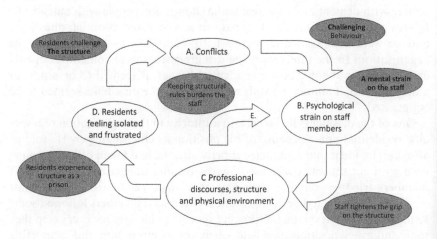

Figure 15.1 Possible consequences of structural pedagogy.

All the residential homes reacted similarly thinking that although they agreed no one else would agree, and definitely not the Ministry of Social Affairs. Eventually, however, they all accepted our conclusion.

The trans-local level

After having reached this point, a closer look at the trans-local conditions seemed to be an urgent obligation for IE to fulfil its purpose. Until now, we had only investigated the internal dynamics at the residential homes and thus the conduct *within* and not *of* the social work. We still missed the linkage between the local level and the trans-local level (Høgsbro et al. 2012). This was included in the follow-up investigation of pedagogical discourses at residential homes for people with dementia and challenging behaviour (Høgsbro and Burholt 2015). Focussing on two residential homes for elderly people with cognitive disorders, we turned to explore the role of management in the balance between mental workload and pedagogical discourse.

When interviewing the managers, we got a picture of the conditions of management within the residential homes. The residential homes in Denmark are positioned in a field characterised by competition between different privatised institutions offering services like residential homes for people unable to live by themselves. The term 'privatised' indicates that the status of the institutions is not entirely clear. They do not have a well-defined owner but are formed in collaboration between several local authorities. The residential homes offer their placements on an open market to local authorities who can choose between those services by looking at the price and quality of the service. When I asked the managers what would happen if they went bankrupt, they did not really know who would be held responsible as no clear ownership was in place. When I asked them what knowledge the local authorities had before choosing one residential home over another, that was also quite unclear. The pressure and the workload in the local authorities were considerable, and the overall impression was that the decisions were based on reputation and personal acquaintances. Thus, the premises for referring social clients to a particular residential home were unclear.

The residential homes are also subject to a kind of accreditation system. This accreditation is carried out by a team of professional social workers. To ensure a so-called neutral judgement in a small country where the professional networks are dense, they come from a different part of the country and have little knowledge of the specialised services they evaluate. Furthermore, they have limited time for investigation, and when we went through the documents, we could see that their data and judgement were rather erratic when compared to our own systematic research. So the premises for the inspection and accreditation decisions were questionable.

Although the managers were dedicated to supporting the staff, their knowledge of the diversity in experiences and the function of the support system (education and supervision) was limited. Despite trying to collaborate with other service providers, the willingness to exchange information and be exact about their specialised competences and divisions of labour were limited because of the competition between residential homes that resulted from 'privatisation'. If they could not get a sufficient number of residents with serious problems they would be forced to dismiss staff members. Indeed, the subsidy provided by the local authorities for each resident depended on how serious the challenging behaviour is evaluated to be. This pressure also resulted in a tendency to accept referrals which were a little outside the specialised competences of the staff, and I knew from interviews with staff members that this contributed to increased mental stress.

IE thus gets us closer to understanding the dilemmas faced by the managers in an institutional field characterised by contradictory demands. This is the essence of the institutional complex. It favours a rather simple dissemination of guidelines for practice and hinders an exchange of experiences between residential homes. It further impedes a coordinated structure of specialised services and stresses the staff members with unclear demands stemming from an unclear definition of the target group of potential residents and the qualification required for taking care of those people. This all together implicates a tendency to orthodoxy and inhibits an open discussion of experiences which might question approved methods, guidelines and discourses.

Making changes that work for people

Our investigation changed the discourses at different levels within 'the institutional complex'. The investigations and reports made us understand the role of 'dissidents' in the development of an institution. Afterwards the reports have been subject to intense discussion among the professionals.

Later on, I was invited to join the advisory board of the Ministry of Social Affairs that were planning to publish new guidelines for tackling challenging behaviour. The board comprised of representatives from several advanced residential services targeting a wide range of social, psychological and cognitive problems such as homelessness, drug abuse, autism and people with reduced IQ. The guidelines were adjusted in a way that was aligned with our critique of pedagogical discourses and local management, and they were rooted in a respect for lifeworlds of residents and the experiences of staff members. It involved a change from a strict structural pedagogy to a broader focus on interaction and meaning. Furthermore, it included a shift from demanding consequent actions to unacceptable behaviour towards a focus on the background and reasons for such behaviour as well as personal relations between staff members and residents.

This advisory board further encouraged me to write a short and condensed presentation of the premises for what now became the principles of pedagogical intervention and management guidelines for meeting challenging behaviour. This book was published in August 2018 aimed at supporting the education of students and young staff members in the field.

Resistance to this new paradigm did not come so much from the Ministry of Social Affairs as from the Ministry of Finance. The Ministry of Social Affairs in Denmark, on the one hand, still has a strong connection to practice and engages with a large network of consultants and advisors in the field. The Ministry of Finance, on the other hand, had very little knowledge of social problems and no realistic means for intervention. The Ministry of Finance firmly believed that new public management was the only way to regulate public services. To do this regulation efficiently, they emphasised the necessity of simple premises for evaluating the quality and resources of the different providers of public services. The development and implementation of the new guidelines seemed to counter the priorities of the Ministry of Finance as these are based on recognition of complexity and difference in professional judgement and relations. The struggle and compromises between the diverging discourses can be seen in the official guidelines, particularly in the use of modifiers such as 'should be', 'may', 'must be', etc., which does not directly challenge the decisions of the advisory board but turns the guidelines into something more acceptable for the Ministry of Finance.

IE investigations do not necessarily change the world, but they has potential to be a catalyst for social change and cultural transformations in the field of social discourses and professional organisation.

References

Fairclough, N. 2003. *Analysing Discourse: Textual Analysis for Social Research.* London: Routledge.

Goldberg, E. 2001. *The Executive Brain: Frontal Lobes and the Civilized Mind.* Oxford, New York: Oxford University Press.

Habermas, J. 1981. *Theorie des kommunikativen Handelns.* [*Theory of Communicative Action*]. Frankfurt am Main: Suhrkamp Verlag.

Happé, F. and U. Frith. 1996. "The neuropsychology of autism." *Brain* 119 (4): 1377–1400. doi: 10.1093/brain/119.4.1377

Høgsbro, K. 2007. "ETIBA": *Evaluation of Preschool Programs for Children with Autism Spectrum Disorders in Denmark, with Particular Emphasis on the Trial of ABA Method (Applied Behaviour Analysis).* Århus: Marselisborgcentret.

Høgsbro, K. 2017. "Institutional Ethnography for people in a vulnerable and oppressed situation." In *Social Work and Research in Advanced Welfare States,* edited by K. Høgsbro and I. Shaw, 117–130. London: Routledge.

Høgsbro, K. and A. Burholt. 2015. *The Demensproblematic: An Institutional Ethnography of a Life-World and a Professional Work.* Aalborg: Aalborg Universitetsforlag.

Høgsbro, K., L. Eskelinen, M. A. Fallov, K. Mejlvig, and N. P. Berger. 2012. *When Boundaries are Challenged: Stress and Pedagogical Challenges at Residential Homes.* København: AKF, Anvendt Kommunalforskning.

Ringø, P. 2012. *Dybder og overflader i styring, viden og praksis i det sociale og psy-kiatriske arbejde. [Depths and Surfaces in the Ruling, Knowledge and Practice of Social and Psychiatric Work]*. Aalborg: Aalborg Universitet.

Schutz, A. and T. Luckmannn. 1989. *The Structures of the Life-world*. Evanston, IL: Northwestern University Press.

Smith, D. 2005. *Institutional Ethnography: A Sociology for People*. Toronto: AltaMira.

Spradley, J. 1979. *The Ethnographic Interview*. New York: Holt, Rinehart and Winston.

Spradley, J. 1980. *Participant Research*. New York: Holt, Rinehart and Winston.

16 Resisting the ruling relations

Discovering everyday resistance with Institutional Ethnography

Majken Jul Sørensen, Ann Christin E. Nilsen and Rebecca W. B. Lund

Introduction

The universalist and egalitarian policies of the Nordic model have historically been foundational for societies characterised by social stability, relatively equal distribution of resources and financial success (cf. Chapter 1 in
this book). As a consequence, the Nordic welfare states still enjoy relatively
strong support among their citizens, in spite of growing inequality. Within
this context, the concept of resistance might seem out of place. What is there
to resist if people agree with the ideology of the welfare states? Yet, as several
of the chapters in this collection bear witness, the perception of the welfare
state as a good agent has indeed been challenged. This is particularly manifest in professional practice and the "impossible mission" (Bourdieu 1999)
of professionals who find themselves squeezed between the well-being of the
citizens and the requirements to abide by the rules and regulations imposed
as a part of the neoliberal turn, and the introduction of principles from new
public management. In addition, the users of the services provided by the
welfare state might resist in various ways, which makes it interesting to ask
what resistance looks like when the power you oppose is a power with intentions to do good.

In this chapter, we address how insights from the field of *everyday resistance* may inform institutional ethnography (IE) studies in a way that
sensitises us to discover acts of resistance when they are tacit, subtle or unexpected. Our argument is that, within the Nordic context, resistance can
be traced in oppositional or critical talk, in tacit acts of non-compliance
or in the "twisting and bending" of regulations, as well as in acts that are
explicitly aimed at opposing ruling. Below, we first introduce resistance
studies and present an outline of the concept of everyday resistance. Next,
we look at similarities between everyday resistance and IE before we explore what resistance may look like in the context of the Nordic welfare
states, drawing on empirical examples from two IE studies. Finally, we
discuss the potential, as well as some of the challenges and paradoxes, of
incorporating the perspective of everyday resistance in IE studies in the
Nordics.

Everyday resistance

Resistance studies is an emerging cross-disciplinary field where researchers work to uncover the nuances and complexities of resistance. While the study of power has a long history and has been debated for centuries, inquiring into resistance has not been equally common. Traditionally, *resistance* has been associated with highly visible phenomena such as organised protests, social movements, revolutions and riots, but with the growing interest in resistance, there has also been an increasing interest in less obvious forms, such as *constructive resistance* (Sørensen 2016) and *everyday resistance*. The latter refers to the ways in which people resist dominance in unorganised and hidden ways. James Scott, who coined the term, writes about it as "infrapolitics", the politics that usually goes unnoticed and unrecorded, under the radar (Scott 1985, 1990). Johansson and Vinthagen (2016) have taken Scott's work further and theorised it in relation to the repertoires of actions, the relationship between agents and the spatialisation and temporalistion of everyday resistance. They understand everyday resistance as a practice that is entangled with (everyday) power and has the potential to undermine power relations. It is intersectional and heterogeneous, dependent on changing contexts and situations.

To date, most studies that use the term "everyday resistance" have been conducted in the Global South or among minority peoples, drawing direct inspiration from Scott's own empirical work among poor peasants in Malaysia (Scott 1985). Scott discovered that the peasants resisted dominance in various ways; for instance, they resisted the tax system by underreporting their harvests and delivering goods of poor quality. To provide an overview of all studies of everyday resistance is beyond the scope of this chapter, but recent studies have used the concept in numerous settings and analyses. Johnsen and Benjaminsen (2017), for instance, were informed by Scott's work in their analysis of the resistance of the indigenous Sami reindeer herders in Norway when they attempted to undermine the "rationalisation" of their traditional way of managing the herds. Jenkins (2017) studied women engaged in anti-mining activism in Peru and Ecuador and found that they did not only participate in organised movements, e.g. blockades and marches, but also "stayed put and carried on" with their traditional farming and handicraft work in spite of the obstacles they faced.

The concept of everyday resistance has also found its way into studies of marginalised groups in Europe and the US. One example of this includes Grenier and Hanley's (2007) study of how elderly women exploit and resist the label "frail" on both an individual level and a collective level. Another example is Frederick's (2017) study of mothers with disabilities. Frederick found that being a disabled woman and becoming a mother is itself a form of resistance towards the stereotypes that label disabled women unfit as mothers. Moreover, when they mother their children, they employ various resistance strategies to appear visible and respectable in a proactive attempt to counter stereotypes. A third example is Ward et al.'s (2016) study of women living with dementia. The authors utilise Johansson & Vinthagen's analytical framework to explore the everyday resistance of women with dementia in terms of looks and physical appearance. They discovered that the women resist the spatial and temporal regimes of the care facilities where there is one standard for all and little time for personal routines and "extraordinary" demands related to hair and makeup.

What these studies have in common is that they explore resistance from the standpoint of actors that are commonly assumed to be under-privileged. One can easily sympathise with their acts of resistance to oppressive power relations. However, as this book bears witness, many Nordic scholars of IE are preoccupied with the work of professionals. Within this context, the very term "resistance" may seem inappropriate. In some research fields, such as feminist studies, work studies, and organisational studies, everyday resistance has been explored through other, but highly related concepts, such as *organisational misbehaviour* and the *micro-politics of resistance* (see for instance Ackroyd and Thompson 1999; Contu 2008; Karlsson 2012; Parsons and Priola 2013; Thomas and Davies 2005). Both in these fields and in resistance studies, there has been debate about what should count as resistance. The most central aspect of this debate has been the question of intentionality.

In his understanding of resistance, Scott includes oppositional *intention*, whereas this is not a requirement in Johansson and Vinthagen's definition of everyday resistance mentioned above. An early critique of Scott's insistence on intentionality came from Bayat (2000), who has studied the everyday resistance of the urban poor in the Middle East. Bayat uses the term "the quiet encroachment of the ordinary" to describe how slum dwellers, street vendors and other marginalised people day by day carve out a place to exist in the cities. They do not organise collectively to demand water supply and electricity for the sheds they have built on public land, but rather illegally tap into the power grid and set up their stalls. They have no intention of changing the landscape of the city; they simply want a better life for themselves. Nevertheless, their practices are reshaping the cities and undermining state power. Such examples of *consequences*, rather than intention, have inspired recent definitions of resistance where intent is not essential. Sørensen, for instance, suggest that acts can count as resistance *either* if there is an oppositional intention (but the results might be limited) *or* if the consequences of practices undermine systems of power (Sørensen 2016).

Bayat warned against romanticising resistance, i.e. reading too much into some acts, so as to find resistance "everywhere" (Bayat 2000). In his opinion, some resistance researchers confuse the awareness of subordinates about, and articulation of, the oppressive situation they live in with resistance to it. Bayat argued that as long as the acts do not undermine the system of power and carve out more space from sources of power like the state, capital or patriarchy, this does not count as resistance. However, such a position raises the question as to whether only those who are successful can be considered resisters? Johansson and Vinthagen's answer to this dilemma has been to include the term *potential* in their definition, arguing that resistance may incorporate acts that have the potential to undermine existing systems of power (Johansson and Vinthagen 2016).

Taken together and adapted to the Nordic welfare states, everyday resistance can be understood as oppositional practices that carry a transformative potential. In other words, acts and talk that are explicitly critical of the current state of affairs and that involve a desire to change or challenge dominant understandings may count as everyday resistance despite not deliberately being referred to as such.

Similarities between IE and everyday resistance studies

The approach to resistance studies described above converges with IE in many important aspects. First of all, both are interested in what people actually do, that is, their everyday activities and practices. The researcher enquires into people's actual everyday/night *doings*. In IE, the concept of *work* (understood as all activities that require time, effort and intention), and *work knowledge*, is the starting point for inquiry into the social organisation of everyday life (Smith 2005). IE studies should result in thick descriptions of actions and the subjective meaning associated with the activities rather than surface descriptions of intentions. As such, "everyday resistance" may be part of the everyday *doings* of people.

Another strong link between IE and everyday resistance is the interest in examining power and an understanding of power as relational. When it comes to everyday resistance studies, many authors have been inspired by Foucault (Baaz et al. 2016). Within IE, the notion of power is based upon an interpretation of Marx's epistemology (Smith 2004). The concept of *ruling relations* draws attention to how people's activities are coordinated with those of other people, located elsewhere elsewhen, and how this coordination is mediated and shaped by texts. Accordingly, IE emphasises that a study always starts from a specific standpoint. In line with the majority of research on everyday resistance, IE studies often take the standpoint of those who are perceived to be at the bottom of the hierarchies in the ruling relations. The aim is one of emancipation and transformation of the social processes that work against their best interests, i.e. to produce knowledge *for* and *with* people, not *about* them. Likewise, many resistance researchers explicitly take a normative approach, advocating that resistance research should be useful for those who practice resistance against domination (Vinthagen 2018). Although it follows from a relational understanding of power that power is complex and cannot be reduced to something some people possess while others do not, power is not evenly distributed throughout society. Scholars of both everyday resistance and IE acknowledge that people are often alienated from their own position and participation in relations of power/ruling in ways that sometimes conceal domination and how power is distributed and exercised in their daily lives.

Although the concept of ruling relations is useful for understanding the operations of power, there is a risk that it encourages a focus on how people reproduce ruling, while downplaying resistance to ruling. We say this knowing that this was never the intention with the concept nor with IE more generally – indeed quite the opposite. The concept is relational, not functionalist or structuralist, and as such agency and ultimately the possibility of resistance, is central to IE discovery. Despite this, it seems to us that many empirical studies drawing on IE are good at meticulously unpacking how everyone – be they in the upper or lower echelons of institutional hierarchies – is caught up in webs of ruling, but they speak in less detail about how people challenge and resist the ruling relations in which they are entangled.

It may seem obvious when starting exploration from people's actual work and work knowledge that one might also discover acts of resistance and ways of challenging ruling relations. However, ensuring that involves careful and active listening, primarily because people may not be aware that their acts constitute a form of resistance, and nor do they explicitly refer to their acts in such terms. Thus, we can learn from everyday resistance studies to become aware of acts that counter ruling institutional intentions. In IE, the notion of *oppositional or critical talk* is suitable to sensitise us to words and acts that imply some kind of resistance. According to Liza McCoy (2006: 120), oppositional or critical talk highlights the differences between the institutional discourse and the forms of knowing and being that the speaker feels to be preferable, or brings with her from elsewhere. It does not imply an ignorance of the dominant discourse but marks a stance of opposition or criticism against it and, as such, it is a good entry point to better understanding the operation of the ruling relations. Explicating acts of buying into, strategically enacting, and/or challenging the ruling relations are all equally important in understanding how ruling works (or fails to work) and the social organisation of everyday life. However, we argue that resistance can also be found in acts of non-compliance or in the silent manoeuvring of institutional regulations. In the next section, we will look more closely at how resistance can be traced within two studies set in a Nordic welfare state; Rebecca Lund's study of junior female academics in Finnish universities, and Ann Christin E. Nilsen's study of early intervention in Norwegian kindergartens.

Tracing resistance in welfare state institutions

In her IE of a Finnish university undergoing neoliberal restructuring and reform from the standpoint of junior female academics, Rebecca Lund identified forms of resistance that did not only work in the interests of those who did not speak the institutional language. A central pillar in the

208   *Majken Jul Sørensen et al.*

university restructuring was the introduction of a US-style Tenure Track System, which involved clearly defined standards and notions of "the good academic". Emphasis was placed on international journal publications in English and the priority of research above teaching, and increasingly, an individualist competitive working culture was encouraged (Lund 2015, 2018; Lund and Tienari 2018). It was argued by the university management that these standardised notions of quality would promote equality because all people – regardless of gender, class, race or sexuality – would be evaluated on exactly the same criteria. The standardised notions of excellence shaped the choices and priorities of early career academics at the university, who were striving for permanent positions, but it quickly turned out that there was gendered and class-oriented backlash to the so-called neutral criteria. While, for the most part, junior female academics, due to gendered divisions of labour within and beyond the university, were systematically disadvantaged in terms of achieving a position, the response to this was surprising. Some women openly resisted standardised notions of "excellence" by speaking derogatively about the institutional intentions of becoming "world class" and about those individuals who had been "seduced" by the institutional language and performed the so-called ideal academic. But people were positioned very differently in terms of engaging in everyday derogatory talk. On the one hand, it seemed that those who were most openly and ardently critical of the standard were also those who were perfectly capable of speaking the institutional language and living up to the excellence criteria. On the other hand, those who were positioned most vulnerably in relation to the new criteria, tended to internalise, individualise and depoliticise the problem; focussing on their own "lacks" rather than critiquing the standards of excellence and university strategy. Thus, it would seem that derogatory talk, as a form of everyday resistance, was a privilege only some could afford. Resistance was revealed as an element in (re)producing hierarchies within academia, because it was used in the enactment of a subtle distinction between "true researchers", driven by passionate commitment to knowledge building, and "instrumental researchers", driven by career building and status more than substantial contributions to knowledge. This example brings together the process of "discovery" which IE affords, with an important discussion within resistance studies – that resistance cannot be understood as dichotomous; as either/or. Those who appear powerful within one relationship might be the resisters in another. And what is today a form of resistance to a system of power might tomorrow be the new dominant system, facing a new type of resistance (Baaz et al. 2016).

Although the ideals and standards were pivotal for aspiring young academics, Lund found that they were actively challenged, particularly by academics in relatively secure positions. For instance, by insisting on writing in Finnish, and dedicating themselves to teaching and offering PhD courses in which participants would learn about and challenge university politics,

senior academics enacted other ways of being academic than those promoted by the tenure track system. For instance, at the university, a PhD
course was explicitly designed to oppose the current university regime. Formally, the course was called "Professional Academics at Work" and thus,
from an outsider perspective, would seem like a course in "best practices or
how to get tenured", but informally the content was very different. Thus, the
course leader used the tools of the master in the attempt to dismantle the
master's house. These acts were important acts of resistance because they
showed younger scholars that the standards of excellence were not inevita-
ble, and that young scholars would learn a language by which they could
speak resistance and *speak their experience* and actively think through how
they would weave their commitments together with whatever they would be
held accountable for. Whereas this is an example of resistance that, albeit
concealed in formal papers, was outspoken and deliberately aimed at transforming the university sector, Ann Christin E. Nilsen's study provides an
example of resistance performed in more covert and tacit ways.

Nilsen (2017) interviewed kindergarten staff about their *concern work* (see
Chapter 7). An important part of this work is to identify children "at risk"
or with "special needs", and in doing so, the kindergarten employees are
expected to use different tools to assess the development or behaviour of
the children. The intentions are explicitly to do good: The children, once
assessed and identified as children of a specific at-risk category, will be subject to some kind of intervention intended to ameliorate their situation. The
idea to "screen and intervene" (White and Wastell, 2017) is part of an international social investment paradigm which increasingly permeates the
education sector. However, critical voices warn against the unintended consequences of labelling children. The quote below is taken from an interview
with the kindergarten teacher "Heidi", who has worked in kindergartens for
more than 30 years. Building on her experience and discretionary knowledge, she finds the requirements to use assessment tools troubling: *"There
are no tests that are good enough. You see that quite easily when you work with
children, that it doesn't work that way. You cannot just sit there and tick off
this and that"*. Later in the interview, Heidi gives an account of a three-year-
old boy in the kindergarten:

> Now, we have this little naughty one. He just cannot take control of
> that hand of his – it is as if he just *has to* hit [chuckles], or pinch or push
> or grab. Last year he used to bite, but fortunately he stopped that. He is
> still so small, and I am thinking that we cannot put him in that "behav-
> ioural disorder" box yet. Because he has so many good sides. But very
> often there is this one child who becomes the one who gets the blame,
> and the other children pick that up immediately. [So even if it was not
> him] he still gets the blame. And that is the worst thing that can hap-
> pen, I think, that it will last. So, I tell the other adults that we have to
> be cautious so that we don't turn him into the scapegoat. Because then

he will get all the blame, and that's not fair. No, he cannot be made into that problem-child that other parents don't want their children to play with.

Heidi knows well that if the kindergarten teachers document the boy's behaviour in line with some predefined assessment criteria (as they are supposed to do, according to the regulations), he will most likely be ascribed a specific category (e.g. a child with "behavioural disorders") or even a diagnosis. In her opinion, however, this is likely to have more harmful effects for the boy than what she assumes will be a gradual behavioural adaptation. She therefore attempts to persuade her colleagues not to "screen" him, out of both a distrust in the assessment technology and a concern for the effects of intervention. Her acts are clearly in opposition to the ideology of early childhood intervention. In the interview she is open about her stance, yet in her everyday work, her acts of resistance are quite covert. She does not openly object to using the assessment tools, but she finds ways to bypass them whenever she finds that necessary.

The professor in Lund's study who explicitly challenges the system by giving a critical PhD course is an example of resistance that is intentionally aimed at undermining the standardised excellence criteria and the university strategy from within. However, acknowledging that the university would not approve of such a course, (s)he deliberately twists her way around the regulations in ways that conceal the resistance. Heidi, on the other hand, disobeys the rules in order to make a difference for one particular boy. Although her behaviour may influence or inspire the actions of her colleagues, her actions are not explicitly aimed at transforming the system of child assessment. Hence, it seems unlikely that her covert resistance and pragmatic adaptation of the rules will contribute to changing the system as long as she acts alone. In order for such actions to be transformative, there has to be some kind of collective action. One may argue, nevertheless, that such acts carry a potential for transformation (Johansson and Vinthagen 2016), and as such count as resistance.

IE and resistance – some challenges and potentials

The examples above point towards some challenges in explicating resistance that are worthwhile discussing. Our first concern is with the term resistance itself, whereas the second concerns ethics. A potential problem with the term *resistance* in an IE study is that what the researcher calls resistance, people themselves might refer to with different words. In neither of the two illustrative examples above was the term "resistance" uttered explicitly by research participants. Some people might not be comfortable being labelled a "resister", for instance if the informants themselves have not articulated their acts as explicitly oppositional, or due to fear of repercussions. This might be something to be especially alert to in a Nordic context where power is frequently associated with good intentions in welfare institutions. The dominant discourse of abiding to rules as something that serves the greater good in the Nordic countries places resistance as marginal activities by individuals on the fringe of society, or more commonly, something which is practised by people elsewhere. In order to discover resistance, we need to pay attention to oppositional talk and to acts that challenge the dominant discourse. However, referring to these acts as resistance involves theorising and requires the researcher to elaborate on the discrepancy between the informants' and researcher's understanding. Such an approach is clearly in line with Smiths's original formulations and should not be problematic in the IE tradition, where mapping the ruling relations beyond what may be immediately visible to the individuals involved is essential. Such a map might also be a tool to guide the emancipation process by pointing towards individual activities that already exist and which might be turned into more organised resistance. Then, IE will be able to contribute to knowledge production which is truly useful for people when they navigate the terrain of the ruling relations.

Another potential problem worth highlighting is that of ethics. People who engage in everyday resistance do it, either explicitly or not, in ways that challenge or undermine the ruling relations. Much of this is hidden and takes place under the radar. But what happens if the researcher exposes everyday resistance and articulates it? An obvious risk is that those who have an interest in minimising and controlling this resistance will know more about it, making it easier for them to do their job. Or maybe, if they already knew about it, they feel forced to act on it when it is made public by the researcher. Do we risk that those responsible for kindergartens become even more insistent that Heidi and her colleagues should assess all children, even when there is just a slight suspicion that one of them does not fit the standard? Will this make it even harder for Heidi to escape the demand to "screen and intervene"? And what about the Finnish academics who organise a course with different content than the title suggests – is there a risk of sanctions once this "misbehaviour" is made public? We believe that these are indeed real risks, but they will always have to be weighed against the potential benefits the openness will provide for those who seek change. One may even ask whether it would be unethical *not* to reveal these dilemmas. Potentially, more focus on resistance makes it easier for Heidi's colleagues to join hands with her in opposing the assessment regime in kindergartens. And perhaps an articulation of the oppositional content of the academic course could give the management of the university a chance to reconsider their reliance on the tenure track system.

Inspired by studies of everyday resistance, we argue that there is also potential to discover resistance in contexts where it seems out of place, such as in the Nordic welfare states. The concept of resistance sensitises us to question how ruling relations are maintained and challenged, whether overtly or tacitly. Resistance does not necessarily lead to transformation, yet discovering acts as resistance brings awareness to the emancipatory and transformational potential of IE.

References

Ackroyd, S. and P. Thompson. 1999. *Organizational Misbehaviour.* London: Sage Publications.

Baaz, M., M. Lilja, M. Schulz and S. Vinthagen. 2016. "Defining and Analyzing "Resistance": Possible Entrances to the Study of Subversive Practices." *Alternatives* 41 (3): 137–153. doi: 10.1177/0304375417700170.

Bayat, Asef. 2000. "From 'Dangerous Classes' to 'Quiet Rebels': Politics of the Urban Subaltern in the Global South." *International Sociology* 15 (3): 533–557. doi: 10.1177/026858000015003005.

Bourdieu, P. 1999. "An Impossible Mission." In *The Weight of the World: Social Suffering in Contemporary Society,* edited by P. Bourdieu, 189–202. Cambridge: Polity Press.

Contu, Alessia. 2008. "Decaf Resistance: On Misbehavior, Cynicism, and Desire in Liberal Workplaces." *Management Communication Quarterly* 21 (3): 364–379. doi: 10.1177/0893318907310941.

Frederick, Angela. 2017. "Visibility, Respectability and Disengagement: The Everyday Resistance of Mothers with Disabilities." *Social Science & Medicine* 181: 131–138. doi: 10.1016/j.socscimed.2017.03.030.

Grenier, A. and J. Hanley. 2007. "Older Women and 'Frailty': Aged, Gendered and Embodied Resistance." *Current Sociology* 55 (2): 211–228. doi: 10.1177/0011392107073303.

Jenkins, Katy. 2017. "Women Anti-Mining Activists' Narratives of Everyday Resistance in the Andes: Staying Put and Carrying on in Peru and Ecuador." *Gender, Place & Culture* 24 (10): 1441–1459. doi: 10.1080/0966369X.2017.1387102.

Johansson, A. and S. Vinthagen. 2016. "Dimensions of Everyday Resistance: An Analytical Framework." *Critical Sociology* 42 (3): 417–435. doi: 10.1177/0896920514524604.

Johnsen, K. I. and T. A. Benjaminsen. 2017. "The Art of Governing and Everyday Resistance: "Rationalization" of Sámi Reindeer Husbandry in Norway Since the 1970s." *Acta Borealia* 34 (1): 1–25. doi: 10.1080/08003831.2017.1317981.

Karlsson, Jan C. 2012. *Organizational Misbehaviour in the Workplace: Narratives of Dignity and Resistance.* Basingstoke: Palgrave Macmillan.

Lund, R. 2015. *Doing the "Ideal Academic": Gender, Excellence and Changing Academia.* Helsinki: UniPress, Dissertation Series.

Lund, R. 2018. "The Social Organization of Boasting in the Neoliberal University." *Gender and Education.* doi: 10.1080/09540253.2018.1482412

Lund, R. and J. Tienari. 2018. "Passion, Care and Eros in the Gendered Neoliberal University." *Organization* 26 (1): 98–121. doi: 10.1177/1350508418805283

McCoy, L. 2006. "Keeping the Institution in View: Working with Interview Accounts of Everyday Experience". In *Institutional Ethnography as Practice,* edited by D. E. Smith, 109–126. Oxford: Rowman & Littlefield Publishers Inc.

Nilsen, A. C. E. 2017. "Bekymringsbarn blir til: En institusjonell etnografi av tidlig innsats som styringsrasjonal i barnehagen." [Concern Children are 'Made Up': An Institutional Ethnography of Early Intervention in Kindergartens]. PhD diss., University of Agder.

Parsons, E. and V. Priola. 2013. "Agents for Change and Changed Agents: The Micro-Politics of Change and Feminism in the Academy." *Gender, Work and Organization* 20 (5): 580–598. doi: 10.1111/j.1468-0432.2012.00605.x.

Scott, James C. 1985. *Weapons of the Weak: Everyday Forms of Peasant Resistance.* New Haven, CT: Yale University Press.

Scott, James C. 1990. *Domination and the Arts of Resistance: Hidden Transcripts.* New Haven, CT: Yale University Press.

Smith, D. E. 2004. "Ideology, Science and Social Relations: A Reinterpretation of Marx' Epistemology". *European Journal of Social Theory* 7 (4): 445–462. doi: 10.1177/1368431004046702.

Smith, D. E. 2005. *Institutional Ethnography: A Sociology for People.* Lanham, MD: AltaMira Press.

Sørensen, Majken J. 2016. "Constructive Resistance: Conceptualising and Mapping the Terrain." *Journal of Resistance Studies* 2 (1): 49–78.

Thomas, R. and A. Davies. 2005. "Theorizing the Micro-politics of Resistance: New Public Management and Managerial Identities in the UK Public Services." *Organization Studies* 26 (5), 683–706. doi: 10.1177/0170840605051821.

Vinthagen, S. 2018. "We Need High Quality Research that is Useful for Resisters." *Journal of Resistance Studies* 4 (1): 5–8.

Ward, R. S. Campbell and J. Keady. 2016. "'Gonna Make Yer Gorgeous': Everyday Transformation, Resistance and Belonging in the Care-Based Hair Salon." *Dementia* 15 (3): 395–413. doi: 10.1177/1471301216638969.

White, S. and D. Wastell. 2017. "The Rise and Rise of Prevention Science in UK Family Welfare: Surveillance Gets Under the Skin." *Families, Relationships and Societies* 6 (3): 427–445. doi: 0.1332/204674315X14479283041843.

Wrapping it all up

Future prospects of IE in the Nordics

Ann Christin E. Nilsen and Rebecca W. B. Lund

The aim of this book has been twofold: To show the multiple ways in which institutional ethnography (IE) is used in the Nordic context and to contribute to a development of IE by bringing it into view and discussing how it can be combined with other approaches and theories. In the first section of this book, we have argued for the need to contextualise IE by drawing attention to the societal conditions under which IEs are carried out and the scientific legacies they become a part of. We believe that the different chapters of this book combined succeed in addressing these issues. The question we raise and reflect on in this final comment is what the future of IE might look like in the Nordic region.

First, let us have a look at some of the characteristics of this book as a whole. In sum, the chapters show that the significant role that the state plays in the Nordic countries cannot be underestimated. Several of the chapters describe the work that professionals within different sectors and organisations of the state do to conform to – or resist – a certain state policy or standard, such as the activation policy that is intended to bring people into employment (e.g. Chapters 4, 11 and 12), maternity healthcare (Chapter 6) and early intervention (Chapter 7). Other chapters explicate how state policy come to inform people's everyday lives, as seen from the standpoint of for instance men who do breadwinning work (Chapter 10) and informal carers (Chapter 13). Even in global development aid work, the significant role of the state is visible (Chapter 14). We believe the attention paid to state policy is rather unique for social research in the Nordic region, given the prominent and comprehensive role of the state here. Nevertheless, when working with this book, it struck us, the editors, that the chapters seldom addressed people's work to deliberately change or transform society. With the exception of Høgsbro's chapter on people with cognitive disorders living in residential homes (Chapter 15), none of the chapters specifically addressed such issues. This made us alert to what we in Chapter 16 together with Sørensen refer to as resistance. Our underlying concern is that unless we pay more attention to rendering visible the agency and power people have to make changes in and of society – and indeed, that includes our own work as social scientists – the important transformative potential of IE becomes derailed.

Related to this is the observation that, with a few exceptions, the IEs in this book do not start from within the standpoints of people that are commonly perceived as underprivileged. Now, it would be a misunderstanding to think that Nordic scholars are uninterested in the situation of the poor, the deprived, the unemployed etc. Quite the contrary, this may very well be their interest, but the lens is turned towards the people who are, in principle, in a position to change the situation of the underprivileged, i.e. the street-level professionals working to put the policy of the welfare state into practice. That being said, the professionals are seldom portrayed as a superior class of individuals, but rather as a category of people squeezed between a state policy from "above" and the needs of citizens who, oftentimes, are aware of their rights, feel entitled to have their needs met and who know how to claim them, at the "bottom". In a (relatively) egalitarian and democratic society, where "all benefit, all are dependent, and all will presumably feel obliged to pay" (Esping-Andersen 1990, 27–28), the authority and trust of professionals is guaranteed by the state, whose power is gained through a democratic process. Yet democracy is at risk and can never be taken for granted, even in the so-called "Scandinavian utopia" (Booth, 2014), which should caution institutional ethnographers to address their research topics from a wider array of perspectives. Of special interest in the Nordic context are the ruling relations involved in the good intentions of the welfare state, which Widerberg discusses in Chapter 2. Public welfare state objectification does not only leave many welfare arrangements immune to critique but may also impede Nordic scholars' ability to question the taken-for-granted assumptions of what works in the best interest of the citizens.

With these warnings in mind, we still believe Nordic scholars will continue to embrace IE. As we have outlined in the first chapter of the book, the Nordic network on IE, which was initiated by Karin Widerberg in 2011, is thriving and growing. Even though the members of the network are still predominantly Norwegian, we notice an increasing interest for IE also from Danish, Finnish, and Swedish scholars. We believe this reflects a global trend which indicates that IE is a method of inquiry that is well suited to explore the current state of affairs in modern societies in the wake of neoliberalism, and that responds well to the linguistic and ontological turn in social sciences (as addressed in Chapter 5). Although modern societies undergo a development that share many of the same characteristics, we cannot assume that the problematics that engage institutional ethnographers, the questions they raise, and the ways in which they go about to conduct their research are similar or even transferable. Hence, we would like to encourage institutional ethnographers across the world to explore the conditions for doing IE in their context. This, we believe, has potential to develop IE as a method of inquiry further and to make it relevant to scholars whose conditions for social research are quite different.

Given the legacy of social research in the Nordic countries, IE arguably does not stand out as an alternative sociology. The majority, if not all, of the authors who have contributed to this book use different methodologies in their research. Rather than taking a script-like approach in how they use IE, notable scholars in the network, such as Karin Widerberg, have been proponents for flexibility in how to conduct IEs (e.g. by combining IE with other methodologies), which problematics to take up and whose standpoint to start from while simultaneously remaining loyal to the ontological premise of IE. We believe that this has nurtured a mindset in which IE is seen as a method of inquiry that has the potential to improve qualitative research in general without rejecting other methodologies.

References

Booth, Michael. 2014. *The Almost Nearly Perfect People: Behind the Myth of the Scandinavian Utopia.* New York: Picador.
Esping-Andersen, G. 1990. *The Three Worlds of Welfare Capitalism.* Princeton, NJ: Princeton University Press.

Index

Note: Page numbers followed by "n" denote endnotes.

collaboration and trust: counsellors and
job agents 142–3; joined-up approach
to social organization 140–1; looking
for ruling in job agents' practices
143–5; Norwegian activation services
140–1; overview 138–40; RiW as case
of co-production 145–7
"collaborative working" 146
Collins, Barbara G. 124
colonialism 109–11
companion species 85n5
*The Conceptual Practices of Power:
A Feminist Sociology of Knowledge*
(Smith) 3, 6, 118
consensual democracy 9–10
conservative regimes 9
constructive resistance 204
Cooperation Agreement on a More
Inclusive Working Life (the IA
Agreement) 141
co-production: governance practices and
146; RiW as a case of 145–7
Cornwall, Andrea 180
counsellors 142–3
Crewe, Emma 184
cultural traits 58–9
"cutting-out" procedure 94
cyborg 85n5

Dalits 183–4
de Bruijn, Mirjam 178
deinstitutionalization 65–6
Denmark: academic work 31; citizenship
rights 102; maternity healthcare
practices in 77; and sociology 16
Derrida, Jacques 108, 112n3
DeVault, Marjorie 106–7
dialectic realism 90
D'Ignazio, Catherine 16
discourses: institutional ethnography of
94–7; T-discourses 109, 112n4
dynamic nominalism 90

early childhood education and care
(ECEC) 98n1
Economy and Society (Hacking) 88
employment segregation: Nordic
countries 102
epistemology: and institutional
ethnography 56–7; and institutional
theory 56–7
equality 11–12
Eriksen, Erik O. 12
Eskelinen, Leena 191

Esping-Andersen, Gøsta 9
Europeanization 24
European Union (EU) 7
everyday resistance: IE and resistance,
challenges and potentials 210–11;
overview 204–6; similarities between
IE and everyday resistance studies
206–7; tracing resistance in welfare
state institutions 207–10
everyday resistance studies: Foucault on
206; similarities between IE and 206–7
*The Everyday World as Problematic. A
Feminist Sociology* (Smith) 6, 118

Facebook 185
family: exploring research on gender in
nuclear 131–3; exploring trans-local
gendering of 134–5; use of money 130
'female drug abusers' 120
femininity 132
feminist studies of technoscience (FT):
and institutional ethnography 76–85;
maternity healthcare services 77–80;
overview 76–7
Finland: academic work 31; immigration
in 105; institutional ethnography
finding its way to 118–19; Inuits
people 8, 101, 110–11; maternity and
child health services in 119; maternity
healthcare in 77–8; Roma people
105, 107, 110; Sami people 7–8, 101,
105, 107–8, 204; unemployment of
non-Western immigrants 102; welfare
service system 120
Finnish welfare state 118
foetus: emotional distancing of pregnant
women from 79; Harawayan politics
of 82; as human life 80–1; moral
value 80–3; personalising 82; *see also*
pregnant women
"folkhemmet" 12
Foucault, Michel 67, 88–92
Frame Analysis (Goffman) 91
Framework Plan for Kindergartens 96–7
Frankenberg, Ruth 105
Frederick, Angela 204
frontstage behaviour 95–6

gender: being captured by concepts
129–30; exploring breadwinning
as work 130–1; overview 128–9;
research on, in nuclear family
131–3; trans-local gendering of
family practices 134–5

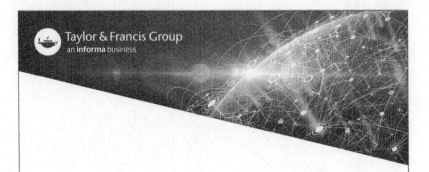